QUICK ESCAPES® SERIES

Quick Escapes®
pacific northwest

getaways from portland, seattle, and vancouver, b.c.

EIGHTH EDITION

Marilyn McFarlane

Revised and Updated by
Christine A. Cunningham

INSIDERS' GUIDE®

GUILFORD, CONNECTICUT
AN IMPRINT OF THE GLOBE PEQUOT PRESS

The prices and rates in this guidebook were confirmed at press time. We recommend, however, that you call establishments before traveling to obtain current information.

INSIDERS' GUIDE ®

Copyright © 1991, 1994 by Marilyn McFarlane
Revised text copyright © 1997, 1999, 2001, 2003, 2005, 2007 Morris Book Publishing, LLC

Photo Credits: pages 1, 139, and 153 courtesy Micky Jones; pages 73, 127, 162, 180, and 199 courtesy Marilyn McFarlane; page 25 courtesy Dick Powers; page 90 courtesy John Parkhurst; page 97 courtesy George White/Salish Lodge; page 113 courtesy North Cascades National Park Service.

Text design by Casey Shain
Maps © Morris Book Publishing, LLC

ISSN 1535-5721
ISBN 978-0-7627-4433-6

Manufactured in the United States of America
Eighth Edition/First Printing

CONTENTS

INTRODUCTION

This guide to brief getaways from Portland, Seattle, and Vancouver is intended for longtime residents, newcomers to the Pacific Northwest, and visitors passing through—anyone who's eager to explore the recreational wonderland that lies beyond the three major cities of the region.

When you want to travel scenic byways and discover their hidden treasures, take this book with you. It will lead you to well-known spots that no tourist should miss and will uncover hideaways that only the local folk know.

The guide provides fully detailed itineraries, much like a customized, organized tour. But they are suggestions only! Don't try to do everything listed on each trip or you'll feel too rushed to enjoy yourself. Pick and choose among the activities, and plan to return for those you missed.

At the end of each chapter, **There's More** provides more reasons to come back. **Special Events** lists regional events and holiday activities. **Other Recommended Restaurants and Lodgings** gives concise descriptions of good places to eat and stay other than those included in the itinerary. Finally, **For More Information** tells you whom to contact to obtain maps and learn about the area you're visiting.

The itineraries are designed as auto tours, but public transport, walking, and bicycling are viable alternatives in many cases. I recommend using them whenever you can.

Consider traveling in the off-season, rather than the high-use summer months. The weather is mild in spring and fall, though rains are frequent. Winter has its own appeal, with the crowds gone and the landscape spare or clad in white.

Wheelchair-accessible facilities are mentioned where appropriate.

Rates and fees are not specifically stated, as they often change, but you may assume that most costs are reasonable. If a place seemed unusually expensive (or amazingly inexpensive), I have so indicated. Museums usually charge a nominal admission fee or request a donation.

Distances are approximate and are expressed in miles (and in kilometers in the Vancouver, British Columbia, section). American standard spelling is used throughout, except for Canadian place-names.

Make reservations in advance at hotels and inns whenever possible. Some are very small, and rooms fill up quickly, especially during the busy season.

The following is a list of standard equipment you'll probably need on your escapes:

Raingear (in the Northwest, the weather is unpredictable)
Jacket
Sturdy walking shoes
Daypack
Water bottle
Insect repellent
Camera
Binoculars
Travel-size umbrella
Regional maps

A great deal of effort has gone into making this book as accurate as possible, but places do change. If you wish to suggest a correction or a special find that should be included in a future edition, please let me know. I'll be glad to investigate. Meanwhile, enjoy your minivacations—all twenty-four of them.

Marilyn McFarlane
Portland, Oregon

PORTLAND
ESCAPES

PORTLAND ESCAPE ONE

Hell's Canyon

Jet-boating through Hell's Canyon / 2 Nights

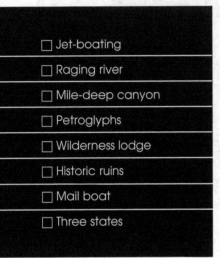

☐ Jet-boating

☐ Raging river

☐ Mile-deep canyon

☐ Petroglyphs

☐ Wilderness lodge

☐ Historic ruins

☐ Mail boat

☐ Three states

Jet boats carry modern travelers, young and old, over the riffles and rapids of the Snake River and through Hell's Canyon, the deepest canyon in North America. The Snake cuts through high desert plateaus of Washington and Oregon, and the craggy mountains of Idaho, before plunging between the narrow walls of the canyon.

Native Americans took refuge here. Miners, ranchers, and steamboaters tried to tame the canyon, but the only permanent residents who survive are a few stubborn ranchers. Some ride 8 miles on horseback to collect their weekly mail.

Beamers Hell's Canyon Tours and Excursions, 1451 Bridge Street, Clarkston, WA 99403 (800–522–6966; www.hellscanyon tours.com), which offers a variety of day and overnight trips, is the largest of several riverboat companies. You can ride the historic mail boat on its weekly Wednesday run. Otherwise, follow the two-day, one-night Copper Creek Overnight tour that leaves Beamers Landing in Clarkston, Washington, across the river from Lewiston, Idaho, daily, and bucks furious water for 70 miles upriver to its overnight stop at Copper Creek Lodge to return the following day. The tours operate daily May through September.

Boats that ride like bucking broncos on the high raging waters of spring offer a gentler swinging ride in summer and fall. Spring and fall are recommended tour times, when crowds are few and temperatures moderate.

Day 1 / Morning

It is worth the time and money to fly from Portland to Lewiston, Idaho, for this Escape, although it is a pleasant and scenic 345-mile drive. If you drive, leave early and follow Interstate 84 down the Oregon side of the **Columbia River** and have lunch 208 miles east in **Pendleton,** Oregon.

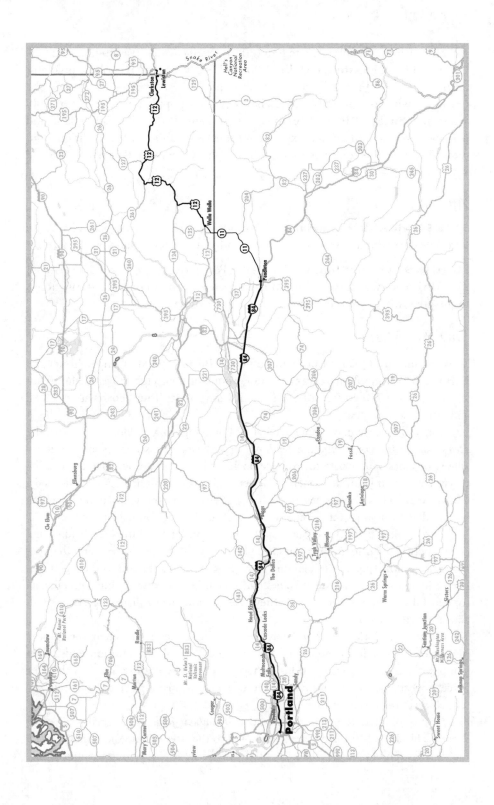

From Pendleton, follow State Route 11 to **Walla Walla,** Washington, and U.S. Highway 12 to **Clarkston,** population about 7,000. Clarkston is Washington's most inland seaport, 450 miles up the Columbia and Snake Rivers. A bridge connects Clarkston with its sister city of **Lewiston,** with a population of about 31,000, across the **Snake River.** The towns were named after William Clark and Meriwether Lewis, the noted explorers of the Lewis and Clark expedition, who camped here at the confluence of the Snake and Clearwater Rivers in 1805 and again in 1806.

Afternoon

DINNER: Bogey's Restaurant, 700 Port Drive, Clarkston, WA; (509) 758–9500. Offers salads, seafood entrees, and chicken and pasta dishes. Overlooks the river.

LODGING: Quality Inn, Clarkston, 700 Port Drive; (509) 758–9500 or (800) 228–5151. The two-story motor inn has a heated swimming pool and easy access to the dock where your jet boat leaves in the morning.

Day 2 / Morning

Walk behind the Quality Inn to the office of Beamers Hell's Canyon Tours and Excursions. You should have a reservation on one of their eight covered aluminum jet boats, each 30 to 40 feet long. The Hells Canyon Day Tour departs at 8:00 A.M. and returns at 6:00 P.M.

You will be sitting, or, more accurately, bouncing on a padded seat aboard the *Hell's Canyon Rose* or maybe the *Spirit of Copper Creek*. Dress warmly and comfortably, with shoes appropriate to riverside docks and rustic pathways. Plan to get a little river water on your face when you open and close the sliding glass windows for a better view! These are regular tour boats, not river rafts, but you will be bouncing up and down on your seat, so sit at the rear of the boat if you have back trouble.

A few jokes from the captain, and you are under the interstate bridge that crosses between Idaho and Washington. One thrust of the jet engines and the boat moves from float speed to full engine. For a few moments the rooftops of the town climb the grassy hills and steep ridges, but you are soon between high, green, flat-topped hills, scored and folded as they rise straight up to plateau pastures high above the river.

Captain Tim Stuart will probably be at the helm, describing the river and the history that is visible to those who know where to look. Civilization ends when you pass the houses and gas stations of **Asotin,** once a wintering place for the Nez Percé, now the last town on our journey. Its name means "a place of eel"; freshwater eels were once caught there.

A rusty old paddle wheel steamer, the **Steamboat Jean,** is snugged against the shore. Its black-and-red stacks are a memorial to the days when gold miners braved the river. As the old wreck recedes behind your boat, the rocky outcroppings dominate the view. The sumac that climbs the steep hills on both sides is green in spring but turns the landscape red in autumn.

The essence of these deep river valleys is, of course, water. In spring, the water partially submerges the riverside trees. The jet boat rides high and hard above the angry river in May; it rides on much shallower water in September.

"We're passing through **Buffalo Eddy**," the captain says. "The water here can be 120 feet deep."

He steers to the far bank of the river and slows so that you can see **petroglyphs** carved by ancient Nez Percé natives. Nobody knows how long ago these figures were made, but the Nez Percé have been in this area for 7,200 years.

The Snake River begins to churn and boil, but this is just the approach to Hell's Canyon, so you are not yet in wild rapids. The first stop of the day is at **Heller Bar,** homesteaded by Cecil Heller.

BREAKFAST: Heller Bar Lodge and Restaurant, where a continental breakfast buffet is provided amid guidebooks and postcards.

A high green hill seems to block the river beyond Heller Bar. This is where the **Grand Ronde River** joins the Snake. Excitement mounts as the boat passes a clutter of houses at the base of a hill and turns left at **Lime Point.** The National Geological Society and the United States Army Corps of Engineers designate this point as the entrance to **Hell's Canyon.**

"We are now at river mile 170, 170 miles from the confluence of the Columbia River and the Snake River at Pasco, Idaho. You can see three states from here," the captain says. "Idaho is to your left, Washington to your right, and Oregon straight ahead. Those cabins clinging to shelves of rock are on original land grants and can be accessed only by water."

Outcroppings pull the mountains up steeply in dark ridges of rock and grass. The river narrows and the water churns as you move into 652,977-acre **Hell's Canyon National Recreation Area,** created under the Wild and Scenic Rivers Act in 1975 to preserve the natural flow of the Snake River. Some private land remains on the Idaho bank, but all the land on the Oregon side is administered by the Forest Service from here to the end of navigation.

The jet boat twists and turns through **Deer Head Rapids** and **Wild Goose Rapids** on the way to **Geneva Bar** and the **Salmon River.** As you ride the wild rapids, you won't be surprised to learn that the explorers abandoned Hell's Canyon as a transportation route. Green hills give way to steep rocky mountains fringed with green. A sheep rancher's cabin sits alone on the draw now, but there was a time when wool was stacked beside the river waiting for the mail boat.

The 429-mile-long Salmon River, which begins and ends in Idaho, is one of the last free-flowing fishing rivers in the West. The 1,000-mile-long Snake River can rise and fall 6 or 7 feet in a day because it is controlled by dams, but the Salmon, which has no dams, can fluctuate 20 to 30 feet in depth over the seasons.

Travel this river in fall, and you will have a swinging water ride, with endangered elk on either bank. Go in the high water of spring, and it is more like a wild roller coaster that crashes on every wave. As the boat is launched out of the water—and you are launched out of your seat—on your way past **High Mountain Sheep Rapids,** think about the steamboats that braved this river at the turn of the twentieth century. Prospectors came because the canyon was full of mineral wealth, but they didn't last long.

A regularly scheduled stern-wheeler, the *Imnaha,* made its way between Lewiston and Eureka by being winched over those rapids by cables anchored to rocks, until the day in 1906 when the cable failed. By some miracle, everybody got out alive, but the steamboating era was over.

By the time you pass the *Imnaha,* the river is at full boil. "Look up that hill and you'll see the foundation of the old hotel at **Eureka Bar,**" the captain says. The town was a tiny version of the Klondike, but these prospectors were looking for that valuable 3-foot vein of copper claimed by the Eureka Mining Company and funded by eastern investors. The copper mine went 580 feet through the ridge to the Imnaha River, but now all that remains are a few visible mining ruins and the laughter of the Imnaha Rapids.

The mail boat still comes up this wild river canyon every Wednesday. You can ride aboard as a passenger. From your bouncing transportation you can see the mailbox hanging over the riverbank of a ranch leased by the Forest Service at **Dug Bar,** also known as **Nez Percé Crossing.** Chief Joseph crossed here with his tribe and his horses. If you think this ride is interesting, imagine being among the women and children pulled on rafts across the river by horses.

There are only a few signs of life in the canyon wilderness today, but many human dramas have played out here. At **Deep Creek,** thirty-two Chinese gold miners were robbed and killed by seven horse thieves in 1887. Deep Creek is at river mile 201.

LUNCH: Picnic at **Kirkwood Historic Ranch and Museum,** a working ranch maintained by the Forest Service as a museum.

Afternoon

Navigation ends upriver at river mile 232, 17 miles below Hell's Canyon Dam. As the jet boat turns back downriver, you will look straight up for 1½ miles to the top of **He Devil Mountain.**

The captain pulls out of the wild river to a dock at river mile 208. You are home for the night, at **Copper Creek Lodge** (800–522–6966), first homesteaded by Billy Rankin, who prospected for gold and copper in 1903.

Deer wander away as you climb the slight slope to a complex of buildings overlooking the river. If you have ever been to summer camp, you recognize the layout: dining hall, cabins scattered along the path. Couples and families may choose cabins with hotel-style beds and private bathrooms; others choose bunk beds.

The sun goes down. Deer drink from the shore. Stars leap out of the skies in the clear air. After all that "water exercise" and fresh air, guests go to bed early.

DINNER: Copper Creek Lodge, 70 miles upriver in the wilds of Hell's Canyon, where you eat a hearty meal around large tables in the dining hall.

LODGING: Copper Creek Lodge. Modern facilities, with cabin decks overlooking the river.

Day 3 / Morning

BREAKFAST: Copper Creek Lodge, which serves an old-fashioned rancher's breakfast.

You can relax at the lodge, or repeat the upriver portion of yesterday's journey to Kirkwood Ranch and the end of navigation.

LUNCH: Picnic at Kirkwood Ranch or lunch at Copper Creek Lodge.

Afternoon

Your jet boat leaves midafternoon for its wild ride downriver, with the captain shouting "Hold on!" as you round every curve at 35 miles per hour.

During the brief steamship period at the turn of the twentieth century, it took five days for an intrepid steam-powered stern-wheeler to go upriver and three and a half hours for it to go back downriver. Nowadays, it takes only about four hours of bucking-bronco jet-boating to go upstream to Copper Creek Lodge, and two or three hours to come down.

By the time they have stopped once more at Heller Bar and made the last long run back to the dock at Clarkston, most passengers have had enough river.

If you flew, you have probably reserved a late-afternoon flight out of Lewiston Airport. If you drove, you may want to drive two hours to Walla Walla, Washington, or another hour to Pendleton, Oregon, before you stop for the night.

There's More

Asotin County Historical Society Museum, Third and Filmore, Asotin; (509) 243–4659. An 1882 log cabin and an exhibit of branding irons and carriages in a nearby pole barn. Open Tuesday through Saturday, March through October.

Chief Looking Glass Park (509–751–0240), 5 miles south of Clarkston on Highway 129 on lower Granite Lake, offers boat launch ramps to the Snake, as well as docks, moorage, and picnic tables. From there you can follow the 16-mile wheelchair-accessible Clearwater and Snake River National Recreation Trail to historic sites and attractions in Hellsgate State Park, Swallows Nest Rock, and West Pond.

Chief Timothy State Park (509–751–0240), 8 miles west of Clarkston off State Route 12, sits on an island in the middle of the Snake River. The Alpowai Interpretive Center offers audiovisual programs and exhibits.

Hell's Canyon Adventures, P.O. Box 159, Oxbow, OR 97840; (541) 785–3352 or (800) 422–3568; www.hellscanyonadventures.com. Offers white-water rafting as well as day or overnight jet-boat tours.

Special Events

April. Dogwood Festival, Lewiston. Three-week-long event that includes garden tours and crafts fair.

Dogwood Festival Invitational Art Exhibition, Clarkston. Includes garden tours and crafts fair.

Late April. Asotin County Fair, Clarkston. Features rodeo, stock show, and sale.

June. I Made the Grade Bicycle Race, Clarkston. Thirteen-mile bicycle ride that climbs 1,000 feet.

Late June. Lewis and Clark Discovery Faire, Lewiston. Commemorates the Lewis and Clark Corps of Discovery with food, entertainment, and arts and crafts vendors.

September. Nez Percé County Fair, Lewiston. Includes agricultural, livestock, and homemaking competitions, carnival and midway, and commercial booths.

September. Lewiston Roundup, Lewiston. One of the largest professional rodeos in the Pacific Northwest.

Mid-December. Christmas Reflections on the Confluence, Clarkston. Lighted boat parade on the Snake River near Swallows Nest Park.

Other Recommended Restaurants and Lodgings

Clarkston, Washington

Best Western Rivertree Inn, 1257 Bridge Street; (509) 758–9551 or (800) 597–3621. Outdoor swimming pool, fitness room, sauna, and hot tub.

Lewiston, Idaho

Red Lion Plaza Hotel, 621 Twenty-first Street; (208) 799–1000 or (800) 325–4000. Full-service motor inn.

Sacajawea Select Inn Motel, 1824 Main Street; (208) 746–1393 or (800) 333–1393. Near scenic river walkway and bike trail.

For More Information

Clarkston Chamber of Commerce, 502 Bridge Street, Clarkston, WA 99403; (509) 758–7712 or (800) 993–2128; www.clarkstonchamber.org.

Hell's Canyon Visitors Association, 504 Bridge Street, Clarkston, WA 99403; (877) 774–7248; www.hellscanyonvisitor.com.

Lewiston Chamber of Commerce, 111 Main Street, #120, Lewiston, ID 83501; (208) 743–3531 or (800) 473–3543; www.lewistonchamber.org.

Lewiston–Nez Percé County Regional Airport; Horizon Air and SkyWest Airlines offer frequent direct flights to and from Portland, Seattle, and Boise; Horizon Air reservations (800) 547–9308.

PORTLAND ESCAPE TWO

Eugene-Florence-Newport

City Culture and Coastal Beauty / 2 Nights

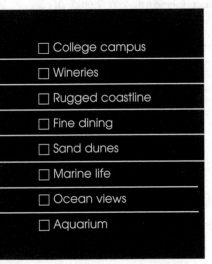

- ☐ College campus
- ☐ Wineries
- ☐ Rugged coastline
- ☐ Fine dining
- ☐ Sand dunes
- ☐ Marine life
- ☐ Ocean views
- ☐ Aquarium

This three-day tour gives you a sampling of some of the best that an Oregon city and the Oregon coastline have to offer visitors. From the restaurants, shopping, and cultural events of Eugene to the rocky coast where waves crash and spray, the variety is exhilarating.

Day 1 / Morning

Travel south on Interstate 5 100 miles to **Eugene,** and stop at the Convention and Visitors Association of Lane County, Oregon, 754 Olive Street, for maps and brochures. Check the calendar for concerts and events taking place at the **Hult Center for the Performing Arts,** Seventh and Willamette Streets (541–682–5000 for ticket information); if the evening's attraction appeals, call for reservations. The Hult Center hosts top artists from around the world in its 2,500-seat, acoustically ideal concert hall. The Eugene-Springfield symphony, ballet, and opera perform on this stage. In June and July the internationally renowned Oregon Bach Festival takes place. Plan on an early dinner if you're attending the theater.

Next, drive north on Lincoln Street to **Skinner Butte Park** and go to the top of the butte. On a clear day you'll have panoramic views of the city, the Willamette River flowing through town, the surrounding green hills and fields, and the mountain on the horizon. Walk through the rose garden and along tree-shaded paths in this grassy park, which was named for the first homesteader in the area; then head back downtown to the Market District.

There are dozens of shops to browse through in the district, but the main complex is **Fifth Street Public Market.** Once a feed mill, it's now a collection of interesting specialty stores selling clothing, gift items, kitchenware, arts and crafts, and foods from around the world. **Casablanca,** a good lunch spot, has Middle Eastern dishes, and **Cafe Yumm** offers a special blend of rice and beans, served with large chunks of bread.

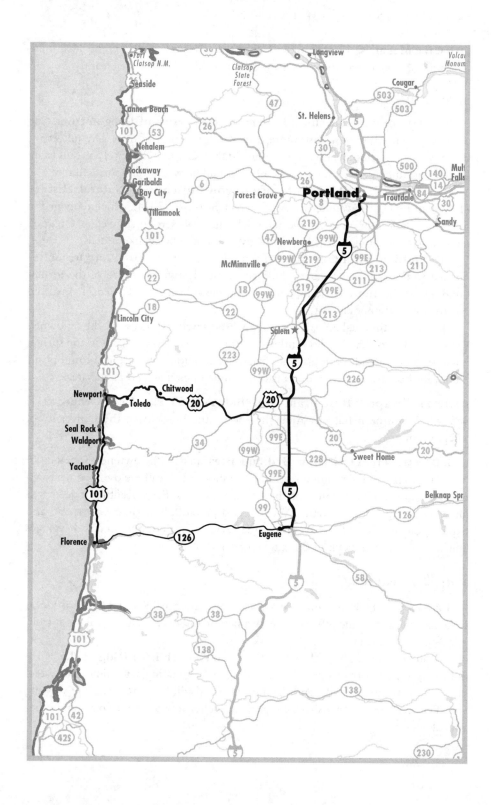

LUNCH: **Mekala's,** 1769 Franklin Boulevard; (541) 342–4872. Good Thai food, hot and spicy or not, as you request, and homemade coconut ice cream.

Afternoon

A short distance from downtown Eugene, the **University of Oregon** covers 250 acres and is an arboretum with more than 2,000 varieties of trees. The university, the city's largest employer, enrolls about 20,000 students. Its lovely grounds are graced with nineteenth-century and modern buildings and outdoor sculpture.

On campus is the **University of Oregon Museum of Natural History** (1680 East Fifteenth Avenue, near Agate Street; 541–346–3024), which reopened in February 2005 after an extensive remodel. The new setting showcases Oregon's cultural history through artifacts, interactive exhibits, and lifelike murals.

The **Jordan Schnitzer Museum of Art** at the University of Oregon re-opened to the public in January 2005 and is nearly twice the size of the former building. Collections include ancient Chinese bronzes, Russian icons, and Northwest contemporary art.

If there is time, take a stroll through **Hendricks Park,** a world-renowned rhododendron garden 2 miles southeast of the campus. Don't miss it in the spring, when the rhododendron displays are magnificent. Thousands of the colorful plants bloom in this park, which also has paths, secluded benches, and picnic areas.

DINNER: **Napoli Restaurant and Bakery,** 686 East 13th Avenue; (541) 485–4552. Southern Italian cuisine. Just down the block from the University of Oregon campus.

LODGING: **The Oval Door Bed and Breakfast,** 988 Lawrence Street; (800) 882–3160. This early-twentieth-century farmhouse is located close to downtown Eugene and the Hult Center for the Performing Arts. Each beautifully decorated guest room has a private bath, TV, VCR, and private phone line. Guests can also expect gourmet breakfasts, evening wine service, and complimentary beverages available around the clock in the kitchen refrigerator.

Day 2 / Morning

BREAKFAST: Early morning coffee and then full breakfast at The Oval Door. Breakfast menu may include pancakes, waffles, or egg dishes, plus cereal, fresh fruit, juice, coffee, and tea.

Head west on Highway 126. In 12 miles you'll reach **Fern Ridge Lake,** a 4½-mile-long reservoir that is popular for sailing, powerboating, jet-skiing, and water-skiing. Shortly after the lake and Peninsula Park, you'll come to a wildlife viewing area. The wetlands and marshes here provide shelter to a variety of birds and other animals.

Continue on to Territorial Highway and turn left toward the Veneta business district and **Hinman Vineyards,** 27012 Briggs Hill Road, Veneta; (541) 345–1945. Hinman, established in 1979 in the foothills of the Coast Range, is a brick winery with graceful arches and a tower. Visitors can sample wines and bring a picnic lunch on the landscaped grounds.

If you turn right instead of left on Territorial Highway, you'll be headed for **Elmira** and **LaVelle Vineyards,** 89697 Sheffler Road, Elmira; (541) 935–7202. This small, family-owned winery is next to groves of fir trees at the end of a mile-long lane.

Continuing on Highway 126 you'll drive through Noti, a timber town where piles of logs are stacked higher than the buildings. The road winds up into the Coast Range, through dense forest where the tree trunks seem to be made of moss, they're so velvety green. In spring the dogwood blossoms float creamy white against the dark firs, and in fall the maples and alders show yellow, brown, and red.

At the confluence of the Siuslaw River and Wild Cat Creek, watch for a **covered bridge** that was built in 1925. The pretty white bridge, a charming addition to the landscape, is easy to miss in summer because it's hidden behind the foliage. Take a sharp right at Whittaker Creek turnoff, pass under Highway 126, and you will see the bridge.

Continue on 126 to **Florence,** at the mouth of the Siuslaw River, and follow the signs to **Old Town.** The historic bayfront here offers quaint shops, boutiques, and restaurants by the harbor, home to a small fishing fleet. It won't take long to look around the area. Check the kite shop, buy a souvenir, have a cappuccino, and head for the dunes.

The **Oregon Dunes National Recreation Area** is a 47-mile stretch of sand dunes, encompassing some 32,000 acres. Walking in these undulating, desertlike hills is an experience not to be missed. South of Florence is **Jesse M. Honeyman State Park,** with convenient access to the dunes. Here a high hill, a favorite spot for climbing and sliding on the sand, meets the edge of a watery gem, Cleawox Lake.

About 10 miles south of Honeyman is the **Oregon Dunes Overlook,** where you can see the dunes from boardwalks and viewing platforms. A short trail leads into the dunes, and interpretive signs explain the natural features such as evergreen islands, beach grass, wildlife, and little lakes. The overlook is wheelchair accessible.

LUNCH: **Traveler's Cove,** 1362 Bay Street, Florence; (541) 997–6845. Riverfront favorite serving coastal classics from chowder to crab or shrimp Caesar salads. Dine on deck (sunglasses provided).

Afternoon

Leaving Florence, drive north on U.S. Highway 101 to **Darlingtonia Wayside.** Walk the boardwalk here to see the exotic-looking cobra lilies growing in the marsh. These plants are carnivorous, luring insects down a tube lined with nectar.

Continue north for 10 miles to **Sea Lion Caves,** and take the elevator down to the caves where Steller's sea lions dwell (admission fee). You can get a close look at the only wild breeding colony of the sea lions on the coast, as well as postcard views of **Heceta Head lighthouse** to the north. Pigeon guillemots and Brandt's cormorants nest by the thousands in the area and can be seen from a path along the cliff.

As you drive north on US 101 along the coast, you'll pass miles of smooth, uncrowded beach. Stop at any parking area to explore the shoreline; all the beaches are open to the public by state law. A park with a sandy cove, lawns, and picnic tables lies at the base of the cliff where the picturesque Heceta Head lighthouse stands (open for tours in summer).

Along the way are landmarks such as Devil's Elbow, Devil's Churn, Muriel O. Ponsler Memorial Wayside, and Captain Cook's Chasm. At **Cape Perpetua** you can enjoy panoramic views up and down the coast. Check at Cape Perpetua Visitor Center for exhibits and information. Walk the trails on this massive basaltic headland to see old-growth forest, tide pools, shell mounds, and chasms of turbulent foam.

When you reach **Yachats** (YA-hots), you're in a charming seaside town nestled between the Coast Range forests and the Pacific Ocean—the perfect spot for a quiet getaway. Visit the **Little Log Church and Museum,** 328 West Third Street, Yachats (541–547–3976), a tiny church built in 1927 and now open as a historical museum. Open from noon to 3:00 P.M. every day but Thursday.

DINNER: La Serre Restaurant and Bistro, 160 South Second Street; (541) 547–3420. Greenery, windows, and skylights give this highly rated restaurant a garden atmosphere. Fresh seafood, tasty salads.

LODGING: Shamrock Lodgettes, 105 U.S. Highway 101 South; (541) 547–3312 or (800) 845–5028. Log cabins on sloping lawns above the beach at the mouth of the Yachats River.

Day 3 / Morning

BREAKFAST: LeRoy's Blue Whale Restaurant, 580 U.S. Highway 101, Yachats; (541) 547–3399. Breakfast, lunch, and dinner offerings make this a popular place for both locals and travelers. Omelets, pancakes, burgers, sandwiches, chili, fish and chips, and salads are available all day. A variety of pies, made on the premises, is another excuse to stop for a break.

Drive north on US 101 to **Waldport** and stop at the **Alsea Bay Bridge Interpretive Center.** Once the bay was spanned by a classic 1937 bridge; it was replaced in 1991, and the interpretive center was opened to provide information and displays on bridge history, early road development, and the settlement of the Alsea Bay area.

A few miles north of Waldport, as you approach Seal Rock, you'll see a sign for **Art on the Rocks.** Stop here for a look at the works of local and international artists in jewelry, paintings, and photography. Semiprecious stones are sold as well.

The heart of the **Seal Rock** community is a collection of shops clustered near the General Store. Close by is **Collector's Choice Antiques** (541–563–4899), which is filled with antiques and collectibles—lots of nice glass and china. Nearby is another intriguing shop called **Purple Pelican Antiques** (541–563–4166).

Don't miss a browse through **Heart Song,** which sells fine glass bead jewelry and has an outstanding collection of ancient and modern beads from all over the world. Even if you're not excited about beads, you'll be fascinated by the information provided on the displays of rare trade beads.

Choose something sweet at SR Fudge N' Stuff (541–563–2766), which sells ice cream and luscious, handmade candies, and see the carved items at Seal Rock Wood Works. Tour Sea Gulch, if you're interested in chainsaw sculpture. This is a western-and-hillbilly theme park, with some 400 red-cedar carvings.

At **Ona Beach State Park,** on the estuary of Beaver Creek, there are picnic tables on the well-landscaped, wooded grounds.

Paved paths curve to a bridge that crosses the creek and leads to a wide, sandy beach with driftwood. Restrooms in the park have wheelchair access.

Continuing north, before crossing the high bridge over Yaquina Bay into **Newport,** stop at the **Oregon Coast Aquarium,** 2820 Southeast Ferryslip Road (541–867–3474), former home to Keiko, the orca whale that starred in the movie *Free Willy.* The state-of-the-art facility replicates the dunes, rocky pools, cliffs, and caves of coastal Oregon. Marine creatures native to the area live in pools and tanks that resemble their wild habitat. You'll see octopuses, tufted puffins, seals, sea otters, and a tank of lavender-pink jellyfish floating through the water in an elegant dance. There's also a touch tank of starfish and other tide-pool creatures. (Open daily except Christmas from 10:00 A.M. to 5:00 P.M. September through May and from 9:00 A.M. to 6:00 P.M. in the summer.)

The **Hatfield Marine Science Visitor Center,** 2030 Southeast Marine Science Drive (541–867–0271), is nearby, with more displays of Northwest sea life. The Center is part of Oregon State University's educational and research program and offers classes, workshops, and field trips. Open daily during the summer; closed Tuesday and Wednesday September through May.

LUNCH: Canyon Way Restaurant and Bookstore, 1216 Southwest Canyon Way; (541) 265–8319. Imaginative entrees, seafood, salads. Deli with soups, salads, sandwiches to go, espresso. Open 10:00 A.M. to 4:00 P.M. Dining room with full lunch and dinner. Lunch 11:00 A.M. to 3:00 P.M. Monday through Sunday and dinner 5:00 to 9:30 P.M. Outdoor terrace, gift shop, and bookstore.

Afternoon

Tour the **Old Bay Front,** where you can watch the fishing boats come and go, buy souvenirs, and, if tourist attractions appeal, see the Wax Works, Undersea

Gardens, and Ripley's Believe It Or Not. Alternatively, you might take a two-and-a-half-hour **whale-watching trip** or go crabbing in the bay with Newport Tradewinds, 653 Southwest Bay Boulevard (541–265–2101 or 800–676–7819). The company also offers longer trips for deep-sea fishing.

Turn east on U.S. Highway 20, a byway that follows Elk Creek to **Toledo.** If you have the time, stop at the Michael Gibbons Gallery and Studio to view the noted artist's landscape paintings. The gallery is in a former church rectory at 140 Northeast Alder (541–336–2797).

Continue on Route 20 to **Chitwood,** where you'll see an old-fashioned **covered bridge,** and on through the wooded hills and farmlands of the Willamette Valley to I–5. Turn north to take the freeway to Portland.

There's More

Dorris Ranch, 205 South Second Street and Dorris Avenue, Springfield; (541) 736–4544. The nation's first filbert orchard, and the oldest commercial filbert orchard still in operation, is also a living history farm on 250 acres. Tours every second and fourth Saturday, April through November. Nominal admission fee.

Drift Creek Wilderness, Waldport. Pocket wilderness in Siuslaw National Forest, contains some of the last of the coastal old-growth forest. Maps available at Waldport Ranger Station; (541) 563–3211.

Golf. Oakway Golf Course, 2000 Cal Young Road, Eugene; (541) 484–1927. Executive eighteen-hole course, no tee times required. Ocean Dunes Golf Links, 3345 Munsel Lake Road, Florence; (800) 468–4833 or (541) 997–3232. Nine-hole course by the sand dunes, "Oregon's biggest sand trap." Sandpines Golf Course, 1201 Thirty-fifth Street, Florence; (800) 917–4653. Eighteen-hole course, one of Lane County's largest, built on sand dunes. Open year-round.

Gwynn Creek Trail, Cape Perpetua, just a few minutes south of Yachats. Easily accessible and beautiful walk from Cape Perpetua Visitors' Center. Climbs Gwynn Creek Canyon, through old-growth stands of Douglas fir and Sitka spruce. Full loop, 6½ miles. Siuslaw National Forest; (541) 563–3211.

Hiking, running, canoeing, white-water rafting. All are available in or near Eugene and Springfield. Check with the Association of Lane County, Oregon, for specific places and arrangements.

Lane County Ice, Lane County Fairgrounds, 796 West Thirteenth Avenue, Eugene; (541) 682–3614. Full-size arena ice rink, open daily.

Lively Park Swim Center, 6100 Thurston Road, Springfield; (541) 736–4244. Indoor water fun in surf of 4-foot waves, 136-foot open flume water slide. Spa, kiddy pool.

Oregon Air and Space Museum, 90377 Boeing Drive, Eugene; (541) 461–1101. Located at the south end of Eugene Airport. The Oregon Air and Space Musuem displays various aircraft and artifacts depicting the history of aviation and space technology. Among the displays are a swept-wing single-seat jet fighter used in Korea; a single-seat three-winged World War I fighter; and a Nieuport 17 World War I single-seat fighter built by the French.

Saturday Market, Eighth and Oak Streets, Eugene. Near the Market District, an outdoor array of booths—a great place to stroll and shop on a Saturday between April and mid-November.

Siuslaw River cruises, P.O. Box 2831, Florence, OR 97439; (541) 997–9691. Aboard the *Westward Ho!,* a half-scale replica of a stern-wheeler that once plied the Columbia River. Frontier theme, costumes, entertainment, dinner cruises. One-hour tours depart from Old Town dock in Florence.

Special Events

February. Oregon Dune Mushers Annual Mail Run, Horsfall Beach to Florence. Dogsled teams run 72 miles through sand dunes.

Late February. Seafood and Wine Festival, Newport.

Summer. Oregon Festival of American Music, Jacqua Concert Hall and Cuthbert Ampitheater, Eugene; (541) 434–7000. Regional performances of American classic music.

June/July. Oregon Bach Festival, Eugene. Two weeks of music by world-famous performers. Concerts, workshops, lectures, dance.

Mid-July. Oregon Country Fair, Veneta. Arts and crafts in the woods near Eugene. Food, music.

August. Jazz on the Water Festival, Newport. Top names in jazz perform at waterfront setting.

September. Chowder, Blues and Brews Festival, Florence. A chowder cook-off, food booths, microbrews, and top blues bands.

Other Recommended Restaurants and Lodgings

Eugene

Café Zenon, 898 Pearl Street; (541) 343–3005. A landmark bistro in downtown Eugene. Eclectic, ever-changing international menu, using fresh local ingredients. Open daily for breakfast, lunch, dinner, and late-night desserts and small plates. Dessert selection is deliciously varied.

Campus Inn, 390 East Broadway; (800) 888–6313. Clean rooms are equipped with dataport phones (with free local calls) and DSL high-speed Internet connections. A Nautilus Fitness Center makes the inn a good choice for those who have been on the road for days. Numerous restaurants and shopping are within easy walking distance, and a complimentary continental breakfast is available.

Pookie's Bed 'n' Breakfast, 2013 Charnelton Street; (541) 343–0383 or (800) 558–0383. Two guest rooms and one suite in nicely restored 1918 home. Residential neighborhood, close to downtown and campus, full or continental breakfast included.

Florence

The River House, 1202 Bay Street; (888) 824–2750. Ideally located on the Siuslaw River in Old Town Florence. Views of boat traffic and river life. Gift shops and restaurants just steps away.

Blue Heron Inn Bed and Breakfast, 6563 Highway 126, P.O. Box 1122, Florence, OR 97439; (541) 997–4091 or (800) 997–7780. A 1940s country home, just five minutes from historic Florence. Offers five nicely decorated rooms with private baths; two with jetted tubs. Spectacular views of the Siuslaw River and wildlife from dining area. Gourmet breakfast might include fresh tropical fruit, homemade yeast waffles smothered with strawberries, or smoked salmon quiche.

Newport

Sylvia Beach Hotel, 267 Northwest Cliff; (541) 265–5428 or (888) 795–8422. Unique hotel on a cliff above Nye Beach, with rooms dedicated to and furnished in accordance with various authors. Restaurant, library, gift shop, ocean views.

The Whale's Tale, 452 Southwest Bay Boulevard; (541) 265–8660. On the bayfront. Known for flavorful omelets and poppyseed pancakes. Light fare and seafood entrees; especially recommended for breakfast.

Seal Rock

Yuzen, 1011 Coast Highway 101 NW; (541) 563–4766. Highly reputed Japanese cuisine. Casual atmosphere, booths and tables, Japanese decor.

Yachats

Adobe Resort, 1555 U.S. Highway 101; (541) 547–3141 or (800) 522–3623. Popular resort at the edge of a rocky shore. Restaurant, lounge, great views.

For More Information

Convention and Visitors Association of Lane County, Oregon, 754 Olive Street, Eugene, OR 97401; (541) 484–5307 or (800) 547–5445; www.cvalco.org.

Florence Area Chamber of Commerce, 290 U.S. Highway 101, P.O. Box 26000, Florence, OR 97439; (541) 997–3128 or (800) 524–4864; www.florencechamber .com.

Greater Newport Chamber of Commerce, 555 Southwest Coast Highway, Newport, OR 97365; (541) 265–8801 or (800) 262–7844; www.newportchamber.org.

Yachats Area Chamber of Commerce, 241 U.S. Highway 101, P.O. Box 728, Yachats, OR 97498; (541) 547–3530 or (800) 929–0477; www.yachats.org.

PORTLAND ESCAPE THREE

Mount Hood Loop

Circling Oregon's Highest Peak / 1 Night

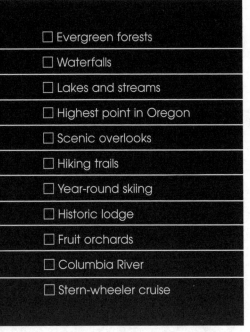

- ☐ Evergreen forests
- ☐ Waterfalls
- ☐ Lakes and streams
- ☐ Highest point in Oregon
- ☐ Scenic overlooks
- ☐ Hiking trails
- ☐ Year-round skiing
- ☐ Historic lodge
- ☐ Fruit orchards
- ☐ Columbia River
- ☐ Stern-wheeler cruise

From Portland, Mount Hood's peak is a familiar presence, looming 60 miles away on the eastern horizon behind hazy, blue-green foothills. At 11,235 feet, its summit is the highest point in Oregon.

Circling around this massive, broad-shouldered volcano takes you through some of the state's most spectacular scenery, from the lush green fir forests west of the Cascade Range to the ponderosa pines, ranchlands, and acres of orchards on the east. On the mountain's north side, the wide Columbia River flows westward, fed by streams from Hood's snowfields.

A two-day loop tour is a satisfying excursion into this world of natural wonder. This itinerary, designed as a summer trip, combines vigorous recreation with restful sightseeing. It takes you up on the mountain, into the orchards, and out on the water. With a few changes, you can enjoy many of its features in winter, substituting ski slopes or groomed trails for forest walks.

Day 1 / *Morning*

From Portland take U.S. Route 26 east toward **Sandy.** Have a light breakfast before you leave home to save room for lunch at **Calamity Jane's Hamburger Restaurant,** 42015 Highway 26, Sandy (503–668–7817). Meals are a real bargain for such enormous portions and consistent quality. Most customers are unable to finish the burgers, and many split these one-pound monsters, which are served in cast-iron skillets with fries.

Five and a half miles east of Sandy, stop at the **Oregon Candy Farm,** 48620 Southeast Highway 26 (503–668–5066), to appease your sweet tooth. For more than fifty years, the candy makers, who began their enterprise in Portland, have been selling handmade chocolates and other candies. Watch the candy-making

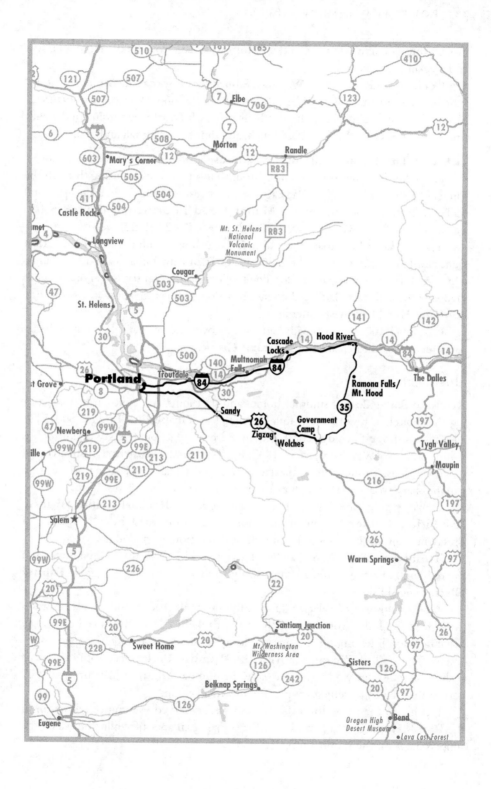

process through glass windows in the factory weekdays from 9:00 A.M. to 5:00 P.M. and weekend afternoons.

Continue on Route 26 to **Welches.** Stop at the Resort at the Mountain, 68010 East Fairway Avenue (503–622–3101 or 800–669–7666). The Resort features a blend of Scottish collectibles, Highland scenery, fresh Northwest cuisine, and a cozy fireside lounge. Open for breakfast, lunch, and dinner during fall and spring.

LUNCH: The Tartans Pub and Steakhouse at the Resort at the Mountain.

From Welches, the road rises into Mount Hood's foothills, cutting through the forests of fir and hemlock to **Zigzag** (18 miles east of Sandy). Pick up maps and trail information along the way at **Mount Hood Information Center,** 65000 East Highway 26 in Welches (503–622–4822 or 888–622–4822).

Take the **Lolo Pass** road north from Zigzag about 4 miles to Road 1825. Turn right and follow the signs to the trailhead for **Ramona Falls,** a 6.8-mile round-trip hike from the lower parking lot. The trail crosses the **Sandy River** and ascends gradually through forestland and open sandy slopes above the river canyon to one of Mount Hood's prettiest waterfalls.

Cascading 100 feet in broad, misty sheets over mossy rocks, Ramona splashes past green ferns into clear, cold **Ramona Creek.**

Afternoon

Return to Route 26 past summer homes and ski cabins, and continue east, ascending the mountain toward the 6-mile spur road to **Timberline Lodge** (800–547–1406; www.timberlinelodge.com). The grand old lodge, built as a Works Progress Administration (WPA) project in 1937, is a **National Historic Landmark.** Its wood carvings, wrought iron, massive beams, and tribal-motif fabrics make it an extraordinary work of art as well as a significant piece of Northwest history.

Don't miss the fine display of craftsmanship in the **Rachael Griffin Historic Exhibition Center** on the main floor. It's accompanied by a recording of President Franklin D. Roosevelt's speech of dedication at the lodge.

Timberline is the second-oldest developed ski area in the United States and the only one offering summer skiing. In mid-July you can ride the lift up **Palmer Glacier** and ski down.

After (or instead of) glacier skiing, stroll the trails that extend in several directions from the lodge. You are literally at the timberline, so if you head down the mountain you'll be among the trees; walk up its slopes and you're in open, rocky terrain. The trail to **Zigzag Canyon** and **Paradise Park** offers both, as well as rushing streams and wildflower meadows in summer. You may have time to walk part of the trail to a scenic viewpoint above the canyon.

Return to the lodge for a shower and well-deserved evening of relaxation in the **Ram's Head Bar,** a perfect spot for enjoying an aperitif while you watch the sunset's glow on the mountaintop.

DINNER: Cascades Dining Room (503–622–7979), Timberline Lodge. American and Continental dinners served by candlelight.

LODGING: Timberline Lodge, Timberline; (503) 222–2211 or (877) 754–6734. For reservations from Portland, call (503) 231–5400; (800) 547–1406 nationwide toll-free number. Classic mountain lodge and ski resort on Mount Hood's south flank.

Day 2 / Morning

BREAKFAST: Cascades Dining Room (503–622–7979).

Drive back to U.S. Route 26, and head east to State Route 35, which winds northeast around the mountain toward the **Columbia River Gorge.** Near the spot where **Pacific Crest National Scenic Trail** crosses the highway, you'll come to **Barlow Pass.** The pass was named for pioneer Sam Barlow, who developed a toll road around the south side of Mount Hood in 1846. Until then, wagon trains on the Oregon Trail took the precarious Columbia River passage to reach the western side of the Cascades.

Crossing the **White River** (the canyon here is a favorite among cross-country skiers), continue on Route 35 to **Bennett Pass** (elevation 4,670 feet) and the road to **Mount Hood Meadows Ski Area** (503–227–SNOW). This is the largest ski development on the mountain, with numerous lifts and runs. It's also a focus of controversy, as developers seek to expand the facilities.

The East Fork of the Hood River runs by the ski area, beginning in a glacier high on the mountain and coursing down the slopes to create **Umbrella Falls** and, closer to the main road, **Sahalie Falls.** Easy walks take you through the forest to either falls; a longer hike of 1.7 miles connects them.

If you take the detour loop road to Sahalie Falls, you'll come to **Hood River Meadows,** the biggest meadow on Mount Hood, spangled with the colors of wildflowers in late spring.

As the East Fork turns due north, so does the road, crossing brooks that rush down ravines into the river. Shortly after passing Sherwood Campground, you'll come to a parking area for East Fork Trail 650, the **Tamanawas Falls Trail.** The 2-mile trail is a classic for Northwest scenery as it follows bouncy Cold Spring Creek, shaded by tall evergreens, through a narrow canyon to a waterfall that cascades 100 feet.

After your two-hour, round-trip hike, take Route 35 to the turnoff to **Cooper Spur** (541–352–6692), a high ridge between Eliot and Newton Clark glaciers. It's about 2¼ miles in from the road.

Drive 6 miles beyond it to **Inspiration Point,** where you'll have a stunning view of the upper **Hood River Valley** and the mountain's north side, with **Wallalute Falls** cascading down from Eliot Glacier.

Still farther—about 11 miles from The Inn at Cooper Spur—is **Cloud Cap Inn,** a starting point for climbers just below Eliot Glacier. The rustic log hotel, constructed in 1889 and now a National Historic Site, is anchored by cables to resist winter storms. The crisp air and incomparable scenery have drawn visitors for over a century. Early travelers to the inn rode the train to Hood River, then paid $12.50 for a six-hour ride in an open coach, with two changes of horses on the way. The first automobile to reach Cloud Cap Inn was a 1907 Cadillac. Now maintained by the Crag Rats, a mountain-climbing and rescue organization, Cloud Cap Inn is not open to the public.

The entire Cloud Cap/Tilly Jane area is a National Historic District. Other points of interest include the Tilly Jane Forest Camp, the American Legion Camp, and the massive public shelter built by the Civilian Conservation Corps in 1939. China Fill memorializes the Chinese laborers who toiled with picks to dig and grade the old wagon road in 1889.

LUNCH: The Inn at Cooper Spur, 10755 Cooper Spur Road, Mount Hood; (541) 352–6692. Homey mountainside restaurant, part of a small resort. Open for lunch Saturday and Sunday. Try the homemade soups and award-winning pie.

A lunch alternative is a picnic on the trail.

Afternoon

Now Route 35, still edging the East Fork, begins its descent into the lush, fertile Hood River Valley, winding through fragrant apple, pear, and cherry orchards. In spring the fields in blossom are as snow-white as the mountain slopes behind them; in autumn the air carries the heady scent of cider.

Stop at **Mount Hood Country Store** (503–352–6024), in the small community of Mount Hood, to browse through an old-fashioned country market. Fresh produce, gourmet foods, Northwest wines, and gifts are sold in a nostalgic setting. It's a good place for ice cream on a hot day.

Farther north, drive 1½ miles off the highway to **Panorama Point** for a wide valley vista, with lofty Mount Hood in the background. It's a froth of white in spring but equally beautiful in autumn, when orchard foliage glows yellow-gold and the maples and tamaracks turn rust and orange, with the occasional scarlet-tinged sumac sparking the fall tones. At harvest time, roadside stands are full of produce.

It's a short drive from Panorama Point to **Hood River.**

Turn west on Interstate 84, and you're in the heart of the **Columbia River Gorge.** In this geological wonder, much of it a designated **National Scenic Area,** the wide Columbia flows on your right. On the left, dancing waterfalls spray from steep cliffs and great basaltic masses exposed by ancient floods. On the ridges around them, thick forests shield a network of hiking trails.

For more activities and attractions in Hood River and for more detail on waterfalls and exploring the gorge, see Portland Escape Six.

Continuing west, you'll pass **Oxbow Salmon Hatchery,** which is open to the public. When you reach **Cascade Locks,** drive to the riverside **Marine Park.** The grassy, tree-shaded park has play equipment, remnants of the old boat locks (used before dam construction made them unnecessary), a museum, and the Oregon Pony, the first steam locomotive built on the Pacific Coast. In the visitor information center there are a gift shop, historic photographs of early stern-wheeler days, and 50-cent showers—a boon to hikers fresh off the numerous trails in the gorge.

The Pacific Crest Trail passes through Cascade Locks in **Bridge of the Gods Park.** The Bridge of the Gods, spanning the Columbia, was built in 1926 and raised in 1938 to provide clearance when Bonneville Dam was built. Indian legend says that long ago a natural bridge of stone stretched across the gorge near here.

From the wharf at Marine Park, the ***Columbia Gorge*** stern-wheeler leaves three times a day in summer for two-hour cruises on the river. A hundred years ago stern-wheelers carried passengers and cargo between Portland and The Dalles. Today a 330-ton, three-deck replica of a river paddleboat provides a chance to step into that colorful bygone era. Dinner, dance, and sunset cruises are available.

DINNER: Aboard the ***Portland Spirit*** (Columbia Gorge stern-wheeler). Dine on an old-fashioned riverboat as it churns past the gorge's magnificent forests and towering basaltic cliffs. Dinner cruises, available June–October, range from ninety minutes to three hours. For information and reservations: 1200 Northwest Naito Parkway, Suite 110, Portland; (800) 224–3901; www.sternwheeler.com.

From Cascade Locks, it's a thirty-minute drive west on I–84 to Portland.

The stern-wheeler Columbia Gorge *navigates the majestic Columbia River.*

There's More

Fishing. Hood River Marina. Smallmouth bass.

Lost Lake, Mount Hood. Picture-perfect mountain lake with rainbow and German brown trout. One of the most photographed lakes in the nation.

Luhr Jensen & Sons, Inc., P.O. Box 297, 400 Portway Avenue, Hood River, OR 97031; (503) 386–3811. Located on the banks of the Columbia River at the Port of Hood River industrial site. Offers a wide array of high-quality fishing equipment and clothing.

Mouth of Hood River. Steelhead run in spring, October, and January.

Mount Hood Railroad. Scenic train excursions through the Hood River Valley, mid-April through November, 110 Railroad Avenue, Hood River; (541) 386–3556 or (800) 872–4661; mthoodrr@gorge.net. Reservations recommended.

Mushroom collecting, spring and fall. Mushrooms grow in profusion in Mount Hood's forests. The ranger station has information on the best locations to search. Chanterelles, shaggy manes, boletus, morels, and other exotic species are easy to find; but several poisonous varieties grow here as well. Do not eat mushrooms unless you're certain they are safe. Permits for mushroom picking are required in Mount Hood National Forest and Columbia River Gorge Scenic Area.

Special Events

April. Blossom Festival, Hood River Valley. Orchard tours, arts-and-crafts sales, train rides on the Fruit Blossom Special.

July. Sandy Mountain Festival, Sandy. Celebration of Sandy's pioneer heritage. Folk music, food booths, arts and crafts.

August. Mount Hood Festival of Jazz, Gresham; (503) 219–9833. Nationally acclaimed jazz series with top musicians playing outdoors at Mount Hood Community College.

October. Hood River Valley Harvest Fest, Hood River. Crafts booths, foods, local produce, wines.

Other Recommended Restaurants and Lodgings

Government Camp

Falcon's Crest Inn, 87287 Government Camp Loop Highway, P.O. Box 185, 97028; (503) 272–3403 or (800) 624–7384; www.falconscrest.com. Chalet-style mountain home and lodge with five suites. Full breakfast. Walking distance to Ski Bowl, largest nighttime skiing area in the United States.

Sandy

The Elusive Trout Pub, 39333 Proctor Boulevard; (503) 668–7884. Pub selling microbrewed ales, lagers on tap, and foods prepared with care.

Wasson Brothers Winery, 17020 Ruben Lane; (503) 668–3124. Open for tastings and tours 9:00 A.M. to 5:00 P.M. daily.

Welches

The Resort at the Mountain, 68010 East Fairway Avenue; (503) 622–3101 or (800) 669–7666. Luxury resort with twenty-seven-hole golf course on Salmon River.

Zigzag

Zigzag Inn, East Highway 26; (503) 622–4779. Delightful, vintage atmosphere in a 1927 log cabin that, by contrast, boasts a covered, heated deck. Serves burgers, steaks, pasta, and pizza.

For More Information

Hood River County Chamber of Commerce, 405 Portway, Hood River, OR 97031; (541) 386–2000 or (800) 366–3530; www.hoodriver.org.

Mount Hood Area Chamber of Commerce, 24403 East Welches Road, Suite 103, Welches, OR 97067; (503) 622–3017 or (888) 622–4822; www.mthood.org.

Sandy Area Chamber of Commerce, 38775 Pioneer Boulevard, Sandy, OR 97055; (503) 668–4006; www.sandyoregonchamber.org.

PORTLAND ESCAPE FOUR

Around Mount St. Helens

Exploring the Volcano / 1 Night

- [ ] Mount St. Helens National Volcanic Monument
- [ ] Volcano museum
- [ ] Devastation area
- [ ] Hiking trails
- [ ] Views of Spirit Lake and crater
- [ ] Scenic lake
- [ ] Picturesque river
- [ ] Longest lava tube in the United States

Before May 18, 1980, Mount St. Helens was a pristine, symmetrical white peak, the queen of the Cascade range. But mighty forces were brewing beneath that serene exterior. After two months of minor explosions and earthquakes, the mountain erupted in a blast of rock, ash, gas, and steam.

Within ten minutes of the eruption, an immense plume of pumice and ash leaped 13.6 miles into the atmosphere and continued roaring upward for nine hours. The volume of ash fall could have buried a football field to a depth of 150 miles. Mount St. Helens' height dropped from 9,677 feet to 8,363 feet, with a crater more than 2,000 feet deep.

When the summit and north flank collapsed in a giant landslide, a huge lateral blast blew sideways, obliterating or knocking down trees. Rock and melting ice created mudflows in the stream valleys, uprooting 150 square miles of trees and tearing out bridges and houses. The devastation left a landscape bleak and gray.

Geologists say the probability of Mount St. Helens producing an eruption of debris or mudflow is small. However, hikers need to exercise caution when crossing the gullies and streams draining the mountain, especially on the north side. Forest visitors near the volcano need to be prepared for potential ash fall. The U.S. Forest Service routinely posts special conditions and closures on its Web site. Before visiting, travelers should either visit www.fs.fed.us/gpnf/mshnvm/ or call (360) 274–0962 for changes in conditions.

The east side of the mountain is open from Memorial Day until snow closes the roads in October, but you can still do a day trip up the west side of the mountain in winter. On the summer loop trip described here, you spend one day on the west side and one day on the east side of Mount St. Helens. This tour touches the highlights and will give you a sense of the awesome power that changed the struc-

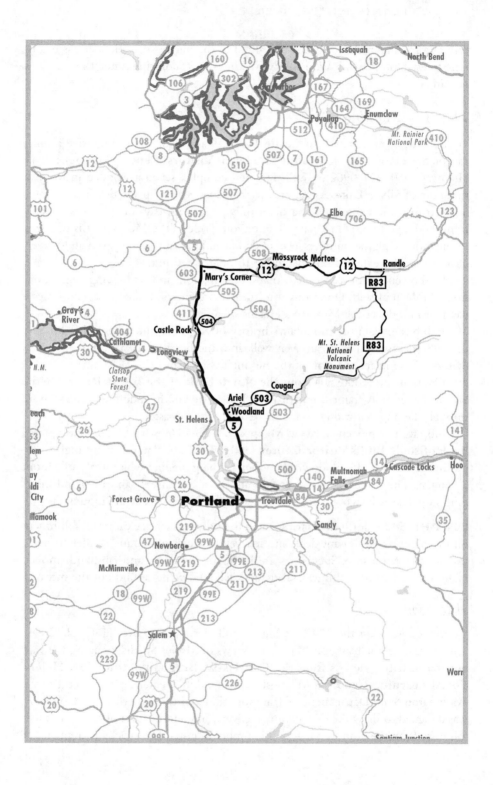

ture of a mountain. As you walk, be careful of the fragile vegetation that is beginning to establish new life. Wear sturdy walking shoes and bring water; there are few resources.

Day 1 / Morning

Head north on Interstate 5 to **Castle Rock,** Washington (exit 49). Drive 5 miles east on State Route 504 to **Mount St. Helens Visitors' Center,** 3029 Spirit Lake Highway (360–274–0962), a well-designed complex set in a wooded grove near the shore of **Silver Lake.** As national park budgets swing up and down with political fortunes, the center may be open only on certain days of the week, usually from 9:00 A.M. to 5:00 P.M. daily. The ongoing rule in the Monument is to check for new times, phone numbers, events, and facilities. Trails (some paved and wheelchair accessible) extend from the center through the forest.

In the center you can obtain maps, information, and sightseeing suggestions from the helpful staff. Don't miss the theater presentation, shown several times a day, that introduces the Mount St. Helens story.

Exhibits explain the mountain's history of eruptions and graphically illustrate the 1980 devastation. You can even walk into the heart of the volcano—a replica that gives a simulated version of the mountain's interior.

Continue on Route 504 along the **North Fork of the Toutle River.** On the way you'll see an A-frame home that was half-buried in the mudflow; you can walk through the dug-out rooms to see the effects of the disaster.

Stop for magnificent views at Milepost 27, where Cowlitz County has opened the **Hoffstadt Bluffs Visitor Center** (360–274–7750). You can stand high above the Toutle River and look down the valley to the glistening white flanks of Mount St. Helens. The center offers a few exhibits, but it is primarily an eating and shopping stop. Take a helicopter ride from here for a closer look at the mountain.

LUNCH: Hoffstadt Bluffs Visitor Center, the only full-service eating establishment on the highway. A pleasant deck and marvelous views of Mount St. Helens make this spot worth a stop. Specialties are barbecued chicken and ribs, and smoked salmon corn chowder. Burgers, salads, and deli sandwiches round out the menu.

Afternoon

Continue east across the 370-foot-high, ½-mile-long bridge over Hoffstadt Creek. You are now in the blast zone. There are views of Mount St. Helens along the way, but the next big view is from the **Charles W. Bingham Mount St. Helens Forest Learning Center** at Milepost 33. This exhibit center, a joint project of the Washington State Department of Transportation and the Weyerhaeuser Company, was designed to show the destruction, recovery, and reforestation of the area. It tells the story from the point of view of the lumber industry. The Rocky Mountain Elk

Foundation has joined this project to help provide views of the elk herds in the valley below the center.

At Milepost 43, which is almost the end of the road, you will find the 6,000-square-foot **Coldwater Ridge Visitor Center** (360–274–2114), facing the volcano crater and with spectacular views of Coldwater Lake. It is open daily year-round, 10:00 A.M. to 6:00 P.M. May through September; until 5:00 P.M. in winter. See the film and learn how many plants and animals have reappeared since the great blast.

Grab an espresso from the adjacent restaurant, and join a ranger for a **Coldwater Ridge Deck Talk.** Follow the ¼-mile **Winds of Change Interpretative Trail** to see how life has emerged from the ashes. Take the barrier-free **Birth of a Lake Trail** to the boardwalk over Coldwater Lake, which was created when debris from the eruption blocked the Coldwater River.

The very end of the road, just beyond the center, has been reserved for the **Johnston Ridge Observatory,** which is open from 10:00 A.M. to 6:00 P.M. in summer.

Ask the park rangers about road conditions on the east side of the mountain. Heavy floods washed out roads and bridges in the mid-1990s, and recovery has been slow. If the east side of the Monument is closed to traffic, you may want to return 43 miles down State Route 504 to Castle Rock and drive an hour home to Portland. This west side of the mountain makes a great day trip.

If you are going on to the east side of the mountain, turn north on I–5 and east again on Highway 12 to **Mary's Corner.** (Shortcut: Turn north off Route 504 before you get to Castle Rock and follow State Route 505 through Toledo to Mary's Corner.) One of the state's first homesteads, **Jackson House,** is in this little community and is occasionally open to the public.

In **Lewis and Clark State Park,** Mary's Corner, you can walk in one of the last stands of **old-growth forest** along the Portland-Seattle corridor. Many of the Douglas fir, hemlock, and cedar trees are 500 years old.

Follow Route 12 east to **Mossyrock,** a small town set in a beguiling valley of farms and rolling green hills. Wild blackberry vines arch over sagging wood fences along this road, and Queen Anne's lace grows tall against red barns. There are acres of Christmas trees, tulip fields, and blueberries. This is logging country, too, and you'll see hills shorn of trees.

East of town there's a view of **Mossyrock Dam;** at 606 feet it's the highest dam in Washington. The dam created **Riffe Lake,** a 23-mile lake stocked with coho and brown trout. Fishing, boating, and sailboarding are popular here.

Morton, a longtime logging town 31 miles east of Mary's Corner, is famous for its annual rough-and-tumble logging show.

D I N N E R: Carter's Country Roadhouse Inn, Highway 12 and Crumb Road; (360) 496–5029. Located 1 mile west of Morton, the inn serves steak and seafood dinners, plus breakfast and lunch.

LODGING: St. Helens Manor House, 7476 Highway 12; (360) 498–5243 or (800) 551–3290. Bed-and-breakfast with four rooms in 1910-era home on wooded grounds at the western end of Riffe Lake.

Day 2 / Morning

Enjoy a full breakfast at St. Helens Manor House. Then explore a few sites in Morton.

The **Lewis County Historical Museum,** 599 Northwest Front Way (360–496–6446), is filled with pioneer relics.

It's 17 miles from Morton to **Randle.** Along the route you may spot hang gliders riding the wind currents on Dog Mountain. At Randle, turn south on Forest Road 25.

In 9 miles you'll come to Forest Road 26. Pass this road by, remaining on Forest Road 25 for 11 miles until you reach Road 99. Turn west on the two-lane, paved road. Starting in deep green forest, it leads into the blast area that appears to be one of total destruction but if you look closely, you'll see evidence of life's beginnings in the small plants.

Your first stop is at **Bear Meadow,** famous as the site where photographs were taken of the 1980 eruption as it occurred. Trails, picnic areas, and restrooms are in this area.

Nine miles in, at the junction of Forest Roads 99 and 26, you'll see the **Miner's Car.** The 1973 Grand Prix, resting atop downed trees, was hurled 50 feet during the eruption and then placed in its present location.

Meta Lake Trail 210 begins 100 yards west of Miner's Car, off Road 99. This is the only trail offering barrier-free access into the blast zone. A naturalist leads a walk and explains the changing environment, usually at midmorning and again in midafternoon. Check the summer schedules for times and events. On the ⅛-mile, level paved path, you'll see small trees that survived the eruption, just 8½ miles away, because they were protected by snow and ice. Birds and insects have returned, and in **Meta Lake,** at the end of the trail, trout, salamanders, and frogs now live.

Three miles from Meta Lake Trail, at **Independence Pass,** Trail 227 leads to striking views of the mountain, the crater with its growing lava dome, and **Spirit Lake.** Ascend to walk the ridge for ¼ mile, and you'll have views in all directions of the blown-down trees and acres of ash-covered slopes.

If you hike 1½ miles to a Spirit Lake overlook, you'll find interpretive signs pointing out the locations of buried campgrounds, Harry Truman's lodge, and cabins on the shores of the lake.

Spirit Lake, once a crystal-clear alpine gem, is regaining its blue clarity. The lateral blast was moving fast when it snapped off thousands of trees. The slower landslide sludge hit the lake and swooshed back uphill to wash the trees back into the basin. Many of those trees still float in the lake; others have sunk and caught on the bottom, perhaps to become a future petrified forest.

Farther on, the trail narrows and passes rock pinnacles, eventually joining **Norway Pass Trail.**

Walk Trail 227 back to Forest Road 99, and drive deeper into the National Monument; in 4 miles you'll reach the end of the road at **Windy Ridge Viewpoint,** which is as close as you can drive to the crater. A parking area is on the edge of the restricted zone, which can be entered only with a permit, but you can hike without a permit if you stay on the trail.

On one side you'll notice a sand-ladder trail against a slope. If you climb the stair-step path to the top of the hill, you'll have a good vantage point into the great, often-steaming crater and devastated area.

Retrace your route back to Forest Road 25, and turn south. Drive 25 miles to join Forest Road 90 at **Swift Reservoir,** a long lake south of Mount St. Helens. The lake has a boat launch, picnic and camping grounds, and some tourist facilities. Take Road 90 to Road 83, turning north to drive 2 miles to the **Trail of Two Forests,** one of the best barrier-free trails for wheelchairs. One forest is an echo of the past; the other is of living, growing lodgepole pines.

An easy, ¼-mile-loop boardwalk (protecting the fragile mosses and plants growing on the lava) passes 2,000-year-old tree molds, formed when a lava flow consumed the forest that once stood here. Interpretive signs tell the tale of the two forests.

Next, take Road 8303 to **Ape Cave,** so called because it was discovered in 1951 by members of a club nicknamed the Mount St. Helens Apes. The cave, formed by an eruption 2,000 years ago, is 12,810 feet long—the longest lava tube in the continental United States. Lanterns and guided trips are usually available. Wear a jacket, carry two light sources, and wear sturdy shoes. It's 42 degrees Fahrenheit year-round.

Ape Cave has two routes to explore. The lower cave, ¾ mile long and fairly level, is easiest and has unique features such as a "lava ball" wedged in the ceiling. Allow one and a quarter hours round-trip. The more challenging upper cave has large rock piles to climb and an 8-foot lava fall.

Back on Road 83, turn northeast and travel 9 miles to **Lahar Viewpoint,** which provides a look at the southeast side of the mountain. A short trail leads to an interpretive sign that portrays the path of the lahar (mudflow).

Drive another ¾ mile past the parking lot to the **Muddy River,** and you'll notice the bright colors of stratigraphy bands on the stream bank. With the hill sliced away by debris racing down the channel of Shoestring Glacier, deposits from previous eruptions were revealed. The lower, bright yellow layer was deposited 8,000 to 13,000 years ago.

Return on Road 83 to Road 90 at the western shore of Swift Reservoir. This is one of three reservoirs created by dams on the **Lewis River.**

Drive 8 miles to the town of **Cougar,** on **Yale Reservoir,** a lake known for its outstanding Dolly Varden trout fishing. Stop in at **Cougar Ceramics,** 16834

Lewis River Road (360–238–5371), where Lynn and Dave Birch create smooth, marbled works of Mount St. Helens ash. They were among the first to use local volcanic ash in ceramics. Many of their pieces have become collectors' items.

Travel 5 miles south to **Ariel** on State Route 503 to **Jack's Store and Restaurant,** 13411 Lewis River Road (360–231–4276). Travelers traditionally purchase supplies here for camping, fishing, and hunting, and it's one of the places where climbers had been able to sign in before beginning their trek up Mount St. Helens.

LUNCH: Jack's Store and Restaurant. This is logger country; omelets and hamburgers are the size of platters. You may also picnic along the way to Cougar or enjoy a snack at the concession stand at Spirit Lake.

Afternoon

Drive Route 503 west, along **Lake Merwin's** northern shore, 23 miles to **Woodland.** The visitor center here sells souvenirs and such gifts as emerald obsidianite, a gemlike stone made from heat-fused volcanic rock; the center also provides maps and helpful information.

From Woodland it's a 30-mile drive south on I–5 to Portland.

There's More

Camping. Beaver Bay Park (503–813–6666), east of Cougar on Lewis River Road. Boat launch, fishing, RV sites.

Cougar Park and Campground (360–238–5224). Tents only. Swimming, boat launch, fishing.

Lewis River RV Park, 3125 Lewis River Road, Woodland, WA; (360) 225–9556. On North Fork Lewis River. Tent sites, swimming pool, picnic supplies, boat rentals. Near golf course.

Swift Camp Pacific Power Company and Recreation Facility (503–813–6666), east end of Swift Reservoir. Tent sites available.

Chief Lelooska Living History Presentation, 165 Merwin Village Road, Ariel; (360) 225–9522. Colorful, evocative, educational programs on Northwest Coastal Indian culture. Ceremonial dances, masks, songs, stories. Afternoon performances for school groups; occasional evening performances. Native American art and artifacts displayed in Exhibit Hall.

Climbing. As long as the growth of the new lava dome inside the crater of Mount St. Helens is in progress, the mountain is closed to climbing. Existing climbing permits have been canceled, and Jack's Store and Restaurant has discontinued issuing new permits. A number of trails in the Mount St. Helens National Volcanic

Monument have also been closed, so call the Climbing Hotline at (360) 247–3961 or visit the Mount St. Helens National Volcanic Monument Web site at www.fs.fed.us/gpnf/mshnvm/.

Hopkins Hill. Four miles west of Morton, the hill provides a commanding view of the Mount St. Helens crater and, often, a column of steam.

Special Events

Mid-August. Loggers' Jubilee, Morton, WA. Parades, carnival, arts and crafts, bed races, quilting exhibition, logging skills competition: tree fallers, logrollers, wood-choppers.

Other Recommended Restaurants and Lodgings

Cougar

Lone Fir Resort, 16806 Lewis River Road; (360) 238–5210. Nothing fancy, but fifteen motel units, five with kitchens, are clean and well kept. Swimming pool, laundry facilities, RV sites with hookups.

Morton

The Seasons Motel, 200 Westlake; (360) 496–6835. New, modern motel with fifty spacious rooms.

For More Information

Mount St. Helens Visitor Center, 3029 Spirit Lake Highway, Castle Rock, WA 98611; (360) 274–0962; www.fs.fed.us/gpnf/mshnvm/. Call for road conditions before attempting to drive into the National Monument area.

PORTLAND ESCAPE FIVE

Astoria and Long Beach Water Pleasures

Explore by River and Sea / 3 Nights

When you cross the bridge from Astoria, Oregon, to the recreational pleasures of Long Beach in southwestern Washington, you become part of the great water show of the West. The native canoes and explorers' boats have gone, but the freighters and pleasure boats still ride the broad, 1,000-mile-long Columbia River across that treacherous bar to the Pacific.

Today's travelers cross the Columbia to play on wide beaches and sand dunes around Long Beach, home to gourmet dining, good fishing, raucous kid fun, and a quiet historic village. A three-day loop trip northwest from Portland to Astoria and Long Beach combines the vivid life of the river with the lazier life of the beach.

- ☐ Columbia River views
- ☐ Sandy beaches
- ☐ Pioneer museums
- ☐ Early explorers' fort
- ☐ Lighthouses
- ☐ 28-mile beach
- ☐ Ocean views
- ☐ Seaside resort town

Day 1 / Morning

Drive U.S. Route 30 west to the 10-block historic district that edges the Columbia in one of Oregon's oldest settlements, **St. Helens.** Visit the handsome Georgian Revival courthouse and pioneer museum. Watch river life from the old-fashioned gazebo, brick viewing platform, picnic tables, or boat facilities at **Columbia View Park.**

Give into temptation, and try the warm Danish pastries, maple bars, and doughnuts at the **Home Bakery Co.,** an authentic Finnish bakery located on the east end of Astoria, at 2845 Marine Drive (503–325–4631). For a full breakfast or brunch, the **Sunnyside Café** (1 Sixth Street, Astoria; 503–325–8642) serves three-egg scrambles with potato pancakes and a biscuit, and a chive-encrusted salmon filet served over potato pancakes and topped with two eggs.

Continue heading northwest on Route 30 to **Astoria,** the Northwest's first European–American settlement. In 1811 John Jacob Astor built his fur-trading post and the Fort Astoria stockade in this rain-washed, fish-rich, hilly corner.

Fishing, logging, and canning drew settlers, many from Finland. By 1900 Astoria was the largest city in the state. It's still a sizable fishing port, keenly aware of its historic position and Scandinavian heritage.

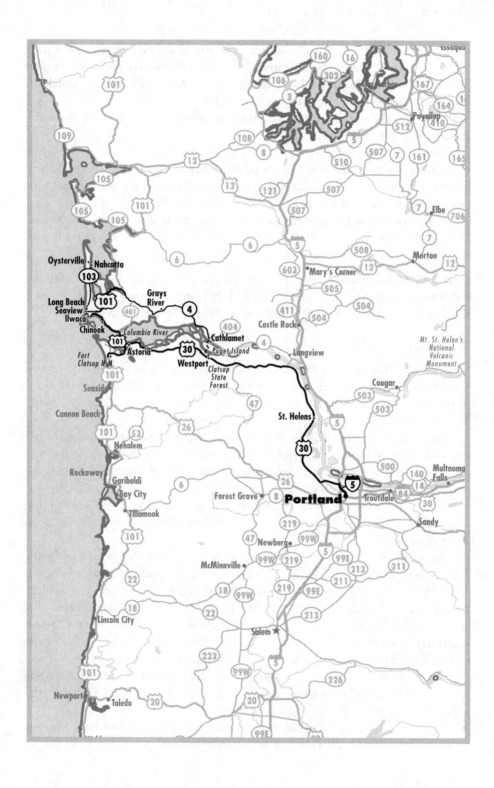

Start your exploration on Coxcomb Hill, where a mural depicting historical highlights spirals up **Astoria Column.** Climb the 125-foot column's 166 steps for a sweeping view of the city, the long bridge, and the hills of Washington. Watch the Pacific Ocean meet the river in a roll of thunder.

Tour a replica of the **Fort Astoria log stockade,** a National Historical Landmark, at Fifteenth and Exchange Streets.

Don't miss one of America's finest nautical displays at the ultramodern **Columbia River Maritime Museum,** 1792 Marine Drive (503–325–2323). It exhibits historic sailing vessels, a river steamer wheelhouse, World War II submarine periscopes, and the historic West Coast lightship *Columbia*.

Next stop is **Josephson's Smokehouse and Specialty Food,** 106 Marine Drive (503–325–2190 or 800–772–FISH), where alder-smoked seafood is produced. It is shipped all over the world—there's none better.

LUNCH: Columbian Cafe, 1114 Marine Drive; (503) 325–2233. Richly flavored soups, vegetarian and seafood crepes, lovely offbeat atmosphere. Open seven days a week for lunch; also open Wednesday through Sunday for dinner.

Afternoon

Park at **Flavel House,** 441 Eighth Street (503–325–2203), an ornate 1883 Queen Anne mansion built for a river pilot. It was saved when a 1922 fire burned much of the town, and the house is now a museum operated by the Clatsop County Historical Society.

Buy a walking-tour map in the museum, and explore seventy gracious old homes bearing historical markers. Check a few shops and galleries along the way. Michael's Antiques and Art Gallery features Asian and Victorian antiques plus the works of Pacific Northwest artists.

Choose your favorite historic clothing style at Personal Vintage Clothing, 100 Tenth Street (503–325–3837), which sells hats, beaded bags, jewelry, linens, laces, and period wear.

Astoria offers a small but satisfying number of galleries for browsing: Pacific Rim Gallery, 1 Twelfth Street (503–325–5450); RiverSea Gallery, 1160 Commercial Street (503–325–1270); and Valley Bronze of Oregon Fine Art Gallery of Astoria, 1198 Commercial Street (800–559–2118). All showcase fine-quality craftsmanship.

Take U.S. Highway 101 and go 6 miles south of Astoria to **Fort Clatsop National Memorial** (503–861–2471 or 800–967–2283), a reproduction of the fort used by the Lewis and Clark expedition during the wet winter of 1805–1806. Enjoy the center, its theaters, and interpretive displays by buckskin-clad rangers who tan hides, cure jerky, make candles, and carry muzzle-loaders just as the explorers used to do.

Follow the coastal road to the northwestern tip of Oregon and **Fort Stevens State Park** (503–861–2471), a military reservation built during the Civil War to guard the river mouth from Confederate attack. It is now a 3,800-acre park with campgrounds, bicycle and hiking trails, beaches, and an interpretive center.

The shipwrecked remains of the **Peter Iredale** have poked through the sand here since 1906. Artifacts from the ship are displayed in the **Clatsop County Heritage Museum,** 1816 Exchange Street (503–325–2203).

DINNER: Ship Inn, 1 Second Street; (503) 325–0033. Watch the ship traffic as you feast on tender, crisply battered fish-and-chips and other British specialties.

LODGING: Rosebriar Hotel, 636 Fourteenth Street; (503) 325–7427 or (800) 487–0224. Large home restored as stylish hotel. Mahogany furniture, fireplaces, televisions, phones. Winner of Astoria's Historic Preservation Award.

Day 2 / Morning

BREAKFAST: A full breakfast is included in the room rate at the Rosebriar Hotel.

Cross the bridge that spans the wide, choppy mouth of the Columbia River. Turn west on U.S. Highway 101 to **Chinook,** once a fabulously rich fishing town, and **Ilwaco,** Washington, where gill-netters and trappers fought ferociously over fishing grounds at the turn of the twentieth century.

Learn about the Northwest heritage, from Chinook Indian life to the logging and fishing industries, at **Ilwaco Heritage Museum,** 115 Southeast Lake Street (360–642–3446). The museum's loop map will guide your scenic 3-mile trip around the southwestern tip of the peninsula. Outdoor murals grace the walls in Ilwaco and other peninsula towns; they are part of a plan to attract visitors.

Stop at **North Head Lighthouse,** located in Fort Canby State Park and built in 1899 to warn boats approaching from the north. From this bluff above the Pacific you have a panoramic ocean view.

The road then curves toward **Cape Disappointment State Park** (360–902–8844) and the **Lewis and Clark Interpretive Center** (360–642–3029; open daily year-round). Inside, you can trace the intrepid explorers' adventures through pictorial displays, which include excerpts from the original journal entries. Ramps take you from the planning of the expedition in 1804 to its final destination here on the Pacific Ocean.

Stormy weather creates surf action at its wildest as monster breakers slam against steep cliffs below the interpretive center. Nearby **Waikiki Beach,** a local picnic favorite, is the only relatively safe swimming beach in the area.

Drive to the Coast Guard station south of the interpretive center and walk the ¼-mile path to the 1856 **Cape Disappointment Lighthouse and Lewis and Clark Interpretive Center,** one of the oldest lighthouses on the West Coast. Far below you lie the churning river mouth and the whitecapped sea. Captain John Meares named Cape Disappointment in 1788, when he was unable to cross the rough Columbia bar. More than 200 ships have been wrecked or sunk in these treacherous waters.

Take the loop drive back to Ilwaco, one of several Northwest towns claiming the title "Salmon Capital of the World." Drive down to the harbor to see the busy tangle of boats and crab pots, charter fishing companies, canneries, and cafes, all mingling on the waterfront. The harbor has moorage for 1,000 boats.

Dockside Cannery and Gift Shop, on the waterfront, sells fresh seafood and gift packs.

LUNCH: McNel's English Pub Steak & Seafood Grill, 107 Spruce Street, Ilwaco; (360) 642–3104. Coats of arms and British flags displayed on dark wood paneling take McNel's diners back to old Britain. Chow down on English favorites such as fish and chips, bangers and bash, corned beef and cabbage, and shepherd pie. The Pub Burger, prime rib, seafood, and chowder are other well-liked menu items.

Afternoon

Head north 2 miles into **Seaview,** once a fashionable resort town. Turn-of-the-twentieth-century Portlanders took a Columbia River steamer and a narrow-gauge railway to the village, which still retains a pleasantly drowsy, old-fashioned atmosphere. Take a quiet walk on the sand. Enjoy art galleries like the Sea Chest, which shows work by watercolorist Charles Mulvey.

Long Beach, just north of Seaview, is a lot livelier and more commercial. Youngsters love its go-kart track, moped rentals, and horseback riding and the oddities and kitschy souvenirs of Marsh's Free Museum (360–642–2188). Climb whimsical wooden sculptures in the miniparks.

Buy a kite at Above It All Kites, 312 Pacific Boulevard (360–642–3541), and spend an exhilarating hour holding a bright dragon, box kite, or bird against the sky as you fly it on the wide, windy beach, said to be the longest (28 miles) in the world.

At the **World Kite Museum** (near the corner of Third Street, Northwest Pacific Highway; 360–642–4020), visitors can learn about kites from around the globe, how they were developed, why they were used during wartime, and what they contributed to the development of airplanes. The museum is open daily.

Drop by Long Beach Coffee Roasters (811 Pacific Avenue South; 360–642–2334) to sip fresh-brewed coffee and check your e-mail on free Wi-Fi. They roast their coffees daily. Buy sweets at Anna Lena's Quilt Shop (111 Bolstad Avenue East; 360–642–8585). Anyone with a sweet tooth will have a tough time deciding which of twenty-four fudge flavors to purchase at Anna Lena's. Always on hand are chocolate, four kinds of cranberry, praline, mint, and Butterfinger. But other flavors—lemon meringue, pumpkin, and Baby Ruth—rotate. Choose a book for the beach at the Bookvendor, 101 Pacific Highway.

Check in at the Shelburne Inn, 4415 Pacific Way (Forty-fifth and Pacific Way, 360–642–2442 or 800–INN–1896). Enjoy a Northwest wine or beer at the inn's Heron and Beaver Pub, which also offers soups, salads, and sandwiches.

DINNER: Shoalwater Restaurant in the Shelburne Inn; (360) 642–4142. Gourmet dining emphasizing regional foods and fine wines. Candlelight, linens, stained glass, quiet atmosphere.

LODGING: The **Shelburne Inn,** 4415 Pacific Way; (360) 642–2442. Antiques-furnished inn, on the National Register of Historic Places. Calico quilts and plenty of charm.

Day 3 / Morning

BREAKFAST: Full country breakfast served family-style in the Shelburne Inn; complimentary for hotel guests.

Drive north up the peninsula, between sand dunes, forests, and cranberry bogs. In this major cranberry-growing center, the roads are bordered with acres of brilliant red berries in the fall. Call ahead to make arrangements for a tour of the bogs (360–642–2031).

At **Briscoe Lake** you'll see the rare, majestic trumpeter swans, which migrate to peninsula lakes and Willapa Bay in December and January.

Pass Klipsan Beach and Ocean Park, which have good beach access, and turn east across the peninsula to **Oysterville.**

Great sailing ships loaded with oysters sailed to San Francisco from here during gold rush days, in the mid-1800s, when oysters cost $1.00 apiece. The industry collapsed and the village faded, but the gracious old homes and the pretty church are on the National Register of Historic Places. Pick up a walking-tour map at Oysterville Church, and amble into a previous century.

Drive Stackpole Road north to **Leadbetter Point State Park** at the peninsula's northern tip, a quiet world of sand dunes, beach grasses, and hiking trails. Thousands of shorebirds feed and rest on the tidal flats and salt marshes during their migrations. The dunes are closed to the public to protect the snowy plover during the April-to-August nesting season, but the rest of the park is open year-round.

LUNCH: Picnic in Leadbetter Park.

Enjoy the beach, surf-fish, go clam digging, or bird-watch on **Eliot Hiking Trail.**

Travel Sandridge Road south to **Nahcotta,** once the northern terminus of the railroad that carried vacationers up and down the peninsula. The town is still active in the oyster business, and mountains of shells whiten the docks at the Port of Peninsula.

Buy oysters shucked or in the shell at **Wiegardt Brothers' Jolly Roger Oysters** (360–665–4111), Nahcotta Boat Basin, or choose a whole range of seafood from a live tank at **East Point Seafood Company** (360–665–6188), Nahcotta Docks; closed Sundays.

DINNER: The Ark, at 273rd Street at the Nahcotta Docks; (360) 665–4133. Nationally acclaimed restaurant featuring regional seafood specialties, homemade breads, and fabulous desserts. Picturesque setting overlooking Willapa Bay. Hours vary seasonally. Call first.

LODGING: The Shelburne Inn.

Day 4 / Morning

BREAKFAST: Another Shoalwater breakfast, perhaps with homemade sausage omelet and buttery pastries.

Follow US 101 and State Route 4 north and west to Grays River. A short detour will take you to the Grays River salmon hatchery and a **covered bridge,** the last such bridge remaining on a public road in Washington.

Travel east on Route 4 to **Skamokawa,** one of the early river settlements, now a National Historic District. **Redmen Hall,** an old-fashioned schoolhouse from 1894, is open to the public on summer weekends. The **River Life Interpretive Center** here tells the history of the area. **Vista Park,** on the Columbia shore, is a worthy stop for its broad river views. The park has picnic facilities, tennis courts, showers, and campsites for recreational vehicles.

You are now on your way to **Cathlamet,** Washington, a peaceful logging and fishing community established in 1846. Visit the **Wahkiakum County Historical Museum,** 65 River Street (360–795–3954; call for hours, which vary seasonally), to see how the early pioneers, loggers, fishers, and farmers lived. The museum has a walking-tour map of the town's historic sites: a pioneer church, settlers' homes, and a cemetery.

Descend a slope to the sheltered harbor and **Elochoman Slough Marina** to watch the sturdy gill-netters come and go, reminders of the region's fishing heritage. This is one of the few full-service marinas on the lower Columbia.

Cross the bridge over the Columbia River to **Westport.** Board the twelve-car ferry (360–268–0047), which departs every hour from 5:00 A.M. to 11:00 P.M. for **Puget Island.** The ten-minute ride will take you to a bucolic world far from city stress.

LUNCH: Picnic on the little beach near the ferry landing on Puget Island.

Afternoon

Spend the afternoon hiking and birding in a nature preserve that is seemingly worlds away. The **Robert W. Little (Puget Island) Preserve** is a thirty-acre peninsula of undiked river floodplain that serves as a habitat for the Columbian white-tailed deer, a threatened subspecies in North America. The preserve also is a sanctuary for beaver, raccoon, and great blue heron. Seasonally, migratory songbird species make this island home. Wetlands of cattails and Sitka spruce trees are under protection here, too.

When you are ready to go home, follow Route 30 east to Portland.

There's More

Boating. Bring your own boat to Long Beach Peninsula.

Boat from Nahcotta to Long Island, in Willapa Bay, and hike up to the last known groves of old-growth cedar in the United States. In this wilderness, home to deer, elk, grouse, bear, and 1,000-year-old trees, you can experience a bit of what the Northwest was like when Lewis and Clark arrived. *NOTE:* The bay is subject to tidal action; consult a tide table and use caution.

Fishing. Tiki Charters, 350 Industry Street, Astoria; (503) 325–7818.

Golf. Peninsula Golf, Ninety-seventh and Highway 103, North Long Beach; (360) 642–2828. Nine-hole course.

Museum. Clatsop County Historical Society Heritage Museum, 714 Exchange Street, Astoria; (503) 338–4849.

Pacific Coast Antiques, 1206 Forty-seventh, Seaview; (360) 642–7199. Several dealers sell wares in a colorful old house.

Special Events

Late April. Astoria-Warrenton Crab and Seafood Festival, Astoria. Carnival, wine tastings, arts, crafts, Dungeness crab.

May. Ragtime Rhodie Dixieland Jazz Festival, Long Beach. Weekend performances of Dixieland jazz.

First Saturday in May. Blessing of the Fleet, Ilwaco. Children's parade, salmon barbecue, flowers cast on the waters.

June. Scandinavian Midsummer Festival, Astoria.

Mid-July. SandSations Sand Sculpture Contest, Long Beach. Cash prizes for winning sand sculptures.

August. International Kite Festival, Long Beach. Annual kite-flying competition on the beach; one of the world's largest kite events.

Late December. Fort Clatsop Living History, Astoria. Dramatic re-creations of the region's history located at this reproduction of Lewis and Clark's winter fort.

Other Recommended Restaurants and Lodgings

Astoria

Franklin Street Station Bed-and-Breakfast, 1140 Franklin Street; (503) 325–4314 or (800) 448–1098. Walking distance from downtown. Tastefully furnished home with antique reproductions and modern comforts. Full breakfast. Closed during winter months.

Grandview Bed-and-Breakfast, 1574 Grand Avenue; (503) 325–5555. Airy, attractive rooms in early-twentieth-century home on a hillside above town. Warm hospitality.

Hotel Elliott, 357 Twelfth Street; (503) 325–2502 or (877) 378–1924. In Astoria's downtown historic district. Thirty-two lovingly restored rooms and suites with heated tile bathroom floors, cedar-lined closets, antique sleigh beds, and period furnishings. Views of the Columbia River or historic downtown from each room and from a sixth-floor roof garden. Complimentary breakfast.

Hood River

Egg Harbor Café, 1313 Oak Street; (541) 386–1127. Everyone—from kids to windsurfers—will find something to please the palate at this cafe. Nine pages of the menu are devoted to breakfast fare, which ranges from pancakes with blueberries and bananas topped with fresh whipped cream, to smoked salmon eggs Benedict. Open from 6:00 A.M. to 2:00 P.M. daily.

Ilwaco

Inn at Ilwaco, 120 Williams Street NE; (360) 642–8686. Former church converted to bed-and-breakfast hotel and performing arts center. Cozily furnished rooms, friendly ambience. Full breakfast.

Seaview

The 42nd Street Cafe, 4201 Pacific Highway; (360) 642–2323. Lunch and dinner in cozy, quiet, nostalgic atmosphere.

Sou'Wester Lodge, Thirty-eighth Place and J Street; (360) 642–2542. Historic home of former U.S. senator Henry Winslow Corbett; very casual, on the beach. Three rooms in lodge plus several cabins and mobile homes.

For More Information

Astoria–Warrenton Area Chamber of Commerce, 111 West Marine Drive, P.O. Box 176, Astoria, OR 97103; (503) 325–6311 or (800) 875–6807; www.oldoregon.com.

Long Beach Peninsula Visitors Bureau, Highway 101, P.O. Box 562, Long Beach, WA 98631; (360) 642–2400 or (800) 451–2542; www.funbeach.com.

PORTLAND ESCAPE SIX

Columbia River Gorge

A National Scenic Treasure / 1 Night

Nature was more than generous in lavishing scenic beauty on the Pacific Northwest. The Columbia River Gorge, with its thick green forests, rocky bluffs, rushing streams, and misty waterfalls, is a spectacular example. Much of the gorge is a federally designated National Scenic Area (Columbia River Gorge National Scenic Area; 541–308–1700).

☐ National Scenic Area

☐ Waterfalls

☐ Wildflowers

☐ Woodland trails

☐ River and mountain views

☐ Bonneville Dam

☐ Orchards

☐ Sailboarding

☐ Wineries

The broad Columbia divides northern Oregon from southern Washington as it slices through the Cascade Mountains on its way to the sea. Streams rush into the river from the foothills of Mount Hood, on their journey from melting snow to waterfalls to tumbling creeks to the river and the sea.

On either side, sheer basaltic cliffs reveal a geologic history of earthshaking violence: rock that twisted like taffy under the onslaught of ancient floods, lava casts where trees fell before streams of molten lava, gaping holes where hillsides slid into the river.

This getaway immerses you in natural splendor. You'll walk forested trails to overlooks and waterfalls, watch boaters and sailboarders (or join them), taste Northwest cuisine, and tour the largest dam on the river.

Day 1 / Morning

Pack a picnic lunch (or plan to eat at Multnomah Falls Lodge), drive east from Portland on Interstate 84 to Troutdale (about thirty minutes), and take the **Scenic Highway** exit. The historic road, much of it edged with moss-covered stone walls, cuts into riverside cliffs for 24 miles. Built in 1915, the road rises from river level to **Crown Point,** a basalt ledge jutting 720 feet above the Columbia. Stop here for one of the most romantic views in the world—a panoply of forest, mountains, and sky, with the mighty river glistening far below. **Vista House,** perched atop Crown

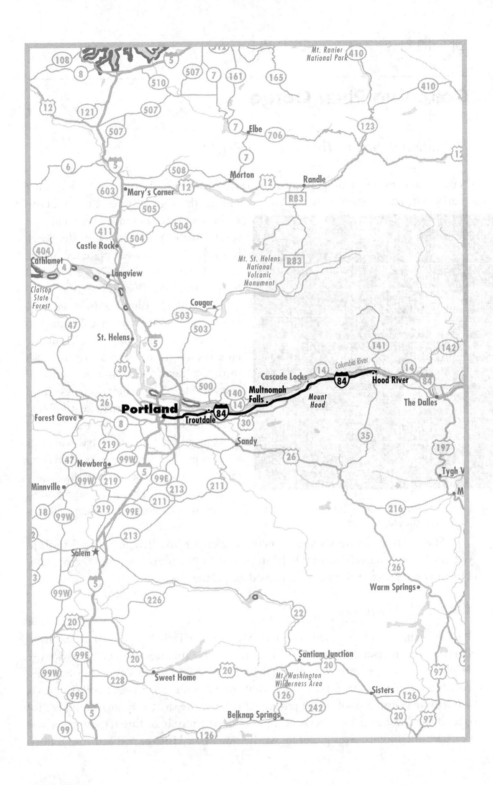

Point, is a circular stone structure built in 1918 as a monument to pioneers. It contains information about the gorge and has a gift shop selling local handicrafts.

Continue 2.4 miles on the Scenic Highway to **Latourell Falls,** where a 2-mile trail curves up through ferns and mossy undergrowth to the 100-foot cascade. Lichens grow a brilliant yellow-green against rock walls. Hawks, crows, songbirds, and sometimes eagles soar overhead, while scolding squirrels scamper underfoot.

East from Latourell on the Scenic Highway, make a brief stop at **Shepherd's Dell.** Here a ¼-mile paved path, edged with a curving, mossy rock wall, descends to expose the spraying tiers of a stream not visible from the road.

The next stop is **Bridal Veil Falls State Park,** fifteen acres of footpaths and camas meadows on an open bluff above the river. Interpretive signs explain how natives and pioneers dug up the bulbs of the sky-blue camas flowers and dried and baked them for winter food.

The park has picnic tables and restrooms and a fenced, paved trail, accessible to wheelchairs, that loops along the bluff. The views of the river and across it to the immense basalt columns called the **Pillars of Hercules** are stunning.

An easy ⅔-mile walk takes you to an observation platform under a canopy of alder and maple trees, where you can see **Bridal Veil Falls,** a double cascade of dancing white water.

LUNCH: Picnic in Bridal Veil Falls State Park.

Afternoon

Continue east on the Scenic Highway, passing lovely **Wahkeena Falls** as you proceed to **Multnomah Falls,** a shimmering, 620-foot ribbon of spray that is the second-highest waterfall in the United States.

Native American legend says that long ago a chief's daughter plunged over the cliff above the falls as a human sacrifice to save her tribe from a devastating plague. Sometimes, people say, when the wind blows through the waterfall, you can see the shape of a maiden in the mist.

For an eagle's-eye view of the Columbia, hike up the paved trail to the fenced platform perched at the top of the falls (about 1 mile). The dizzying, over-the-edge view is what the legendary princess saw.

Rather than heading back down on the paved route, take the main trail into the woods along **Multnomah Falls Creek.** Then follow well-marked **Perdition Trail;** it will give you a two-hour walk through the ferny forest, over streams, and across a ridge to the top of Wahkeena Falls.

Along the trail are picturesque staircases, quaint bridges, and breathtaking glimpses of the river. To the north, on the Washington side, you'll see the snowy slopes of **Mount Adams** and **Mount St. Helens.** At Wahkeena, take the path downward toward the road, and connect with the final ¼-mile segment of the walk, which will lead you back to your car at Multnomah Falls.

If you did not bring a picnic, order lunch in **Multnomah Falls Lodge,** 50000 Historic Columbia River Highway, Bridal Veil (503–695–2376). This may be the only place in the world where you can sip a huckleberry daiquiri as you relax in a glass-enclosed lounge and gaze up at a waterfall as high as a sixty-story building.

Your next stop is **Oneonta Gorge Botanical Area.** In summer, you can walk upstream in a cool, narrow canyon, which ends at a waterfall. Fifty species of wildflowers, shrubs, and trees grow in this fragile habitat; six grow nowhere else.

Just beyond Oneonta is **Horsetail Falls,** then **Ainsworth State Park,** where the Scenic Highway ends.

If this is a day trip, you may decide at this point to head back to Portland on I–84.

To continue exploring the gorge, travel eastward on I–84 and stop at **Bonneville Dam** (541–374–8820), the oldest and largest hydroelectric project on the Columbia. Open daily for tours, the dam has a visitor center with exhibits that explain the structure's operation. Underwater windows overlook fish ladders so that you can watch migrating salmon on their way back to their native spawning grounds.

A mile east of the huge dam is **Eagle Creek Trail,** probably the most scenic in the gorge. As the fir needle-strewn path climbs and twists along steep cliffs, Eagle Creek tumbles beside and then below it, bouncing over boulders on its way to the river. Next to the trail are high cliffs, where thick, spongy moss drips showers of silver.

Two miles in from the trailhead you'll come to **Punchbowl Falls.** There's a viewing point above this lovely deep pool, and a short spur path leads down to its pebbled shore. From a rocky cleft, the falls plummet into the pool, while ferns clinging to the cliffs around it tremble in the mist. The stream plunges northward in a broad cascade at Punchbowl's wider end.

You can either make this your turnaround point, thereby retracing your route back down the Eagle Creek Trail, or continue another 4 miles to **Tunnel Falls.** Such a hike (12 miles round-trip) would obviously take much of the day and mean excluding some of the other suggested walks.

At Tunnel Falls, another impressive waterfall, you'll pass through a 25-foot-long tunnel cut into the cliff. Eagle Creek Trail continues to **Wahtum Lake,** 14 miles in from the highway; it's an all-day hike.

When you return to your car and are back on I–84, drive east another 22 miles to the **Hood River Valley.** On the dry side of the Cascade Range, the valley's orchards produce fruit for world markets. In spring, Hood River's apple, pear, and cherry trees provide a glorious display of bloom. Mount Hood, mantled in glaciers, rises steeply behind them on the southwest, while northward across the river Mount Adams and Mount St. Helens are snowy sentinels against the sky.

Take the 35-mile, scenic **Hood River Fruit Loop** drive through Hood River Valley's orchards and farmlands. Sample and purchase succulent fruits, homemade preserves, and fresh-baked breads and pastries. Visit a winery. Inhale fields of fragrant lavender. Farms and attractions along the Hood River Fruit Loop are open from at least 10:00 A.M. to 5:00 P.M. Fruit Loop route maps are available at the Hood River Visitor's Center off exit 63 on I–84 and at the Mount Hood Country Store on Highway 35 at the south end of the Hood River Valley.

Take exit 62 from I–84, and curve around toward the imposing yellow stucco inn that stands on a precipice high above the river. The **Columbia Gorge Hotel,** 4000 Westcliff Drive, Hood River (541–386–5566 or 800–345–1921), is a fine place to relax with a drink in the **Valentino Lounge.** The historic hotel, built in 1921, harks back to the Jazz Age in its furnishings and decor. Adjoining the hotel is **Hood River Vineyards'** tasting room and art gallery, where you can sample local wines.

Continue on I–84 to the next exit, which will take you into downtown Hood River and your hotel.

DINNER: Stonehedge Inn, 2375 Montello Avenue; (541) 386–3940. Once a summer home with lovely gardens; now a fine restaurant with a classic continental menu.

LODGING: Hood River Hotel, 102 Oak Avenue, Hood River. Small-town hotel with thirty-two rooms and nine suites in downtown Hood River. Local craftspeople have modernized the facilities with saunas, Jacuzzis, and a fitness room, while restoring the European charm of the original hotel, including a brass elevator gate and a marble-faced lobby fireplace. Rooms with river views are well worth the price difference.

Day 2 / Morning

BREAKFAST: Corner Stone Cuisine at the Hood River Hotel. Open for breakfast, lunch, and dinner. Even packs picnic lunches for Columbia Gorge outings.

After the preceding day's vigorous activity, this is a slower-paced morning for exploring Hood River and its peaceful valley. Start with the visitor center in **Port Marina Park** (503–386–1645), which has information on area attractions.

The **Hood River County Historical Museum,** 300 East Port Marina Drive (exit 64 off I–84; 503–386–6772), is also in Port Marina Park and holds intriguing displays of Native American artifacts and relics from early settlement days. The museum is open daily; call for hours.

The park has swimming and boating facilities and is a good place to watch sailboarders skim over the waves. On a clear, windy day hundreds of the brilliantly colored sails dot the river. Hood River, widely considered the "sailboarding capital of the world," draws fans of the sport from around the country. The best spot for close-up views of sailboarders is the Hood River Event Site, at the north end of Second Street. The site, under development for sailboarding events, has a rigging area and bleachers. Other good viewing sites are the West Jetty and Rushton Park, west of the Columbia Gorge Hotel.

If you want to try sailboarding, several shops in Hood River rent equipment and provide a variety of lesson packages.

Drive up to **Panorama Point** (the turnoff is just south of town on Route 35) for a memorable view of the valley and Mount Hood. The view is most striking in spring, when the orchards are frothy with pink-and-white blossoms. Five miles south of Hood River, at the Odell turnoff on Route 35, is **River Bend Farm and Country Store,** 2363 Tucker Road (800–755–7568; www.gorge.net/river bend). Country gifts and gourmet foods are sold in a quaint setting.

LUNCH: **Carolyn's Restaurant,** 1313 Oak Street; (541) 386–1127. Begin the day with breakfast here and views of Mount Adams and the Columbia River. Breakfast and lunch are served all day.

Afternoon

Check the shops of Hood River, watch the sailboarders, fish, golf, or just relax on the beach.

You might take a self-guided tour of the **Full Sail Brewing Company,** 506 Columbia Street (541–386–2247). There, you can watch traditional brewing techniques. Taste Full Sail Ale in the adjacent **White Cap Pub** (541–386–2281), which overlooks the Columbia River.

If you're feeling ambitious and the cool forests and waterfalls of the gorge look inviting, hike one of the dozens of trails that wind from the road up to Mount Hood's lower slopes. Or continue on into Portland.

There's More

Cascade Locks. A park and museum are located on the site of the river locks that were used for river navigation before Bonneville Dam inundated the rapids. (See Portland Escape Three for more information.)

Cascade Salmon Hatchery. Near Eagle Creek campground.

Hood River Golf Course; (541) 386–3009. Scenic, nine-hole public course 5 miles southwest of Hood River.

Mount Hood Railroad, 110 Railroad Avenue, Hood River; (541) 386–3556 or (800) 872–4661; mthoodrr@gorge.com. Old-fashioned train excursions (summer only) through Hood River Valley on the Fruit Blossom Special. Dining car, restored historic depot, children's photos with the engineer—and free rides on your birthday.

Swimming and picnicking, at pools of Eagle Creek.

Windsurfing is seen in local and international events near Hood River Expo Center, off I–84, exit 63.

Special Events

April. Hood River Valley Blossom Festival, Hood River Valley. Arts-and-crafts fairs, dinners, orchard tours, train rides.

May. Hood River Pear and Wine Festival. A three-day festival of the senses that includes wine tasting, cooking demonstrations, food, fine art, music, and, of course, Hood River Valley pears for sampling.

July. Sternwheeler Days, Cascade Locks. A family event that includes stern-wheeler rides, a salmon feed, and arts and crafts.

Late August. Gravenstein Apple Days, Hood River. Wine tasting, food, and a "Volkswalk" to help walk away consumed calories.

Mid-October. Harvest Fest, Hood River Valley. Two days of entertainment, crafts sales, freshly baked goods, fresh produce.

Day after Thanksgiving. Light Up the Gorge!, Columbia Gorge Hotel. Historic hotel illuminates grounds for the holidays with more than 65,000 lights.

Other Recommended Restaurants and Lodgings

Bridal Veil

Bridal Veil Bed and Breakfast, 46650 East Historic Columbia River Highway; (503) 695–2333; in Portland, (503) 284–8901. Bed-and-breakfast home, built in the 1920s, across the road from Bridal Veil Falls State Park. Two cozy rooms and a guest cottage in knotty pine, shared bath. Full breakfast.

Hood River

Columbia Gorge Hotel, 4000 Westcliff Drive; (541) 386–5566 or (800) 345–1921. Classic country inn with forty-two rooms, 1920s motif, and river view. Full farm breakfast included. Dining room open to public.

Lakecliff Bed and Breakfast, 3820 Westcliff Drive; (541) 386–7000. Former grand summer home, now on the National Register of Historic Places, has four rooms with forest or river views. Full breakfast included.

Oak Street Hotel, 610 Oak Street; (541) 386–3845. Within walking distance to several nice restaurants and shops. Nine small, tastefully decorated rooms that include hand-forged queen bed frames, bedside tables with oak leaves, and steel counters with bronze finishes and porcelain sinks in the bathrooms. Homemade pastries from the hotel kitchen are served buffet-style at breakfast, along with fresh fruit and beverages.

Vagabond Lodge, 4070 Westcliff Drive; (541) 386–2992 or (877) 386–2992. On the outskirts of Hood River, this forty-two-room lodge is a handy place for establishing a home base while exploring the Gorge area. Most rooms have stunning views of the Columbia River, and the mossy courtyard and picnic area are filled with indigenous trees and wildflowers.

Troutdale

Tad's Chicken 'n' Dumplings (503–666–5337), on 1325 East Historic Columbia River Highway, a mile east of Troutdale, overlooking the Sandy River. Popular for its country cooking and fried chicken.

For More Information

Columbia River Gorge National Scenic Area, USDA Forest Service, 902 Wasco Avenue, Suite 200, Hood River, OR 97031; (541) 386–2333; www.fs.fed.us/r6/columbia.

Columbia River Gorge Visitors Association, PMB 106, 2149 West Cascade 106A, Hood River, OR 97031; (800) 984–6743; www.crgva.org.

Hood River County Chamber of Commerce, 405 Portway Avenue, Hood River, OR 97031; (541) 386–2000 or (800) 366–3530; www.hoodriver.org.

Port of Cascade Locks Visitor Center, P.O. Box 307, Cascade Locks, OR 97014; (541) 374–8619; portofcascadelocks.org.

PORTLAND ESCAPE SEVEN

John Day Fossil Beds to Shaniko

Fossils and Falls / 1 Night

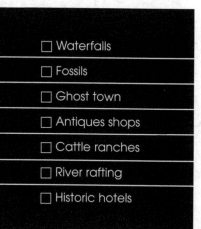

☐ Waterfalls

☐ Fossils

☐ Ghost town

☐ Antiques shops

☐ Cattle ranches

☐ River rafting

☐ Historic hotels

If you appreciate nature's artistry, history on the grand scale, and a bit of adventure, you'll enjoy this tour. In two days you'll travel through millions of years of geologic change, visit a frontier town, raft on a river, and ride through cowboy country. It's all a comparatively short distance from the city but a long way from urban living.

Day 1 / Morning

From Portland, drive east on Interstate 84 to the Bridal Veil exit. Leave the freeway here, and at the top of the hill turn left on the **Scenic Highway.** This was the first federally designated scenic highway in the United States; only a short section remains, but the views are spectacular. In spring colorful wildflowers bloom beside the winding old road; in all seasons it's surrounded by greenery. Below, on the north, lies the freeway and beyond it the broad **Columbia River** and the hills of Washington.

After passing through the quiet Bridal Veil community, you'll come to **Wahkeena Falls,** a 242-foot series of falls pouring down the boulder-strewn basaltic cliff. It's a short distance from here along the Scenic Highway to the famous **Multnomah Falls.** Stop for a close look at the long, double cascade and perhaps have coffee and breakfast in the historic, stone **Multnomah Falls Lodge,** 50000 Historic Columbia River Highway (503–695–2376).

Next is **Oneonta Gorge Botanical Area,** a narrow canyon with rare plants and dense greenery; then comes picturesque **Horsetail Falls,** twisting 176 feet into a pool behind a low stone wall. **Ainsworth State Park** is the last stop on the Scenic Highway, a pleasant place for camping and picnics.

Rejoin I–84 at this point and continue east along the Columbia River toward the town of Hood River, another 28 miles (for more on Hood River, see Portland Escape Six). You're driving through the great cleft in the Cascade Range, with Mount Hood rising immediately on the south and brawny Mount Adams and chopped-off St. Helens across the river on the north. On a clear day you'll see the peaks of Rainier in the distance. East of the Cascades, the scenery changes. The fir

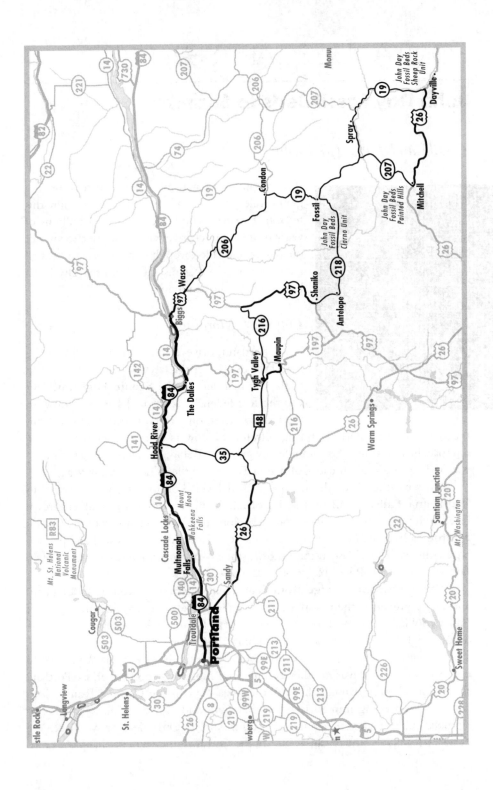

forests, waterfalls, and rugged cliffs are left behind, with rounded hills, sere and brown in summer, lying ahead.

After Hood River, take the Mosier/Rowena exit to travel a scenic byway, where cherry orchards grow on the hillsides and balsamroot and lupine carpet the fields with yellow and blue in April and May. As you climb the hill you'll have sweeping, panoramic views of the river and mountains.

Six miles after you leave I–84, you'll come to **Rowena Dell.** Stop to admire the view from **Rowena Crest View Point** and walk the paths of the **Tom McCall Preserve at Rowena Plateau.** This scenic area offers stunning displays of wildflowers on a plateau above the river. You might also walk the 1½-mile footpath that leads to **McCall Point,** a high overlook.

The cliffs here, composed of dark Columbia basalt, were formed in a series of massive lava flows about fifteen million years ago. Ten million years ago, as the great basalt plain crumbled, erosion carved out Rowena Dell. Later floods and ash from volcanic eruptions created the steep cliffs and landscape visible today.

You can rejoin I–84 after descending from Rowena Dell, or continue on the country byway to Rowena and Mayer State Park, joining I–84 at **The Dalles.** In spring the countryside around The Dalles is a pastel sea of cherry blossoms, as this is a prime fruit-growing area.

If time allows, take a look around the history-steeped town. For centuries it was a Native American trading center and then the end of the overland Oregon Trail. A walking-tour map points out the original **Wasco County Courthouse,** 420 West Second Place (541–296–4798 or 800–255–3385), now an interpretive center. Tours are led mid-morning and mid-afternoon from the Chamber of Commerce, 404 West Second Street. The courthouse was built in 1859 when Wasco was the largest county in the United States, extending into present-day Idaho, Montana, and Wyoming.

Old St. Peter's Landmark, West Third and Lincoln (541–296–5686; closed on Monday and major holidays), dates from 1898. In it, you'll see brilliant stained-glass windows, Italian marble, rich woodwork, and the church's original organ. The former **Surgeon's Quarters** is all that remains of Fort Dalles. In the mid-1800s it was part of the only military post between Fort Vancouver and Fort Laramie; today the quaint structure is a museum with displays on pioneer life.

Leaving The Dalles, you find rocky hills dotted with fragrant blue-gray sagebrush, while willows and wildflowers grow by the water. From I–84, take exit 97 to State Route 206. **Celilo Park,** between the river and railroad tracks, is a green oasis here, with lawns, trees, and restrooms.

Traveling on Route 206, you'll cross the Deschutes River and come to **Deschutes River Recreation Area.** This large, attractive riverside park is a popular gathering spot. It has boat launches, grassy slopes under locust trees, and campsites. An **Oregon Trail Historic Marker** tells of pioneers crossing the Deschutes on their way west.

At the FULTON CANYON/WASCO sign, Route 206 heads inland, away from the river. You're driving up a winding road into a steep canyon, where sheep paths crisscross the treeless hills. Then you're up and out of the canyon, surrounded by vast grain fields, with cottonwood trees where there is water. By the roadside, in a grove of locust trees, you'll see Locust Grove Church, with its high steeple and arched windows. Now deserted, gray, and weathered, the quaint little church was built in 1895 and last used for a funeral in 1914.

Crossing U.S. Highway 97, you'll arrive in **Wasco,** a small, intensely quiet town dominated by big grain elevators. There are brick buildings and lilacs, a small city park with play equipment, a city hall, a post office, and the Wasco Market, where the community goes to learn the latest happenings. Recent signs in the window advertise garage sales, a junior rodeo, the high school sports schedule, a gun show, and an annual rummage and plastic flower show.

Continue through ranch country, where grain and cattle are the mainstays, to the sagebrush of Cottonwood Canyon, and on to the **John Day River.** At J. S. Burres State Park, a simple wayside with a couple of picnic tables and toilets, boaters often put in to the river.

From the John Day, ascend out of the canyon to a hilltop with a "Mountain Identifier," which names the visible mountains: Jefferson, Hood, St. Helens, Adams, and Rainier.

Forty miles after leaving the Columbia River, arrive in **Condon,** a historic oasis in the middle of Oregon's scenic wheat country. The small town is charming and picturesque, from the restored Country Flowers Soda Fountain to the restored Liberty Theatre.

Several historic buildings are well preserved. Condon's city hall, built in 1899, housed the hose cart of the city fire department and was used as the city jail. The building, with its barred windows, is still standing in the original site, just off Main Street on Summit Street.

The Condon railroad was completed in 1905, and the Union Pacific depot was built a few years later. Now the **Gilliam County Historical Society Museum** (541–384–4233), the building was moved in 1975 to its present site on Highway 19, adjacent to Burns Park and Fairground. The museum complex houses antique farm equipment and vintage buildings, such as the Rice Cabin, which was built in 1884 from hand-hewn logs hauled 20 miles by wagon team; a one-room schoolhouse; and a 1890s frame building from Main Street that has been restored as a barber shop. The museum is open May 1 through October 31, from 1:00 to 5:00 P.M.

Condon's school neighbors a pretty green park with play equipment and has a pool and tennis courts.

LUNCH: Country Flowers Soda Fountain, 201 South Main; (541) 384–4120. Soups, thick sandwiches, taco salad, Italian sodas, frozen yogurt, ice cream, espresso. Open daily until 5:00 P.M.

Afternoon

Leave Condon on Route 19 headed south, driving through old lava flows covered with a thin layer of topsoil that supports sagebrush and a few juniper trees. The town of **Fossil** (population 469) is 20 miles south of Condon. Fossil has several points of interest, including the **Fossil Museum,** 401 Main Street (503–763–2698), with well-displayed nineteenth-century artifacts and exhibits on early-twentieth-century fossil hunters, a **car museum** where you can see a collection of vintage autos, and the **Wheeler County Courthouse,** 701 Adams (503–763–2400). The courthouse has fish-scale shingles, two towers (one with four stories, making this the tallest building around), and a curved brick entrance.

Arthur Glover Park has a playground and picnic tables. Fossil Mercantile sells groceries and sundries.

Turning southwest on Route 218, you'll drive 20 miles to reach **John Day Fossil Beds National Monument,** a journey that reaches far into the past. The National Monument, established in 1975, encompasses 14,000 acres in three separate units: Sheep Rock (541–987–2333), Painted Hills (541–462–3961), and Clarno (541–763–2203). This visit to the northernmost site, the **Clarno Formation,** explores the oldest fossil beds, fifty-four million to thirty-seven million years old. They are some of the best preserved on earth. Beds spanning more than five million years are rare, yet the John Day Fossil Beds show more than forty million years of diverse plant and animal life.

Evidence of ancient subtropical forests abounds, as well as fossils of mammals that roamed the region thirty-four million years ago.

Visitors usually pick up a trail map and hike the short walk to the cliffs, or palisades. The **Clarno Palisades** are high rocks exposed by erosion after volcanic mudflows over millions of years inundated the forests again and again. One trail is fairly steep and leads to a high arch in the rocks; the other is an easier nature trail, with fossils identified.

Nearby is the **Hancock Field Station,** 39472 Highway 218 (541–763–4691), operated by the Oregon Museum of Science and Industry. It offers field trips and study courses on the geology, paleontology, and ecology of the area.

After you've explored the Clarno Unit, consider spending an evening winding down in the affable, sleepy town of **Fossil.** The same owner operates **Bridge Creek Flora Inn Bed & Breakfast,** 828 Main Street (541–763–2355), and the **Fossil Lodge** next door at 808 Main Street (541–763–2355). The hosts offer an optional full breakfast for guests at both the inn and the lodge—an all-you-can-eat country-style breakfast served in the lodge dining room from 5:00 to 8:30 A.M.—that will fuel even the largest appetite for the entire day. The spread might contain blueberry or marionberry pancakes and honey-glazed ham or Irish potato sausage, as well as eggs, potatoes, and homemade pastry.

Walk off a bit of your breakfast by wandering around town. Explore the one-room Pine Creek Schoolhouse and Asher Car Museum. Browse around the old-fashioned Fossil General Mercantile, the Little Country gift shop, and the Outpost General Store.

Many people visit this area primarily to investigate all three stations in the John Day Fossil Beds National Monument. In that case, you will want to continue southeast on Highway 19 to the tiny town of Spray (population 140), where you will receive a warm welcome with your coffee at the **Coyote Cafe & Rimrock Room,** Willow Street, Highway 19-207 (541–468–2861).

Near the junction of Highways 19 and 26 is the **John Day Fossil Beds National Monument Sheep Rock Unit,** where the Thomas Condon Paleontology Center houses both the monument's fossil collection and the Cant Ranch Historical Museum.

The town of Dayville is approximately 9 miles east on Highway 26. You can also hang your hat for the evening at the **Fish House Inn** (541–987–2124 or 888–286–FISH), nestled among the Rocky Juniper Canyons of the John Day Valley. The inn has five guest rooms and a seven-space RV park. Comfortable, well-tended outside sitting areas, barbecue grills, and horseshoe pits make weary travelers feel right at home.

Within walking distance is the John Day River, a sparse beauty of a river that is undammed along its entire length, making it the second-longest free-flowing river in the United States. The river provides an exceptional habitat for many plant and animal species, including wild salmon.

After a full day or more of exploration, head west on Highway 26, to the **Painted Hills Unit of John Day Fossil Beds National Monument,** near the town of Mitchell. This unit showcases 3,132 acres of spectacular yellow, gold, black, and red painted hills. Many believe the colors are most vibrant in late afternoon, perhaps because the claystone transforms with ever-changing light and moisture levels.

From here, drive north on Highway 207 toward Fossil, where you might choose to visit the John Day Fossil Beds National Monument Clarno Unit, before driving to **Antelope.**

Once in Antelope, a bit of heaven awaits you in a dish of marionberry cobbler at the **Antelope Store and Café,** Main and Union Streets (541–439–3413). The friendly cafe, which serves breakfast, lunch, and dinner, specializes in organically raised lamb and beef entrees from the nearby, historic Imperial Stock Ranch.

From Antelope, the road turns north for 8 miles to U.S. Highway 97, at the crest of a hill, and the ghost town of **Shaniko.** With twenty-seven people, it's not quite a ghost town, but that is how it's labeled, as the residents strive to attract tourists to this slice of the Old West.

Amble through town and notice a rustic old water tower, a shed full of vintage wagons and automobiles, and the original city hall and jail. Sample the wares at Shaniko's Old Fashioned Candy Store, and look around the Juniper Creek Gallery and Studio. At the brimming antique store, Ghosts from the Past, you will find everything imaginable—from a fine, old framed photograph of Celilo Falls, to a book on repairing farm equipment.

Shaniko was once a busy place, the wool shipping capital of the world. Millions of pounds of wool from regional sheep ranches were stored in the big warehouse and shipped out on the rails at the turn of the twentieth century. But eventually the train bypassed the town, the economy dropped away, and Shaniko was nearly deserted. In recent years, though, new owners have taken over the old **Shaniko Historic Hotel** and brought it to life again.

For an afternoon treat, stop by the End of the Rail Ice Cream Parlor, next door to the Shaniko Historic Hotel.

The mood in Shaniko is disturbed only by the rumble of trucks on busy Highway 97, which runs by the edge of town.

DINNER: The **Shaniko Cafe,** Fourth and E Streets; (541) 489–3415. Shaniko Historic Hotel's bright and cheerful restaurant features steak, meatloaf, stew, and hamburgers. Try the crispy-tender fried chicken with home fried potatoes—hearty and delicious.

LODGING: Shaniko Historic Hotel, 93489 Fourth Street, P.O. Box 86, Shaniko, OR 97057; (541) 489–3441. Brick hotel with twenty simple but clean and comfortable second-floor rooms and one ground-floor room. Lace curtains hang at high windows; the atmosphere is updated frontier. On the National Historic Register.

Day 2 / Morning

BREAKFAST: Three breakfast choices are included in the room rate at the Shaniko Hotel—bacon and eggs, French toast, or continental. Or you can order from the menu at additional cost. Portions are generous.

After you've poked around the ghost town, head north on US 97 and take the first right, Bakeoven Road. At this 3,500-foot elevation you can look back toward John Day country, while ahead of you lies the **Deschutes River Canyon.** Mount Hood and Mount Jefferson tower on the horizon, and you can see Mount Adams and Olallie Butte. The near landscape is festooned with power lines, carrying hydroelectric power from The Dalles Dam on the Columbia River.

From the plateau, twist down into the valley where **Maupin** nestles against the Deschutes River. Here you'll meet your river-rafting guides and board the van that will take you to a put-in point on the river. Central Oregon's rivers draw rafters from all over the country. There are several rafting outfitters in the Maupin area. Many offer deli or barbecue lunches. Review the many possibilities at www.maupinoregon.com/rectour.htm#raft.

The Deschutes is a popular rafting river, with weekends, especially in July and August, very busy. It's carefully regulated, but you'll find that off-season weekdays are considerably less crowded. In the 14-foot raft you'll float the Scenic Waterway back to Maupin, encountering several rapids on the way, and have lunch in the park.

LUNCH: Several river rafting companies cater either barbecue or deli lunches at the riverside city park in Maupin along the river itinerary, so check first. Or consider stopping at Henry's Deli-Mart, Highway 197 and Third in Maupin (541–395–2278), where, as the name suggests, you can buy ready-made picnic provisions or the ingredients to prepare your own lunch. Henry's also has a shuttle service that drives visitors to put-in points along the river.

Afternoon

Climb into the raft again and continue down the river to **Sherar Falls,** a series of cascades that pour over rocky ledges. This is a traditional fishing ground, where local tribal members still stand on wooden platforms built out over the falls and dip long-handled nets into the water. Other fishers cast their lines from the shore.

You'll be shuttled back to Maupin when the four-hour ride is over.

From Maupin, travel north on Deschutes River Road, a National Scenic Byway, and parallel your river ride. There are camping and fishing areas all along the road here. Blue Hole Recreation Site has a fishing ramp with wheelchair access.

On your left, the river rushes by and above it rise steep, rocky cliffs topped by a flat plateau. Past Sherar Falls, where you have a good view of the fishing activity, cross Sherar Bridge. It's often crowded near here, with RV campers parked by the bridge and along the shore. Now you're on Route 216, headed for Tygh Valley.

Three miles from the bridge, watch for the state park sign and turn left at **Tygh Valley Wayside,** where there's an attractive, well-tended day park with lilacs and maple trees, grass, and picnic tables. As soon as you arrive you'll hear the roar of the water—**White River Falls,** the most spectacular sight for miles around.

In a series of three cataracts, the falls drop 90 feet through a steep basalt canyon. The White River begins in a glacier on Mount Hood and flows to join the Deschutes. In spring, when there's abundant snowmelt, the falls is at its most powerful, plunging into pools that roil with action. You can see the falls from a fenced viewpoint or walk down a fairly steep dirt trail in order to view all three sections at once. On the site are also the concrete remains of an abandoned hydroelectric plant.

From the wayside, drive on to **Tygh Valley,** home of the All-Indian Rodeo (see "Special Events") and head west on the road to Wamic. This becomes Route 48, the White River Road. The pioneers who chose to travel overland, rather than float their covered wagons down the Columbia from The Dalles, came this way and often traded with the Tygh Indians. Sam Barlow forged a trail around Mount Hood and set up a tollgate to charge travelers coming through on his road.

You can drive part of the Old Barlow Road, which parallels White River Road and goes all the way to Barlow Pass and Highway 35. There are several turnoffs and signs pointing the way from Route 48.

Now you've left the sagebrush and ponderosa pines of central and eastern Oregon and entered the thick fir forests of the western Cascades and **Mount Hood National Forest.** Continue into the foothills of Mount Hood, crossing several creeks, with the great mountain looming directly before you.

When you reach Highway 35, you have two choices: Turn west toward Route 26 and head for Portland around the mountain's south side, or go north on 35 to Hood River and take the freeway, I–84, west to Portland. If you choose the latter course and have time, stop at East Fork 650, just north of Sherwood Campground, for a two-hour walk up to **Tamanawas Falls,** another cascade of breathtaking beauty.

There's More

Fishing. The John Day is noted for its smallmouth bass, salmon, and steelhead. The Deschutes is famous for its summer steelhead and trout.

John Day River. The John Day, much less used than the lower Deschutes, offers solitude and quiet within its dramatic canyon walls. It's also good for rafting, especially in spring. The 47-mile run from Service Creek to Clarno is a two-day trip with some rapids. For more information on the John Day River system, visit www.nps.gov/joda/planyourvisit.

Special Events

April. Northwest Cherry Festival, The Dalles. Orchard tours, cherry cook-off, street fairs, parade, runs.

April and October. Celilo Mid-Columbia River Powwow and Salmon Feed, The Dalles. Tribal dancing, feast of salmon, venison, root potatoes. Celebrates long Native American fishing tradition in the Columbia.

May. All-Indian Rodeo, Tygh Valley. Bronc riding, wild-horse race, team roping, bulls, Buckaroo breakfast, Native American crafts, fun runs, kids' carnival, dances, beer garden.

Early June. Pioneer Days, Shaniko. Three-day event with parade, Old West shoot-outs, dances, pie social, stagecoach rides, mountain man camp.

Mid-August. Wasco County Fair, Wasco. Rodeo, parade, music, food.

September. The Dalles Historic Days, The Dalles. Celebrating the historic legacy of The Dalles, incorporated in 1857. Activities occur at historic venues across town.

Other Recommended Restaurants and Lodgings

Condon

Country Café, 211 South Main Street; (541) 384–7000. Open daily at 6:00 A.M. Not open for dinner on Sunday, Monday, or Tuesday. Visitors like the friendly service and the satisfying breakfasts here.

Hotel Condon, 202 South Main Street; (541) 384–4624 or (800) 201–6706. Renovated in 2001. Eighteen large and comfortable rooms, with bed mattresses so comfortable that people go out of their way to stay in this classy small-town hotel. Pretty sitting areas on each floor, for reading, chatting, or playing a round of dominoes. Complimentary continental breakfast.

Maupin

Imperial River Company, 304 Bakeoven Road; (541) 395–2404 or (800) 395–3903. While renowned for its guided white-water rafting excursions, this establishment doesn't hold back on its hospitality services either. Thirty-eight Oregon theme rooms, all with coffeemakers, refrigerators, and—for rafters and fishermen—wader dryers. Newer rooms have full views of the Deschutes River.

Riverview Restaurant at Imperial Lodge, which sits right on the edge of the Deschutes riverbanks, serves lamb and beef raised at Imperial Stock Ranch, a 100-square-mile ranch well known for its sustainable livestock production practices. The ranch's range-raised Angus beef is the mainstay of the Imperial River Company dining menu, although lamb, fresh seafood, and salads are also available.

The Oasis Resort and Guide Services, 609 Highway 197 South, P.O. Box 365, 97037; (541) 395–2611; www.deschutesriveroasis.com. Eleven small vintage cabins, most with kitchens, on a grassy, tree-shaded slope near the Deschutes River. Campground also available. Reasonable rates. The Oasis Cafe, the resort's restaurant, is known for its old-fashioned milkshakes, burgers, ribs, and enormous farm-style breakfasts.

For More Information

The Dalles Area Chamber of Commerce, 404 West Second Street, The Dalles, OR 97058; (800) 255–3385; www.thedalleschamber.com.

Greater Maupin Area Chamber of Commerce, P.O. Box 220, Maupin, OR 97037; (541) 395–2599; www.maupinoregon.com/chamber.

Superintendent, John Day Fossil Beds National Monument, 32651 Highway 19, Box 126, Kimberly, OR 97848; (541) 987–2333; www.nps.gov/joda.

PORTLAND ESCAPE EIGHT

Central Oregon

High Desert Country / 2 Nights

- ☐ Mountain wilderness
- ☐ Lava fields
- ☐ Caves
- ☐ Panoramic views
- ☐ Wildlife
- ☐ Frontier-style town
- ☐ Native American museum
- ☐ Boutique shopping
- ☐ Fine dining
- ☐ Hiking
- ☐ Bird-watching
- ☐ Fishing
- ☐ Golf

Sunny central Oregon is a popular weekend getaway for rain-weary Portlanders. On the dry side of the Cascade Range, its weather is predictably pleasant in summer and clear, crisp, and cold in winter. In this land of rugged mountains with powder-snow ski slopes, 235 miles of streams, and more than a hundred lakes, outdoor recreation is a way of life. You can grab a good bite of it in three days and taste a bit of luxury on the way.

This itinerary emphasizes summer activities. In winter, if you're a skier, you know how you'll spend the weekend: on the lifts and runs of Mount Bachelor or Hoodoo, or slicing through the silent forest on cross-country trails. Other winter recreation includes ice skating, sleigh rides, snowshoeing, dogsledding, and relaxing by a cozy fire.

Day 1 / Morning

Drive U.S. Route 26 east from Portland to the 640,000-acre **Warm Springs Indian Reservation.** As you cross the pass at Mount Hood, you'll leave the cool green rain forests behind and enter a dry landscape of sagebrush and ponderosa pine, steep cliffs, and rocky canyons, backdrops to many western movies.

A must on this route is a tour of the **Museum at Warm Springs,** 2189 Highway 26 (541–553–3331). The innovative museum, constructed of native stone and timbers and designed to resemble an encampment among the cottonwoods along Shitike Creek, shows the heritage of the Confederated Tribes of the Warm Springs Reservation. Using petroglyph replicas, song, photographs, family heirlooms, and trade items, it tells of native traditions and how they were affected by the settlers. Open daily from 9:00 A.M. to 5:00 P.M.

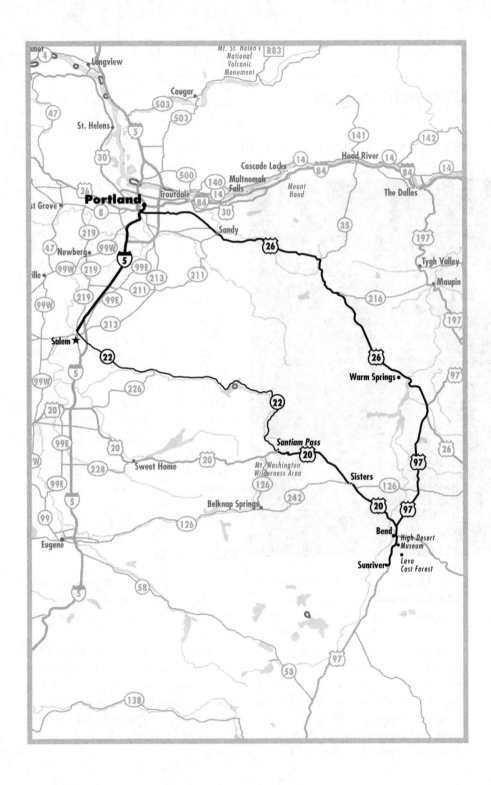

Just past the reservation border, take the **Pelton Dam** exit south for the 25-mile scenic route along the **Deschutes River Canyon.** Overlooks along **Rim Road** present panoramic views across the canyon to cliffs of gray columnar basalt and a wide, sage-covered plain that reaches to the snow-cloaked Cascades. **Mount Jefferson, Three Fingered Jack,** and the **Three Sisters** seem to float on the horizon, white against a deep blue sky.

South of **Round Butte Dam** and the overlooks, a winding road leads down to a bridge that crosses the Crooked River arm of **Lake Billy Chinook.** The lake, formed by dams holding back the waters of the Deschutes, Squaw Creek, and Crooked River, lies at the heart of 7,000-acre **Cove Palisades State Park.**

Walls of rock, carved by volcanic eruptions ten million years ago, tower above the deep green Billy Chinook and line its 72-mile shore. The lake and its watery arms are favorites with boaters and fishers.

Back on Rim Road, head for Culver and Highway 97, and turn south to Bend.

The subtle beauty of the high desert, a vibrant downtown, and the attractive nearby burgs of Redmond, Prineville, Sisters, and Sunriver have drawn tourists and transplants alike to Bend and its environs. Originally a logging town, Bend has become an increasingly popular destination with golfers, camping enthusiasts, hikers, rock climbers, and skiers. And in the past five years, the area's small-town, yet sophisticated lifestyle has encouraged an unsurpassed population growth. In fact, Bend is now the sixth-fastest-growing metropolitan area in the United States, with a 12.2 percent increase between 2000 and 2003, to 129,000 residents today. With that growth have come new amenities and services.

LUNCH: Deschutes Brewery and Public House, 1044 Northwest Bond Street, Bend; (541) 382–9242. Dark woodwork, light menu, locally brewed beers. A microbrewery with style.

Afternoon

Take Greenwood Avenue east to **Pilot Butte,** and drive—or, if the gate is closed, walk—to the top. A twenty-minute walk to the cinder cone's summit will present you with a 360-degree view of Bend, the valley, and the mountains that surround it. Under clear skies you can see virtually all the Oregon Cascades.

Next pay a visit to **Deschutes Historical Center,** 129 Northwest Idaho Street (541–389–1813); the center is housed in a former stone school building on Idaho Street, between Wall and Bond. Displays include pioneer memorabilia, arrowheads, thunder eggs, and a book of biographical sketches of early settlers. Open Wednesday through Saturday afternoons.

DINNER: Merenda Restaurant and Wine Bar, 900 Northwest Wall Street (541–330–2304), a favored eatery, is one of several trendy new restaurants in Bend. A recent *Gourmet* magazine review applauded the establishment's casual sophistication, reasonable prices, and artfully prepared, scrumptious lunch and dinner items.

Ingenious salads and sandwiches make the most of local produce. The restaurant's wine bar and delectable appetizers make this a favorite local meeting spot too.

LODGING: Lara House, 640 Northwest Congress Avenue; (541) 388–4064 or (800) 766–4064. Bed-and-breakfast home near Drake Park. Well-furnished, comfortable guest rooms, cozy sunroom.

Day 2 / Morning

BREAKFAST: Lara House serves a full breakfast.

Drive 6 miles south on Route 97 for a tour of the **High Desert Museum,** 59800 South Highway 97 (541–382–4754; www.highdesert.org). This outstanding center of natural and cultural history shows wildlife (beavers, otters, owls) in natural settings, re-creations of historic events, and interpretive programs that help to increase your knowledge of the high desert country. Open daily, 9:00 A.M. to 5:00 P.M.

Continue south on Route 97 for 5 more miles to **Lava Lands Visitor Center,** 58201 South Highway 97 (541–593–2421). Watch an introductory slide presentation; then follow interpretive trails through the rough black lava and adjoining pine forest. From here, shuttles carry visitors to the summit of **Lava Butte,** a cinder cone formed 6,160 years ago, for stunning views of the lava flows and Cascade Mountains. You can see Newberry Volcano and the Blue Mountains of eastern Oregon.

Drive a few more miles to **Sunriver,** a self-contained resort community with a lodge, tennis courts, three full golf courses, an airport, and shopping malls. This is one of the Northwest's major planned recreational and retirement developments.

LUNCH: Sunriver Bella Cucina Italian Café, Village Mall, Building #3, Sunriver; (541) 593–6440. Open for lunch and dinner. Italian-style meat, chicken, and seafood entrees and, of course, pasta and gourmet pizza. Home-baked focaccia bread, Italian desserts, special children's menu.

Afternoon

Rent a bicycle at the Sunriver shop, and ride the numerous paved, winding paths; or stroll to **Sunriver Nature Center and Observatory** (541–593–4394), a private, not-for-profit scientific and educational organization. The entire family will appreciate the interpretive exhibits and hands-on educational programs about mammals, reptiles, amphibians, and birds that live in central Oregon. A botanical garden and nature trail through forest and marsh habitat offer a thoughtful view of the region's natural environment.

If you'd prefer a game of golf on a sprawling green course traversed by streams and surrounded by high mountain peaks, club rentals are available at **Sunriver Lodge.**

An alternative to the Sunriver trip is to bring a picnic with you to Lava Lands Visitor Center. After your tour, drive 4 miles west past the center to a picnic area for lunch. Then take the mile-long path that leads downstream, across a footbridge, and on to beautiful **Benham Falls.**

For other short hikes through the spectacular central Cascades, take Route 97 south 22 miles from Bend and turn east at the signs to Paulina and East Lakes. From here, walk the **Peter Skeen Ogden Trail** to cascading waterfalls, or take the **Newberry Crater Obsidian Trail** (a fifteen-minute walk) to see one of the world's largest obsidian flows.

Drive back to Bend and relax before dinner.

DINNER: Pine Tavern Restaurant, 967 Northwest Brooks Street; (541) 382–5581. Bend's oldest eatery. Prime rib, lamb, barbecued ribs in a warm, natural wood setting. Windows view tree-shaded lawn and the Deschutes River.

LODGING: Lara House.

Day 3 / Morning

BREAKFAST: Lara House.

Watch the ducks and Canada geese that claim ownership of **Drake Park,** then head north on U.S. Route 20 toward **Sisters.** You're likely to see llamas behind ranch fences along the way; this is the llama capital of North America. The exotic animals are used for show competition, pack trips, and pets, and their wool is prized by spinners and knitters.

The town of Sisters looks like a scene from the Old West, with its wooden boardwalks and false storefronts. Behind them, boutiques and art galleries sell gifts, trendy clothing, Native American and wildlife art, carved burl furniture, frozen yogurt, and whimsies of all kinds.

Because the frontier town churns with activity in summer, chances are strong that you will find yourself in the midst of one of the many festivals.

Fill your water canteen and buy picnic foods at a deli—there are several—then drive north of Sisters toward **Camp Sherman** and **Black Butte,** a symmetrical cinder cone 6,436 feet high.

The two- to three-hour hike up the butte will present you with splendid views of the pine-covered foothills and jagged white mountains. The trail is an easy grade through the woods and up to open clearings. It culminates in a flat summit with a lookout station. From here, the western views of the Three Sisters, Mount Jefferson, and Mount Hood are breathtaking. To the east you can see the steep, sheer **Smith Rocks** rising from the desert.

For a longer hike (about four hours) and an even higher perspective, drive 11 miles west of Sisters on Route 242 to **Black Crater Trail.** It's open from July through mid-October. Steep in spots, the hike is challenging but not unreasonable. And the vista is worth the effort.

After climbing wooded slopes and ridges to a 7,251-foot summit of rough lava, you'll see Mount Washington, Three Fingered Jack, the Three Sisters, Mount

Jefferson, Olallie Butte, and Mount Hood's snowy cap rising 11,235 feet on the north—all the major peaks of the Oregon Cascades. Clearly evident is the Belknap Crater flow of black lava, spreading below.

LUNCH: Pick up a picnic lunch for the trail at **Depot Deli,** 250 West Cascade Street (541–549–2572), or grab some handcrafted baked goods at **Angelina's Bakery and Cafe,** 121 West Main Street (541–549–9122), which even carries dairy-free cupcakes.

Afternoon

Return to your vehicle, and travel north on Route 20 over **Santiam Pass,** which lies between the Mount Jefferson and Mount Washington wilderness areas. When you reach State Route 22, angle northward to follow the curving, cascading **Santiam River.** On either side of the mountainous road are evergreen and decid-uous forests dotted white with dogwood blooms in spring.

The Santiam flows into the deep green, dammed reservoir of **Detroit Lake.** Past the dam, rocky cliffs rise sharply on your right. Waterfalls bounce over them, occasionally splashing the road.

Descending from the mountains, passing small timber towns, you'll eventually reach the lush farmlands of the **Willamette Valley.** Continue on to Salem and the juncture with Interstate 5 for the forty-five-minute drive north on the freeway to Portland.

There's More

Cascade Lakes Highway. This 89-mile scenic loop road provides glorious views of lakes, meadows, Mount Bachelor, the Three Sisters, and Broken Top. At Crane Prairie Reservoir, stop to walk a ¼-mile nature trail to see one of the few osprey nesting sites in the United States. (Cascade Lakes Highway is closed to autos in winter.)

Crooked River Dinner Train and Entertainment Company, 4075 Northeast O'Neil Road, Redmond; (541) 548–8630. Dinner trains weekend evenings, plus Sunday brunch. Murder mysteries and Western hoedowns on two-and-a-half-hour scenic rides.

Horseback riding. Eagle Crest Resort, (541) 595–2061 or (541) 549–6765 (winter only); Nova Stables, Inn at the Seventh Mountain, (541) 382–8711; Sunriver Resort, (541) 593–1000 or (800) 547–3922 (not available during winter months); Smartass Ranch, Redmond, (541) 280–9356.

Lava Cast Forest, 14 miles south of Bend. From Route 97, turn east on Forest Road 9720, opposite the Sunriver turnoff. This is the world's largest grouping of lava tree molds. A paved, self-guided nature trail leads through the lava flow.

Lava River Cave, Newberry National Volcanic Monument, 12 miles south of Bend on Route 97; (541) 593–2421. In summer months, lanterns are rented for tours of the mile-long lava cave. Bring walking shoes and a warm jacket. Open early May to mid-October.

Operation Santa Claus, 4355 West Highway 126; (541) 548–8910. Two miles west of Redmond on State Route 126. World's largest commercial reindeer ranch, with one hundred reindeer. Visit newborns in May and June. Open daily.

Petersen Rock Garden and Museum, 7930 Southwest Seventy-seventh Street; (541) 382–5574. Ten miles north of Bend off Route 97. Four-acre park of miniature bridges, towers, and buildings, all made with various types of rocks. Picnic area, lily ponds, peacocks. Open daily.

Pine Mountain Observatory, 30 miles southeast of Bend off Highway 20; (541) 382–8331. Observe the skies on Friday and Saturday evenings in spring and summer; reservations required.

Rock climbing. Smith Rock State Park, north of Redmond in Crooked River Canyon, has massive, colorful rock formations that present a steep challenge to climbers and a fascinating spectator sport for watchers. There's First Ascent Climbing Service, Inc. (800–325–5462), a climbing school and guide service in Terrebonne.

White-water rafting. Imperial River Company, Maupin, (800) 395–3903; Ouzel Outfitters, Box 827, Bend, OR 97709; (800) 788–7236.

Special Events

Late January. Gallery Art Walk, downtown Bend. Evening walking tour to get acquainted with the arts. Showings, demonstrations.

May. U.S. Bank Pole-Pedal-Paddle Race, Bend. Downhill and cross-country ski, run, bicycle, and canoe on the Deschutes River.

June. Pi-Ume-Sha Celebration, Warm Springs. A lively Native American celebration with authentic music and dancing.

July. Sisters Outdoor Quilt Show, Sisters. Quilters from all over show their work. Largest outdoor quilt show in the country.

Late August. Cascade Festival of Music, Bend. Eight-day series of concerts in Drake Park. Jazz, classical, chamber music, Broadway favorites. Concession stands, strolling minstrels, open rehearsals, student workshops. Call (541) 382–8381 for ticket information.

Other Recommended Restaurants and Lodgings

Bend

Hans Restaurant, 915 Northwest Wall Street; (541) 389–9700. Conveniently located in the heart of downtown Bend. Originally a small coffee shop and European-style bakery, Hans is now a full-scale restaurant, bakery, and wine cellar with its own following. Lunch and dinner menus highlight European cuisine at reasonable prices.

Legends Publick House, 125 Northwest Oregon Avenue; (541) 382–5654. American regional cuisine in casual upscale setting.

McMenamins Old St. Francis School, 700 Northwest Bond Street; (541) 382–5174 or (877) 661–4228. Right in the heart of downtown Bend. These classrooms–turned–lodging rooms are gigantic and, with their vintage-style upholstery and furnishings, a far cry from the stark classrooms of yesteryear. Inside the same building is a movie theater with sofas and reclining chairs, where it's OK to eat pizza and burgers. The complex also boasts a Turkish-style soaking pool and McMenamins Old St. Francis Pub, with indoor and outdoor seating, and nicely prepared food at reasonable prices.

Westside Cafe and Bakery, 1005½ Northwest Galveston Avenue; (541) 382–3426. Highly popular for breakfast and lunch. Natural foods, great muffins and sandwiches, reasonable prices.

Black Butte

Black Butte Ranch, P.O. Box 8000, 97759; (541) 595–6211 or (866) 901–2961. Quiet retreat and top-quality contemporary resort in spectacular setting of wide meadows surrounded by mountains. Golf, tennis, restaurant. Eight miles west of Sisters on Highway 20.

Sisters

Conklin's Guest House, 69013 Camp Polk Road; (541) 549–0123 or (800) 549–4262. Homey, friendly bed-and-breakfast on four and a half acres with mountain views. Five guest rooms with private baths. Romantic setting for weddings.

The Lodge at Suttle Lake, 13300 Highway 20; (541) 595–2628. Offers three historic cabins, six rustic cabins, and eleven lodge suites, most with fabulous lake views. Relaxing in front of the large stone fireplace in the great room with a hot cuppa and an engaging book is a welcome treat for hikers, skiers, or exhausted travelers. Gourmet dining is available in the Lodge on Friday and Saturday nights during winter months, with expanded hours in the summer.

Sunriver

Sunriver Lodge and Resort, P.O. Box 3609, 97707; (541) 593–1221 or (800) 801–8765; www.sunriver-resort.com. Major resort community, with lodge rooms and rental homes. Many amenities and recreational facilities.

Warm Springs

Kah-Nee-Ta High Desert Resort, P.O. Box 1240, 97761; (541) 553–1112 or (800) 554–4SUN; www.kahneeta.com. Resort and convention center on a hilltop in Warm Springs Indian Reservation. Tribal culture and heritage displayed through-out lodge. Swimming, golf, fishing, mineral baths. Breakfast, lunch, and dinner served at the Chinook Room; dinner at the more formal Juniper Restaurant. Look for the traditional Native American salmon bake that begins in May and continues through Labor Day weekend. Comfortable accommodations.

For More Information

Bend Chamber of Commerce, 777 Northwest Wall Street, Suite 200, Bend, OR 97701; (541) 382–3221; www.bendchamber.org.

Central Oregon Visitors Association, 661 Southwest Powerhouse Drive, Suite 130, Bend, OR 97402; (541) 389–8799 or (800) 800–8334; www.visitcentraloregon .com.

Sisters Area Chamber of Commerce, P.O. Box 430, Sisters, OR 97759; (541) 549–0251; www.sisterschamber.com.

Wilderness maps and trail information available from Deschutes National Forest, 1001 Southeast Em Kay Drive, Bend, OR 97702; (541) 383–4000; www.fs.fed.us/r6/centraloregon.

SEATTLE
ESCAPES

SEATTLE ESCAPE ONE

San Juan and Orcas Islands

Islands In the Sun / 2 Nights

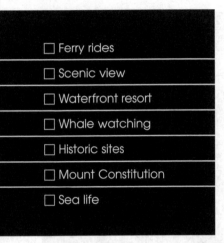

- ☐ Ferry rides
- ☐ Scenic view
- ☐ Waterfront resort
- ☐ Whale watching
- ☐ Historic sites
- ☐ Mount Constitution
- ☐ Sea life

You will see all kinds of sea life when you ferry to the San Juan Islands: seagulls, whales, seals, eagles, boaters, fishers, islanders, and tourists in funny hats. With luck, you'll see some of the three pods of black-and-white orca whales that live year-round in these waters.

Not all of the 172 islands of the San Juan Archipelago are accessible by ferry. We'll see the four biggest islands. Our Washington State ferry leaves from Anacortes, on Fidalgo Island, and stops at Lopez and Orcas Islands on its way to San Juan Island. Friday Harbor, on San Juan Island, is the only real town in the archipelago and has all the necessary facilities.

This escape is by car but can be adjusted for other transportation, including bicycle, taxi, and van shuttle. Go off-season or as a foot passenger to avoid long car-ferry waits in summer, when 50,000 island travelers swell to 250,000. Call (800) 84–FERRY for schedules.

Day 1 / Morning

From **Anacortes,** 85 miles north of Seattle, catch a ferry west for a one-and-a-quarter-hour ride through island-dotted waters to **Orcas Island.** Orcas was named not for whales but for the Mexican viceroy who charted the island along with Spanish explorer Francisco Eliza in 1791. He saw what you'll see, a 57-square-mile U-shaped island of thickly forested hills, with fjordlike inlets and 125 miles of pebbled shoreline.

Drive Horseshoe Highway 13 miles north from the ferry dock to **Eastsound,** a snug community at the head of the island's largest bay and the only commercial settlement.

Much of the valuable tribal collection housed in the **Orcas Island Historical Museum** (181 North Beach Road, P.O. Box 134, Eastsound, WA 98245; 360–376–4849) was saved by Ethan Allen, the San Juan Islands' superintendent of schools around the turn of the century. His hand-built boat, used to row among the

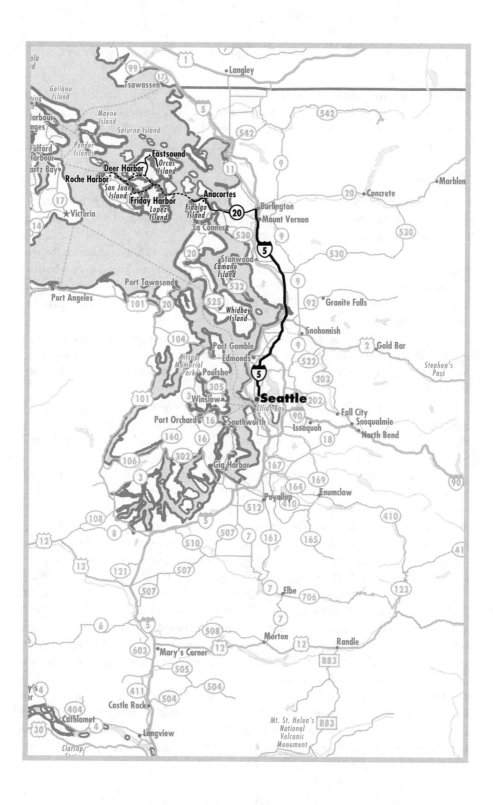

islands when he visited the schools, is in the exhibition, which is set in six homestead cabins.

LUNCH: Rose's Bakery and Café, 382 Prune Alley, Eastsound; (360)
376–5805. Artisan breads are baked in-house and waft through the cafe, which
incorporates seasonal, local produce in soups, salads, and sandwiches. Located in the
old Eastsound fire station next to Library Park.

Afternoon

Browse through Eastsound shops, especially **Darvill's,** a combination bookstore–
rare print shop. It's the oldest art gallery in the San Juan Islands and has an extensive
collection of antique and contemporary prints.

Drive Horseshoe Highway 5 miles southeast to 5,175-acre **Moran State
Park,** where a narrow, steep road leads another 5 miles to the top of **Mount
Constitution,** the highest point in the San Juans at 2,409 feet. From the 50-foot
stone lookout tower, built in 1936 by the Civilian Conservation Corps, there's a
see-forever view.

At your feet the forested mountain, lakes sparkling on its slopes, drops to a blue
ocean and an archipelago of green islands that stretch to the horizon. To the east,
on the mainland, you can see the snowy peaks of **Mount Baker** and **Mount
Rainier.**

An afternoon in or near the park can include biking, fishing, sailing, or kayaking. (See "There's More.") **Cascade Lake,** the biggest lake on the island, offers
three campgrounds, a playground, picnic tables, restrooms, and rental boats.
Swimming is good, but the area is crowded in summer.

Rent a rowboat and fish for trout in the stocked lake. Or hike the 2½-mile
loop trail that starts west of the picnic area. It winds along a bluff above the lake,
crosses a log bridge, and curves through forests of Douglas fir before circling back
to the starting place. You may spy ducks, muskrat, otters, and great blue herons.

Continue east down Horseshoe Highway 2 miles beyond the state park to
Olga. The tiny community is centered by a post office and a combined art gallery
and cafe. **Cafe Olga's** (103 Olga Road; 360–376–5098) is open every day from
10:00 A.M. to 5:30 P.M. Homemade cinnamon rolls and blackberry and lemon
Shaker pies are Cafe Olga's trademark. Smoked salmon salad and roasted eggplant
and hummus sandwiches are inventive lunch favorites. A limited breakfast menu
offers baked eggs, eggs rancheros, hearty granola, and breakfast milkshakes. And at
Orcas Island Artworks (360–376–4408), more than fifty artists display their wares
daily from March through December.

Or you can drive south past the Olga turnoff to Doe Bay Road and begin a
kayaking adventure at **Doe Bay Village Resort and Retreat** (107 Doe Bay
Road, P.O. Box 437, Olga, WA 98279; 360–376–2291), where **Shearwater Sea
Kayak Tours** (360–376–4699; www.shearwaterkayaks.com) offers several kayak

trips, encompassing all skill levels. No experience is necessary. On one ride that's suitable for all ages, you'll paddle to **Doe Island Marine Park** and **Gorilla Rock,** returning via Rosario Strait. You're likely to spot dolphins, whales, and bald and golden eagles.

Follow the signs on Horseshoe Highway to **Rosario Resort,** which faces Cascade Bay on the edge of the sound. The centerpiece of the resort is the mansion built by Robert Moran, a shipbuilder and onetime mayor of Seattle. Consider attending the regular organ concert and a lively talk on the history of the estate. Moran came here in 1905 thinking he had only a short time to live. In his fifty-four-room home he installed a swimming pool, a bowling alley, and a music room containing an enormous pipe organ. Moran then lived on to a ripe old age. In 1920 he donated much of what is now **Moran State Park** to the state of Washington.

DINNER: Rosario Resort, 1400 Rosario Road, Eastsound; (360) 376–2222 or (866) 801–7625. Multilevel restaurant overlooking the sheltered waters of Cascade Bay. Serves a variety of American and continental dishes. Separate lounge on premises serves light meals and breakfast, lunch, and dinner.

LODGING: **Turtleback Farm Inn,** 1981 Crow Valley Road; (360) 376–4914 or (800) 376–4914. Take Horseshoe Highway back through Eastsound to this classic farmhouse-turned-country-inn. Seven comfortable rooms with private baths, common room with fireplace, and expansive deck overlooking eighty acres of pasture and woodland. This renowned bed-and-breakfast fills up quickly, so book your room early.

Day 2 / Morning

BREAKFAST: A full and fortifying breakfast at Turtleback Farm Inn.

Take a scenic drive down **Deer Harbor Road** to the lighthouse, then circle back around West Sound and down Horseshoe Highway to the ferry terminal. Park your car and choose between two great morning adventures: biking and whale watching.

Orcas Island Eclipse Charters, at Orcas Ferry Landing on Orcas Island (360–376–6566 or 800–376–6566), tracks whales for its four-hour whale-watching trips that leave the Orcas Ferry Dock at approximately 9:00 A.M. and 2:00 P.M. seven days a week, March through October. Take this opportunity to see killer and minke whales, harbor seals, porpoises, bald eagles, ospreys, and other marine animals and wildlife. Pass by many of the spectacular 172 San Juan Islands.

Dolphin Bay Bicycles, located at Orcas Ferry Landing (360–317–6734 or 360–376–4157), rents bicycles near the ferry terminal. Bill Fletcher of Turtleback Farm Inn suggests a two-hour route. Circle east on White Beach Road, go northwest on Dolphin Bay Road, take a brief detour to West Sound, and then go south down Horseshoe Highway back to the ferry. You can do this circle either clockwise or counterclockwise, but time it to avoid heavy traffic going on or off the ferry.

LUNCH: Try the seafood chowder at either the **Westsound Cafe** (360–376–4440) at the corner of Crow Valley Road and Deer Harbor Road or at the historic 12-room **Orcas Hotel** (P.O. Box 369, Orcas, WA 98280; 360–376–4300 or 888–672–2792), across the road from the ferry landing.

Afternoon

Ferry schedules change but the forty-five-minute direct ferry to San Juan Island typically leaves at 10:45 A.M. and 4:40 P.M. A midday ferry via Shaw and Lopez Islands might take an hour and a half.

You will land in **Friday Harbor,** a bustling wharfside village on San Juan Island. Pick up maps and brochures at the visitor center in the nearby Cannery Landing Building, behind the open-air market.

For a casual in-town lunch with good salads, sandwiches, and baked goods, stop by the **Garden Path Café,** 135 Second Avenue (360–378–6255). Popular items are homemade meatloaf sandwiches and Reuben panini.

The **San Juan Island National Historic Park** office, 650 Mullis Street, Suite 100 (360–378–2902; open daily in summer), and the **San Juan Island Historical Museum,** 405 Price Street (360–378–3949; open 1:00 to 4:30 P.M. Wednesday through Saturday in summer), offer historic exhibits that explain the island's contentious past and an extensive oral history collection of the island's Native Americans and Japanese settlers.

During the mid-1800s, Britain and the United States shared the island in an uneasy truce. When an American farmer shot a British pig that was disturbing his potato patch, the British authorities threatened to arrest the U.S. citizen. The farmer appealed for help, and soon both sides were lined up for war (not solely because of the pig; San Juan Island has a most strategic location).

The dispute was settled peacefully, however, with the two camps establishing headquarters at opposite ends of the island. Through arbitration they finally agreed to American rule. Now the incident is remembered as the **Pig War.**

San Juan Transit (360–378–8887 or 800–887–8387) will take you on an island tour in season. **Susie's Moped,** 125 Nichols, just up from the ferry landing (360–378–5244 or 800–532–0087), rents mopeds by the hour or day. If you're driving yourself, head northwest for 10 miles on Roche Harbor Road to a historic complex that combines resort, marina, church, and cottages in **Roche Harbor.**

Walk the docks and photograph the old church, and then turn south again to **British Camp,** at Garrison Bay. This portion of San Juan Island National Historical Park is where British troops were stationed during the infamous Pig War. Four restored buildings house interpretive exhibits. From the small formal garden, a trail rises to an overlook where officers were quartered.

Walk the **Bell Point Trail,** a level 1-mile hike above Garrison Bay, to reach a beach and a view of neighboring Westcott Bay. Or walk from the barracks exhibit to a cemetery for servicemen who died during the British occupation. Another ½-mile trail leads up 650-foot Mount Young for a far-reaching view of the sea, scattered islands, and the Olympic and Cascade Mountains.

From British Camp, drive south to **Lime Kiln Point State Park,** where a trail leads to picturesque **Lime Kiln Lighthouse,** built in 1919 and now on the National Register of Historic Places.

Head south again to **Whalewatch Park,** the best location on the island to observe the three pods of black-and-white orcas that live in the waters around the San Juans. This is the nation's only whale-watching park. Signs and pictures tell you how to identify porpoises and orca and minke whales.

If you sight whales, call the toll-free Whale Hotline (800–562–8832) in Washington. Reports of sightings help the Moclips Cetological Society to further its research.

Continue south to the southern tip of the island and **American Camp.** This section of the National Historical Park may seem bleak, with its windswept shores and open fields, but it, too, played an important part in island history. From the Exhibit Center an interpretive loop trail leads to the **Officers' Quarters** and the **Hudson's Bay Company** farm site. Farther down the road you'll find a parking area and several more walking paths. The hike to **Jakle's Lagoon,** along the old roadbed, passes through a grove of Douglas firs, and a walk up **Mount Finlayson** (290 feet high) presents another broad seascape and mountain vista.

On **South Beach,** the longest public beach on San Juan Island, bird-watchers will spot terns, plovers, greater and lesser yellowlegs, and bald eagles. Tide pools hold an abundance of marine life. You can salmon-fish from the beach if you have a license. Return to Friday Harbor.

DINNER: Duck Soup Inn, 50 Duck Soup Lane; (360) 378–4878. Fresh seafood and a varied wine list. Entree choices change regularly. Located north of town; closed in winter. **Vinny's Ristorante,** 165 West Street; (360) 378–1934. Make reservations for a window seat, and feast on crab chiappino or tender calamari. An epicurean sensation, just perfect for a special-occasion celebration.

LODGING: Longhouse Bed and Breakfast, 2187 Mitchell Bay Road; (360) 378–2568 or (360) 378–9728. Five rooms in a historic building that was a Native American longhouse. The space still exudes much of its dignity from yesteryear.

Day 3 / Morning

BREAKFAST: Guests at the Longhouse rave about the breakfasts, which begin with espresso drinks and homemade scones and continue with entrees such as quiche and locally made chicken sausage, and Dutch Baby pancakes with crème fraîche and fresh-cut strawberries. Dinner is also available with prior arrangement.

Visit the **Whale Museum** (62 First Street North, P.O. Box 945, Friday Harbor, WA 98250; 360–378–4710), one of the great attractions on the island. Life-size models of orca whales and numerous exhibits provide a quick education on whale life and habits.

Wander through the art galleries and gift shops. In Churchill Square's Atelier Gallerie, monoprints and finely detailed scrimshaw work are displayed. Calohan Studio exhibits marine art and sculpture. Waterworks Gallery has changing shows, usually themed (flowers, landscapes, and mythology are examples), with works by regional artists.

The **Island Dive and Watersports,** 2A Spring Street Landing (800–303–8386), offers snorkeling and scuba diving classes as well as charter diving boats and guides. You can also go whale watching, fishing, or sailing with various skippers who operate out of these docks. (See "There's More.")

LUNCH: Front Street Cafe, 7 Front Street; (360) 378–2245. Simple, cafeteria-style eatery serving sandwiches, chili, soups, and ice cream.

Afternoon

Watch for your ferry while you have lunch. It is a one-and-a-half-hour ferry ride back to Anacortes. Expect to pass through U.S. Customs when you disembark; since you haven't been across the border into Canada, it's a momentary procedure.

From Anacortes, drive east on Highway 20 to Interstate 5, or return to Seattle via **Whidbey Island.**

There's More

Lopez Island

The ferry stops between Orcas and San Juan Islands at Lopez Island, popular with bicyclists because of its level roads.

Orcas Island

Bicycling. Dolphin Bay Bicycles, Orcas Ferry Landing, Eastsound; (360) 376–4157 or (360) 376–3093.

Island Bicycles, P.O. Box 1609, 380 Argyle Avenue, Friday Harbor, WA 98250; (360) 378–4941.

By air. Magic Air Tours Inc., P.O. Box 223, Eastsound, WA 98245; (360) 376–2733 or (800) 376–1929; www.magicair.com. Scenic guided tour flights with music in a yellow-and-red vintage biplane. Leather helmet, goggles, and scarf provided. Hangar with aeronautic memorabilia and hands-on activities for children.

Cruises. Sharon L. Charters, Box 10, Orcas, WA 98280; (360) 376–4305. Picnic and three-hour sunset/moonlight sail in classic wooden boat.

Shopping. Crow Valley Pottery (2274 Orcas Road; 360–376–4260); Howe Art Gallery (360–376–2945), located ¼ mile west of Eastsound, featuring indoor and outdoor copper and stainless-steel sculptures.

Whale watching. Deer Harbor Charters; (360) 376–5989 or (800) 544–5758. You can sail bareboat or with a skipper, rent small boats by the hour or day, take a water taxi to any island destination, go whale watching, charter a guided fishing trip, or take a sunset cruise.

A list of other whale-watching tours is available at www.san-juan.net.

San Juan Island

Bicycling. Experience Plus Bicycle Tours; (360) 685–4565.

By air. Kenmore Air (6321 Northeast 175th Street; 425–486–1257 or 800–543–9595; www.kenmoreair.com) flies to San Juan Island from the Seattle suburb of Bellevue.

Cruises. San Juan Boat Tours, 355 Harris Avenue, #104, Bellingham, WA 98225; (360) 378–8099. Wildlife and whale-watching tours.

Western Prince Cruises, P.O. Box 418, Friday Harbor, WA 98250; (360) 378–5315 or (800) 757–6722. Call for hours. Narrated by Whale Museum naturalist.

Fishing. Trophy Charters, P.O. Box 2444, Friday Harbor, WA 98250; (360) 378–2110. Fishing, sailing, powerboat charters.

North Shore Charters, P.O. Box 316, Eastsound, WA 98245; (360) 376–4855. Fishing charters for ling cod, halibut, and rock fish. Takes up to six people.

Kayaking. Sea Quest Kayak Expeditions, P.O. Box 2424, Friday Harbor, WA 98250; (360) 378–5767 or (888) 589–4253. Biologist guides on kayaks share their expertise on whales and Orcas tide-pool creatures. Half-day tours to Lime Kiln Whale Watch Park and two- to five-day camping trips to smaller islands.

San Juan Safaris (800–450–6858) leads whale-watching and kayaking trips April through October. Three- and five-hour-long kayak tours in the San Juan Islands.

San Juan Kayak Expeditions, 3090B Roche Harbor Road, P.O. Box 2041, Friday Harbor, WA 98250; (360) 378–4436. Three- to four-day sea-kayak expeditions around the San Juans and Canadian Gulf Islands.

Special Events

May. International Orca Fest of the San Juan Islands, a street fair with music, a whale symposium, and whale tours.

Memorial Day Kids Fest, Eastsound. Salmon barbecue, quartet competition, live performances.

July. Fourth of July. Historical Day, Eastsound, Orcas Island. Parade, pie-eating contest, games, music, fireworks.

August. Orcas Island Chamber Music Festival. World-class musicians performing in a series of concerts.

September. Anacortes Jazz Festival. Scenic wharfside concerts featuring top-notch jazz talent and local seafood.

Other Recommended Restaurants and Lodgings

Orcas Island

Bartwood Lodge, 178 Fossil Bay Drive, Eastsound; (360) 376–2242 or (888) 817–2242. Eighteen rooms, all with private bathrooms, minifridges, and microwave ovens. Some rooms have water views. Three suites also available.

Christina's, 310 Main Street; (360) 376–4904. Famous (and expensive) restaurant serving imaginative, well-prepared Northwest cuisine. Ask for a table on the porch for the best views of East Sound.

Orcas Hotel, 1 Waterfront Street, P.O. Box 155, 98280; (360) 376–4300 or (888) 672–2792. Remodeled twelve-room historic hotel with Victorian flavor. Overlooks ferry landing.

Otters Pond Bed and Breakfast, 100 Tomihi Drive, P.O. Box 1540, Eastsound, 98245; (360) 376–8844 or (888) 893–9680. Five rooms with private baths overlook a pond and wetlands. Amenities such as thick bathrobes, a hot tub, library, and an exquisite garden create a quiet and comfy respite for visitors. Each day begins with a lavish five-course breakfast.

Rosario Resort, 1400 Rosario Road; (360) 376–2222 or (800) 562–8820. Former private estate on gorgeous Cascade Bay. Rooms in outlying buildings have basic motel amenities; the mansion has a restaurant and lounge, indoor and outdoor pools, and spa facilities.

Friday Harbor

Blue Dolphin, 185 First Street; (360) 378–6116. Breakfast served from 5:00 A.M. to 2:00 P.M. and lunch from 11:00 A.M. to 2:00 P.M. Nice atmosphere for families.

Clay Café, 10 First Street North; (360) 378–5544. Sells espresso, baked goods. Living up to its name, ceramicware is available for purchase.

Lonesome Cove, 416 Lonesome Cove Road; (360) 378–4477. Secluded retreat on Speiden Channel. Six log cabins, all with kitchens and fireplaces.

Olympic Lights, 146 Starlight Way; (888) 211–6195. Bed-and-breakfast in 1895 farmhouse on five acres at south end of the island. Three rooms with contemporary furnishings, white carpets. Full vegetarian breakfast included.

Trumpeter Inn Bed and Breakfast, 318 Trumpeter Way; (360) 378–3884 or (800) 826–7926. Quiet country inn of charm and grace. Several rooms recently remodeled; one is wheelchair accessible. Full breakfast.

Wildwood Manor, 3021 Roche Harbor Road; (360) 378–3447 or (877) 298–1144. Surrounded by forest, wildlife, and San Juan Channel water views. Sits on nine acres, with immense lawns and lovely gardens. Impeccably decorated rooms. Serves homemade baked goods, fresh fruit, and hot entrees.

For More Information

Orcas Island Chamber of Commerce, P.O. Box 252, Eastsound, WA 98245; (360) 376–2273; www.orcasisland.org.

San Juan Island Chamber of Commerce, P.O. Box 98, Friday Harbor, WA 98250; (360) 378–5240; www.sanjuanisland.org.

Washington State Ferries, 2901 Third Avenue, Suite 500, Seattle, WA 98121-3014; (206) 464–6400 or (888) 808–7977; www.wsdot.wa.gov/ferries. The ferries all depart from Pier 52.

SEATTLE ESCAPE TWO

Strait of Juan de Fuca

Touring the Northern Olympic Peninsula / 2 Nights

Between the Olympic Peninsula's verdant wilderness and the southern rim of Vancouver Island lies the Strait of Juan de Fuca, dividing the United States from Canada. The sometimes-treacherous, always-fascinating waterway separates Puget Sound and the San Juan and Gulf Islands from the wild Pacific.

- [ ] Ferry rides
- [ ] Views of Puget Sound and Strait of Juan de Fuca
- [ ] Historical museums
- [ ] National Wildlife Refuge
- [ ] Native American museum
- [ ] Northwest corner of United States
- [ ] Makah Indian reservation
- [ ] Hiking trails
- [ ] Rugged coastline
- [ ] Waterfalls

The 110-mile road edging the strait takes you through a microcosm of the variety found on the peninsula. From its eastern tip, where a quaint town clings to its Victorian heyday, to the native fishing village and fog-shrouded coast on the far western corner, the peninsula provides glimpses of great diversity.

Day 1 / Morning

Take the Winslow ferry from Elliott Bay, Seattle, to Bainbridge Island, and head for the Hood Canal Bridge. Cross the bridge to the **Olympic Peninsula,** and turn north on Paradise Bay Road, which follows the coastline (passing Port Ludlow Golf Resort and housing development) and curves inland toward U.S. Route 20. Through the trees you'll catch glimpses of pleasure boats on **Admiralty Inlet** as you continue north to **Port Townsend.**

Much of this attractive town, which is divided between a downtown waterfront district and a residential area on a bluff above it, is a designated **National Historic District.** Victorian homes and commercial buildings, built in the late nineteenth century when Port Townsend was expected to become a great seaport, have been restored with pride.

The town was named in 1792 by Captain George Vancouver in honor of an English marquis, but it wasn't officially established until 1851, when the first set-

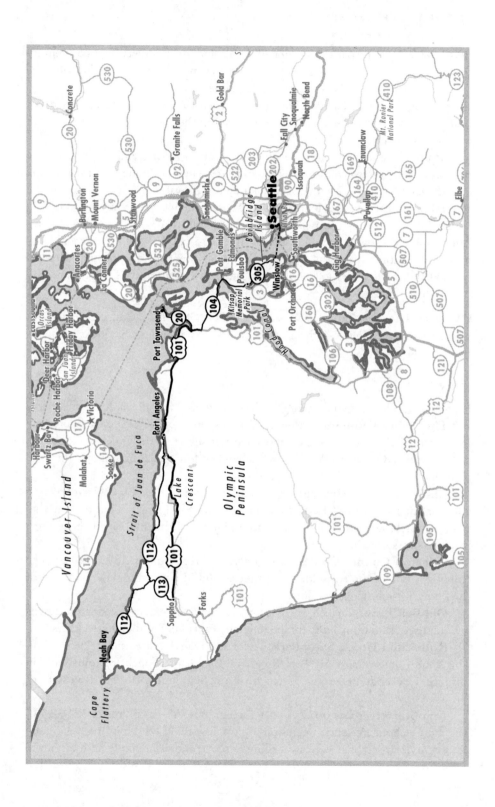

tlers built a log cabin at the corner of Water and Tyler Streets. The community grew, and its prospects as a center of commerce seemed limitless until the transcontinental railroad was laid—and stopped at Seattle.

Out on the peninsula, Port Townsend was left to languish until its charm as a little-changed Victorian seaport was recognized in the 1970s. Now it booms with tourism and as an arts center.

At the chamber of commerce office, pick up brochures and a tour map that points out seventy-two historic homes and sites. Then continue into town to the end of Water Street and the city hall newly renovated to accommodate the **Jefferson County Historical Society Museum,** 540 Water Street (360–385–1003). Well-conceived and well-preserved exhibits on the region's Native Americans and early Chinese inhabitants, the Victorian era, and military and maritime memorabilia make this a worthwhile stop. Open Friday through Monday from 11:00 A.M. to 4:00 P.M. Park your car in this area; most of the tour is easy walking from here.

LUNCH: **The Landfall,** 412 Water Street; (360) 385–5814. Casual, friendly spot serving hamburgers, alder-barbecued seafood, Mexican dishes. Overlooks marina at Point Hudson.

Afternoon

Highlights you'll see as you explore this history-steeped town include the following:

The Haller Fountain, Taylor and Washington Streets. The bronze figure, variously named Galatea, Venus, and Innocence, was shown at the Chicago Exhibition of 1893. It was donated to Port Townsend by Theodore Haller in honor of the early pioneers.

Chinese Tree of Heaven, a spreading tree, nearly 150 years old, said to be a gift from the emperor of China. It was intended for San Francisco, but the ship carrying it was blown off course near Port Townsend. In thanks for his happy stay here, the ship's captain left the tree.

Jefferson County Courthouse, Jefferson Street. Built in 1892, the castlelike building is one of the two oldest courthouses still in use in the state. Its 100-foot clock tower is a beacon to sailors.

Old Bell Tower, on a bluff at Tyler and Jefferson Streets, overlooking the downtown district, dates from 1890. It's the only one of its kind in the United States.

Rothschild House State Park, Taylor and Franklin Streets (360–385–1003). This 1868 home of an early Port Townsend merchant is open for tours daily in summer, weekends in winter. Listed on both State and National Registers of Historic Places.

Ann Starrett Mansion, 744 Clay Street (360–385–3205 or 800–321–0644). The most elaborate Victorian mansion in Port Townsend was built in 1899 in classic stick style. Its circular staircase, ceiling frescoes, and elaborate furnishings make afternoon tours popular with visitors. The house is now in use as a bed-and-breakfast inn.

After your walking tour of this waterfront town, check the myriad shops of Water Street and "Uptown," a business district on Lawrence Street that was originally begun so that respectable ladies would not have to venture to the rougher waterfront area to shop.

Sooner or later everyone stops for ice cream or a delectable espresso-chip brownie at **Elevated Ice Cream,** 627 Water Street (360–385–1156). The bright little shop is reputed to have the best ice cream in the state.

A drive out to **Fort Worden State Park** will take you to the location where *An Officer and a Gentleman* was filmed. Built at the turn of the twentieth century as a base to defend Puget Sound, Fort Worden is a 330-acre estate with an army cemetery, officers' quarters, theater, parade grounds, gun emplacements, bronze foundry, and Point Wilson Light Station.

The Centrum Foundation, a nonprofit arts organization, is based here. Numerous workshops, classes, and programs are presented regularly.

At the **Port Townsend Marine Science Center,** Fort Worden State Park, 532 Battery Way (360–385–5582), in a historic building on the public fishing pier at Fort Worden, visitors can touch and handle sea creatures at open "wet tables." Starfish, sea cucumbers, tube worms, and other marine life live in the touch tanks. The center holds classes in marine ecology, shows informative slide shows, and runs workshops. It's open afternoons in summer, Tuesday through Sunday, and weekends in fall and spring.

On the return trip into town, stop at **Chetzemoka Park** to stroll the grassy grounds and enjoy the fragrant rose garden. The park is named for a Clallam Indian chief who assisted the community in its earliest days. Chetzemoka Park has a bandstand, picnic tables, playground equipment, and access to the beach.

DINNER: The Fountain Cafe, 920 Washington Street; (360) 385–1364. Small, unpretentious restaurant on a hillside above the downtown area. Sublime chowder, pastas, dinners, and desserts.

LODGING: James House, 1238 Washington Street; (360) 385–1238 or (800) 385–1238. Grand Victorian home built in 1891. Three floors with ten antiques-furnished rooms, all with private baths.

Day 2 / Morning

BREAKFAST: Fruit, yogurt, and granola, plus a basket of hot scones and muffins, served in the kitchen at James House.

Drive 13 miles south on Route 20 to U.S. Highway 101; turn right to curve around Discovery Bay and Sequim Bay. Continue 17 miles west to **Port Angeles.** On your right is the **Strait of Juan de Fuca,** a wide channel that defines the border between Washington and Vancouver Island, British Columbia. On the left the Olympic Range rises 7,000 feet, snow clad and craggy, in Olympic National Park.

Drive to **Port Angeles Fine Art Center,** 1203 East Lauridsen Boulevard (360–417–4590). This gallery is in an award-winning home on five parklike acres overlooking the city, with views of the mountains and water. Visual arts exhibitions are shown year-round. The center is open from 11:00 A.M. to 5:00 P.M. Tuesday through Sunday.

If it's a weekday, tour the **Clallam County Historical Museum,** 223 East Fourth Street (360–417–2364; open 10:00 A.M. to 4:00 P.M. Monday through Friday). On the second floor of the brick, Georgian-style courthouse are photographs of early Port Angeles, maritime exhibits, and a replica of an old-fashioned country store complete with a checkers game set up on a barrel.

The courthouse itself is interesting. Built in 1914 and now on the state and national historic registers, it has a stained-glass skylight, a clock tower, and a view of **Port Angeles harbor** 4 blocks down the hill. On a clear day you can see across the strait to downtown Victoria. Hike or bike the 6-mile waterfront trail past the port district.

LUNCH: **Chestnut Cottage,** 929 East Front Street; (360) 452–8344. Big salads, fresh pasta in a light, airy, smoke-free atmosphere. Owner Diane Nagler also owns First Street Haven (360–457–0352), a delightful little place at 107 First Street.

Afternoon

Drive west on US 101 for 5 miles, and branch onto Route 112, which skirts the rim of the peninsula. Far less traveled than the main highway, the route has a greater sense of wilderness. On your right is the rolling surf of Juan de Fuca and beyond it Vancouver Island, its hills looming hazily green and peaked with frost. Eagles perch in the trees and soar above the water; smoke from wood stoves drifts through the air.

At **Salt Creek Recreation Area,** stop to explore the tide pools among the rocks. Now a county park, Salt Creek was once a World War II defense site. You can still see bunkers and gun emplacements. The park has hiking trails, a kitchen shelter and picnic area, showers, a playground, a softball field, and horseshoe pits.

Farther west, **Clallam Bay** and **Sekiu,** neighboring communities divided by a harbor, host thousands of visitors yearly who come in search of salmon and immense halibut. Resorts and charter companies offer boat rentals and ocean trips. Scuba divers seek abalone off the coast.

The tide pools at **Slip Point** are particularly interesting for their teeming sea life. You may encounter scuba divers in search of octopus. Around the point are ancient fossil beds exposed by natural erosion.

Continue to the **Makah Indian Reservation** and the village of **Neah Bay**

(67 miles west of Port Angeles). This is the home of the **Makah Cultural and Research Center,** Bayview Avenue and Highway 12 (360–645–2711), a highlight of the trip.

The $2-million museum, built in 1979, contains a superb collection of Northwest Indian artifacts—more than 55,000. Most were found in the Makah archaeological dig at **Lake Ozette.** There are canoes, intricate weavings of cedar and bird feathers, whale and seal harpoons, baskets, and a replica of a native long-house. One striking exhibit is a cedar carving of a whale's fin inlaid with more than 700 otter teeth.

The museum, which has a gift shop selling the works of Makah artists, is open daily in summer from 10:00 A.M. to 5:00 P.M. Mid-September through May it's closed Monday and Tuesday.

From Neah Bay, it's an 8½-mile drive to **Cape Flattery.** Walk the wooded (often muddy) trail to the tip of the cape (a thirty-minute trip), and you are stand-ing at the northwesternmost point in the contiguous United States. The tree-clad cliff, 150 feet high, faces **Tatoosh Island.** Far below, ocean waves crash against jagged rocks, sending plumes of spray skyward. Whales and sea lions swim these waters, and seabirds nest in rock hollows.

Retrace your drive on Route 112 east to Route 113 and onto the Sappho turnoff and turn south. At Sappho head east on US 101, along the **Sol Duc River** toward Olympic National Park and **Lake Crescent.** The deep blue, glacier-formed lake has some 4,700 surface acres and varies in width from ½ mile to 2 miles. The lake is completely surrounded by national parklands.

DINNER: Log Cabin Resort restaurant, 3183 East Beach Road, on the north shore of Lake Crescent; (360) 928–3325. Rustic and casual, serving family fare with a great view. After dinner, enjoy a stroll by the lake or relax before the big stone fireplace in the antiques-furnished lobby.

LODGING: Lake Crescent Lodge, 416 Lake Crescent Road; (360) 928–3211. Historic, peaceful hotel facing the lake and forested mountains. Old-fashioned lodge rooms, modern motel units, and separate cottages available. Some fireplaces, no kitchens. Open May through October.

Day 3 / Morning

BREAKFAST: Substantial, tasty breakfasts are served in Lake Crescent Lodge restaurant, which overlooks the lake. (The restaurant kitchen will prepare a box lunch if you request.)

There are many ways to enjoy a morning at Lake Crescent. You can rent a rowboat, fish for Beardslee trout, sit in a lawn chair and read, or go hiking. Don't miss a walk up to lovely **Marymere Falls.** The ¾-mile trail can be reached from the lodge or from the nearby Storm King Ranger Station. The path winds through

Lake Crescent Lodge is a classic hotel on the Olympic Peninsula.

ancient fir and hemlock trees, over a stream on rustic wooden bridges, past mush-rooms and flowering plants, and finally ascends sharply to an observation point with a full view of the 90-foot cascade. The first ½ mile of the trail is wheelchair accessible.

From the Marymere Falls Trail, you can continue on **Mount Storm King Trail** for a 2¾-mile climb that offers high views of Lake Crescent.

LUNCH: Picnic by the lake or in the forest, or return to Lake Crescent and eat in the restaurant.

Afternoon

For a different perspective on the lake, drive to the northeast shore and take East Beach Road. Park at the end of the road; from here you can hike all or part of **Spruce Railroad Trail,** which travels for 4 miles through the only roadless wilderness area around Lake Crescent.

Then retrace your route back to Seattle, 144 miles from Lake Crescent.

There's More

Arthur D. Feiro Marine Life Center, City Pier at the foot of Lincoln and Railroad Streets, Port Angeles; (360) 417–6254. Displays of local marine specimens, includ-ing a large octopus. Starfish and other creatures in the touch tank. Open daily 10:00 A.M. to 8:00 P.M. mid-June through Labor Day. Call for off-season hours.

Bicycling. The city of Port Townsend lends bicycles; find them at various downtown locations such as the corner of Quincy and Water Streets.

Boating. Boat rentals at Lake Crescent, Port Angeles, and Sequim.

Kayak Port Townsend, 1017-B Water Street, P.O. Box 1387, Port Townsend, WA 98368; (360) 379–3608 or (888) 754–8598.

City Pier, Port Angeles. This shoreline park has an observation tower, lawns, picnic area, boat moorage, and promenade decks.

Dungeness Spit, near Sequim. Longest sand jetty in the United States, 7 miles of sand, agates, and driftwood. National Wildlife Refuge with waterfowl, shorebirds, seals.

First Saturday Gallery Walk, Port Townsend. On the first Friday evening of the month, galleries and studios are open late.

Fishing. Port Angeles Charters, 1014 Marine Drive, represents three charter fishing companies in the area; (360) 457–7629.

Salmon season starts in late spring, closes September. Bottom fishing from February to November. Fish for the famous Beardslee trout in Lake Crescent.

Golf. Dungeness Golf Course, 1965 Woodcock Road, Sequim; (800) 447–6826. Eighteen-hole course, driving range, clubhouse, restaurant.

Port Ludlow Golf Course, 751 Highland Drive, Port Ludlow; (360) 437–0272 or (800) 455–0272. Twenty-seven holes on hillside above Admiralty Inlet, east Olympic Peninsula.

Hiking. Olympic National Park has 600 miles of hiking trails. Before hiking on beaches, consult a tide table. Headland crossings can be dangerous. The *Strip of Wilderness* pamphlet, available at visitor centers, is helpful.

Hurricane Ridge, 17 miles inland from Port Angeles. Mountain ridge with forest and meadow trails, breathtaking views.

Special Events

May. Irrigation Festival, Sequim. Oldest festival in Washington; features parade, fireworks, logging show.

Mid–May. Rhododendron Festival, Port Townsend. Parade, bed race, flower show, arts-and-crafts fair, dancing, fireworks.

Mid–July. Clallam–Sekiu Fun Days, Clallam Bay. Parade, fun run, logging show, arts-and-crafts booths, salmon bake, fireworks, salmon derby.

Late July. Port Townsend Jazz Festival. Musicians from around the country perform on the Fort Worden main stage and in the downtown pubs.

Last weekend in August. Makah Days, Neah Bay. Traditional Makah Indian salmon bakes, costumes, dances, canoe races, parades.

Early September. Port Angeles Strait Bluegrass Festival. Features top bands from Pacific Northwest and Canada.

Late September. Historic Homes Tours, Port Townsend. Self-guided tours of the city's Victorian architecture: mansions, cottages, country inns, public buildings.

Other Recommended Restaurants and Lodgings

Port Angeles

Tudor Inn, 1108 South Oak; (360) 452–3138 or (866) 286–2224. Voted "2006 Best Bed-and-Breakfast in Clallam County." Five guest rooms, all with private baths and views of the Olympic Mountains or the Strait of Juan de Fuca. Gourmet breakfasts and late-night snacks. Innkeeper packs a sack breakfast for visitors taking the early-morning ferry to Victoria.

Port Ludlow

The Inn at Port Ludlow, 200 Olympic Road; (877) 805–0868. Inspired by New England's classic coastal summer homes, the veranda-wrapped inn features rose and herb gardens, guest rooms with private balconies, fireplaces, sitting areas, and over-sized Jacuzzi tubs overlooking a spectacular waterfront.

Port Townsend

Ann Starrett Mansion, 744 Clay Street; (360) 385–3205 or (800) 321–0644; www.olympus.net/starrett. The most opulent bed-and-breakfast in town. Historic home with Victorian gingerbread, eleven guest rooms. Full breakfast.

Bread and Roses Bakery, 230 Quincy Street; (360) 385–1044. Home-baked pastries, soups, sandwiches, espresso.

Fort Worden State Park, 200 Battery Way; park (360) 344–4434; hostel (360) 385–0655. From campsites and hostel dorm wards, to rooms in Officer's Row with Victorian decor and modern comforts, Fort Worden has options for everyone. Two campgrounds, one in a forested area and the other at Point Wilson beach. Both have restrooms and showers. All are very popular accommodations; make your reservation early.

Ravenscroft Inn, 533 Quincy Street; (360) 385–2784 or (800) 782–2691; www.ravenscroftinn.com. Eight spacious rooms in a hillside inn with a colonial-style look. Peaceful atmosphere, full breakfast.

Salal Cafe, 634 Water Street; (360) 385–6532. Healthy, home-style foods; vegetarian entrees available. Plant-filled solarium. Voted region's "Best Breakfast" for the past four years.

For More Information

North Olympic Peninsula Visitor & Convention Bureau, 338 West First Street, No. 104, P.O. Box 670, Port Angeles, WA 98362; (360) 452–8552 or (800) 942–4042; www.olympicpeninsula.org.

Olympic National Park, 600 East Park Avenue, Port Angeles, WA 98362; (360) 565–3130.

Port Angeles Chamber of Commerce, 121 East Railroad Avenue, Port Angeles, WA 98362; (360) 452–2363 or (877) 456–8372.

Port Townsend Visitor Information Center, 2437 Sims Way, Port Townsend, WA 98368; (360) 385–2722.

Washington State Ferries, 2901 Third Avenue, Suite 500, Seattle, WA 98121-3014; (206) 464–6400 or (888) 808–7977; www.wsdot.wa.gov/ferries. The ferries all depart from Pier 52.

SEATTLE ESCAPE THREE

Snoqualmie Falls and Fall City

Waterfall of the Moon People / 1 Night

Long before the explorers and hop growers reached Snoqualmie Valley, Native American tribes met for trade and council beside the thundering torrent now called Snoqualmie Falls. Early settlers referred to the natives who lived along the riverbanks as the "moon people," for their name was said to be derived from Snoqualm, meaning "moon."

☐ Dramatic waterfall

☐ Steam train ride

☐ Luxury resort

☐ Golf courses

☐ Winery

☐ Bicycling

☐ Hiking

☐ Antiques shopping

☐ Zoological park

The first white settlers arrived in 1855. By the early twentieth century, hops, timber, and electrical power that harnessed the falls' tremendous energy were important segments of the local economy. Today it's tourism.

The scenic valley, just 30 miles east of Seattle, is webbed with quiet backroads that pass farmlands, forests, mountains, and gurgling streams on their way to the Snoqualmie River. This getaway offers both a chance to refresh the spirit and a variety of recreation.

Day 1 / Morning

Travel on Interstate 90 east from Seattle to exit 27, a thirty-minute drive. Follow the signs to **Snoqualmie.** Plan to arrive about 10:00 A.M. so that you'll have an hour to explore the little town and its quaint, restored train depot (38625 Southeast King Street) and **Northwest Railway Museum** before your train ride. The depot, built in 1890, is on the National Register of Historic Places. Its displays include a sizable collection of rolling stock from steam, electric, and logging railroads. The museum is open daily from 10:00 A.M. to 5:00 P.M.

Now board the old-fashioned steam- or diesel-powered train for a 10-mile trip through the scenic valley. (Departure times vary by season; call 425–888–3030 for schedule information.) The vintage coaches pass by the base of rugged **Mount Si,** the top of **Snoqualmie Falls,** and through dense forests. They clickety-clack over bridges and through lush green fields to a scenic viewing point before making the return trip to the Snoqualmie depot.

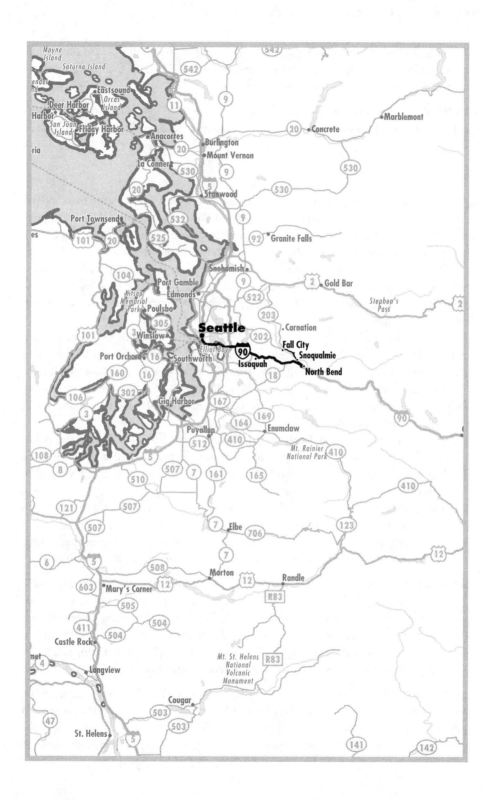

Trains run July through October. Fares are $8.00 for adults, $7.00 for seniors over sixty-two, and $5.00 for children three to twelve. The ride takes seventy minutes. For information, call (425) 888–3030.

LUNCH: Isadora's, 8062 Railroad Avenue; (425) 888–1345. Cafe serving homemade soups, quiche, sandwiches, tea, espresso, scones. Also a gift, antiques, and book shop.

Afternoon

After lunch, or carrying your picnic, continue on 384th Avenue to the freeway on-ramp and Winery Road (watch for the sign to Snoqualmie Winery; the road goes under the freeway). At the winery you can sample local wines while enjoying your picnic and a panoramic view of the Cascades and Snoqualmie Valley.

Turn back toward Snoqualmie and follow the signs to Snoqualmie Falls, which are 1 mile from town. Fenced, paved paths along the cliff offer viewing points for watching the great cascade—100 feet higher than Niagara—as it roars to a misty pool at the bottom.

To get closer to the falls, walk the ½-mile trail that descends to a rocky beach at the falls' base. Behind the powerhouse that stands above the beach you'll find a plank walk leading to an elevated platform, which provides a satisfying overlook.

The trails and landscaped park on the cliff near the lodge were developed by Puget Power, which has received awards of recognition for park design and environmental contributions.

Check in at the **Salish Lodge and Spa,** a resort hotel perched at the brink of the falls. Borrow a bicycle—Salish lends mountain bikes—and wheel along the area's country roads. The lodge also lends fishing gear, if you'd rather try your luck at casting for steelhead in the river.

Golfers can head for one of the four nearby courses (for details, see "There's More" at the end of the chapter). If your top priority is simply relaxation, you'll enjoy lounging on the hotel terrace while the Snoqualmie torrent thunders below, or you could take a health treatment at the largest resort spa in the Northwest.

DINNER: Salish Lodge and Spa, 6501 Railroad Avenue Southeast; (425) 888–2556 or (800) 272–5474. The lodge's dining room receives accolades for serving succulent smoked game and salmon, while the Attic Bistro's king salmon chowder and fire-roasted rib-eye steaks tantalize the taste buds in a less formal setting. In fair weather the outdoor Kayak Café Bistro serves Dungeness crab salad and gourmet sandwiches—a perfect accompaniment to the stunning Snoqualmie Falls.

LODGING: Salish Lodge and Spa. On Condé Nast's Traveler Gold List in 2005, Salish Lodge and Spa has earned kudos as a haven, for both celebratory events and personal retreats. Reservations are a must (800–272–5474). Step into one of eighty-nine guest rooms, each with its own whirlpool tub, wood-burning fireplace, feather

Salish Lodge amd Spa, a luxury inn, perches on the cliff above thundering Snoqualmie Falls.

bed, and custom-built furniture. No small detail goes unnoticed, from the luxury soaps to the bedtime chocolates.

Day 2 / Morning

BREAKFAST: Salish Lodge and Spa. The highly popular breakfast is a five-course extravaganza that includes fresh fruit, hot oatmeal, sourdough biscuits with honey, pancakes, and a main course such as trout with game sausage, eggs Florentine, or smoked salmon in scrambled eggs.

Drive south to **North Bend,** turn left at the traffic signal (the only one in the valley), continue to Mount Si Road, and turn north. Follow this road across the **Snoqualmie River** to 432nd Avenue SE, and park at a gravel area near the bridge. Walk a few yards on 432nd Avenue to the trailhead for **Little Mount Si.**

The 2-mile trail, forested to the top of the mountain, leads to a 1,000-foot summit with sweeping views of the valley, Mount Si, and the Cascade Range in the distance. The hike up Mount Si itself is more time consuming and a greater challenge. The trail zigzags to the top of the great monolith, 4,190 feet high. A panoramic summit view makes the 4-mile trip worthwhile and popular; Mount Si is the second-most-hiked mountain in the state.

If you (or someone in your party) are not interested in hiking, you might visit the **Snoqualmie Valley Historical Museum** at 320 Bendigo Avenue South (425–888–3200). In this former private home, volunteers maintain exhibits of pioneer memorabilia.

A few blocks from the museum is a large, village-style complex of factory discount outlets. The stores represent numerous brand-name manufacturers.

Cougar Mountain Regional Wildlife Park, 19525 Southeast Fifty-fourth Street, Issaquah (425–392–6278), is a five-acre facility that provides a home for almost 300 animals, most of which are either threatened or endangered species. Open daily year-round for prearranged tours.

LUNCH: Tantalus Greek Bistro, 317 Northwest Gilman Boulevard, #37, Issaquah; (425) 391–6090. An extensive menu includes Greek appetizers, soups, sandwiches, salads, meat and vegetarian entrees, and a selection of children's entrees. Open daily for lunch and dinner.

Afternoon

Take I–90 west to exit 17 and leave the freeway for **Issaquah,** a pretty village with a tree-shaded creek running through it. Signs direct you to the state fish hatchery, where you can see thousands of salmon fingerlings being reared with loving care.

Also treated with great care are the hand-dipped chocolates at **Boehm's Candies** (425–392–6652). The Edelweiss Chalet on Gilman Boulevard is the headquarters for the renowned candy company.

Drive north on Gilman and you'll find **Gilman Village,** a complex of fifty-odd shops, restaurants, and tearooms, many of them in old homes that were moved to the site. They're connected by boardwalks.

A short distance past Gilman Village is **Gilman Antique Gallery,** a must for antiques lovers. Here 170 exhibitors display thousands of antiques of all kinds.

If you'd like a stroll on a sandy beach to finish the journey, stop at **Lake Sammamish,** northwest of Issaquah off I–90. By then you'll probably be ready to head the last few miles into Seattle.

There's More

Golfing. There are four eighteen-hole courses in the valley:

Carnation Golf Course, 1810 West Snoqualmie River Road NE, Carnation; (425) 333–4151 or (877) 205–6106.

Mount Si Golf Course, 9010 Southeast Boalch Road, Snoqualmie; (425) 391–4926.

Snoqualmie Falls Golf Course, 35109 SE Fish Hatchery Road, P.O. Box 790, Fall City, WA 98009; (425) 392–1276.

Tall Chief Golf Course, 1313 West Snoqualmie River Road SE, Fall City; (425) 222–5911.

Snoqualmie Falls Forest Theatre and Family Park, P.O. Box 249, Bellevue, WA 98024; (425) 222–7044. Fall City. Outdoor dinner theater, weekends June through Labor Day.

Special Events

June. Annual Greenway Days, North Bend. A weekend celebration that brings people together to enjoy the scenic, recreational, and historic treasures in the area.

Early August. Snoqualmie Days, Snoqualmie. Arts-and-crafts booths, parade, music, food concessions, children's games, helicopter rides.

Other Recommended Restaurants and Lodgings

Carnation

Alexandra's River Inn Snoqualmie Valley, 4548 Tolt River Road; (425) 333–4262. Luxurious solar villa on seven riverside acres. Sauna, banquet facilities, some balconies. Complete breakfast, with vegetarian option.

North Bend

The Roaring River Bed & Breakfast, 46715 Southeast 129th Street; (425) 888–4834 or (877) 627–4647. Three rooms and a cabin. Full breakfast delivered to rooms. Situated on 2.6 acres at the Middle Fork of the Snoqualmie River, outside of North Bend. Offering spectacular views of the mountains, forests, and the rushing river.

Robertiello's, 101 West North Bend Way; (425) 888–1803. Located in the McGraths Building, an award-winning historic preservation project. Open for dinner. Serving pastas, seafood, chicken dishes—all Italian style.

Snoqualmie

House in the Trees at Bethabara Farm, 35909 Southeast 94th; (425) 888–2549. Offers two rooms in a tranquil country setting. Views of the majestic Cascade Mountains and contemplative spaces by a woodland pond. Access to a swimming pool and spa.

For More Information

Greater Issaquah Chamber of Commerce, 155 Northwest Gilman Boulevard, Issaquah, WA 98027; (425) 392–7024; www.issaquahchamber.com.

Snoqualmie Valley Chamber of Commerce, P.O. Box 357, North Bend, WA 98045; (425) 888–4440; www.snovalley.org.

SEATTLE ESCAPE FOUR

Leavenworth to Ellensburg

Apple Orchards and Ranch Country / 2 Nights

One of Seattle's great attractions is its proximity to magnificent mountainous wilderness. You can breakfast in a cosmopolitan restaurant and be deep in a silent forest by lunchtime. This three-day getaway will take you east through the rugged North Cascades, into the softer valleys where 60 percent of the nation's apples are grown, and on to dry ranching country. On the way you'll encounter breathtaking scenery, rivers that invite white-water adventure, beckoning trails, and a few surprises.

☐ Mountain scenery

☐ Waterfalls

☐ Pioneer village

☐ Wild rivers

☐ Apple orchards

☐ Bavarian town

☐ Historical museums

☐ Hiking

☐ Boating

☐ Horseback riding

☐ Columbia River

Day 1 / Morning

Drive north from Seattle to State Route 202, headed toward **Woodinville,** and stop for a tour of the famed **Chateau Ste. Michelle Winery,** 14111 NE 145th Street (425–415–3300 or 800–267–6793). The state's leading winery is in a turreted chateau.

Tours and tastings are available every day. Stroll eighty-seven acres of landscaped grounds. There are trout ponds, manicured lawns, formal gardens, experimental vineyards, and picnic tables.

North of the winery, join State Route 522 headed northeast toward U.S. Route 2. Traveling east on the scenic highway, you'll follow the **Skykomish River,** a ribbon of clear blue water that flows west from the high lakes of the Alpine Wilderness. Popular with rafters for both its rapids and its serene stretches, the Skykomish offers steelhead fishing, riverside trails, and gold panning, as well as float trips. Eagles soar above all the activity, indifferent and majestic.

Amid the new-growth forests found on either side of the river are the stumps of virgin old growth, long since logged. The stumps indicate the size of these giants; some are 6 feet in diameter.

Two miles east of Gold Bar, at **Wallace Falls State Park,** stop to hike the trail, which climbs to 1,200 feet and affords grand views of **Wallace Falls,** a 365-foot

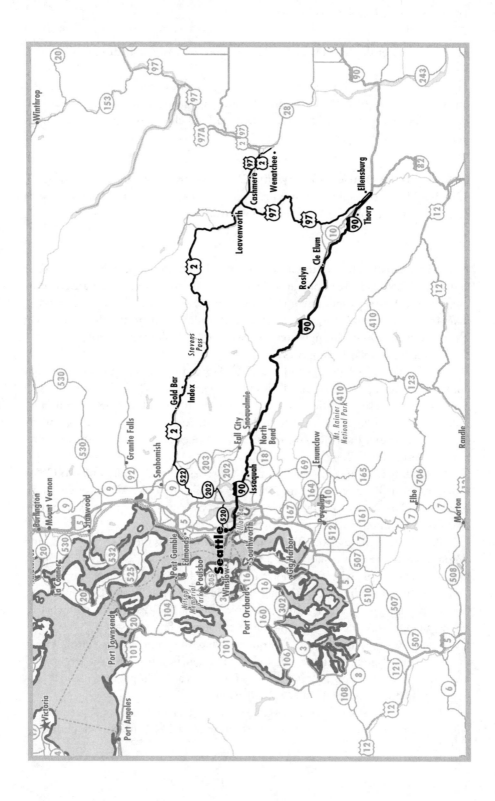

cascade. South of the Skykomish you'll see imposing **Mount Index,** nearly 6,000 feet high.

The next stop on the highway is the village of **Index** (population 150). It is a quaint assortment of dark-red clapboard buildings that include a historic tavern, museum, general store, city hall, and pioneer park, all clustered around the first corner as you cross the bridge into town. Go to the second corner, and you're ready for lunch.

LUNCH: Bush House Country Inn, 300 Fifth Street; (360) 793–2312 or (800) 428–BUSH. Rustic dining room with river-rock fireplace. Soups, sandwiches, salads, light entrees, homemade desserts. Open daily.

Afternoon

Near **Skykomish,** a timber town that fills with hikers and backpackers in summer and with skiers in winter, you can take a short walk to **Deception Falls,** a tumbling waterfall that splashes down the mountainside and under the highway bridge. The **Iron Goat Trail,** signed on Route 2, follows the route that the Great Northern Railway cut through Stevens Pass in 1893. Walk past old collapsed snow sheds, tunnels, and work campsites.

Continuing on Route 2, you'll leave the Skykomish River and drive through coniferous forest, passing Alpine Falls and rising into the Cascade Mountains to **Stevens Pass,** at an elevation of 4,061 feet. One thousand feet below runs a 7-mile tunnel, the longest railroad tunnel in North America. If you walk from the summit to **Stevens Pass Ski Area,** you'll have a peerless view of the snowy peaks of the Cascade Range.

Descending now on the east side of the Cascades, drive 20 more miles to **Coles Corner.** From here, State Route 207 leads 4 miles to **Lake Wenatchee State Park** (888–226–7688). This busy recreation area on the edge of **Lake Wenatchee** offers skiing, fishing, boating, and beaches.

Take Route 2 through the **Tumwater Canyon,** along the bouncing, cascading **Wenatchee River** as it rushes toward the Columbia. In any season the landscape is lovely, but in autumn, when the woodlands blaze with color, it's particularly glorious.

Sixteen miles south of Coles Corner, in **Icicle Valley,** you'll enter **Leavenworth.** Almost the entire town is designed to resemble a quaint Bavarian village, with chalets, carved railings, peaked gables, and hundreds of hanging flower baskets.

In the 1960s, when the local economy was rapidly fading, the townsfolk began the Bavarian village project as a way to stimulate tourism. It has succeeded beyond imagining, drawing visitors by the thousands every year to shop, gawk, eat, and participate in the lively festivals (see "Special Events").

The alpine setting is an even-greater draw. Leavenworth is a gateway to wilderness adventure, white-water rivers, mountain lakes, fishing, rock climbing, and skiing.

For the rest of the afternoon you might choose to hike or bird-watch, play golf, or linger in the dozens of quaint shops. Browse through the handpainted country pine items in **Pie in the Sky,** the many cuckoo clocks at the **Cuckoo Clock Shop,** and see artisans at work in the **Woodcarver Gallery.** There are many fascinating shops, but be sure to see the Northwest artifacts at **Cabin Fever Rustics,** the quilts next door at **Dee's Country Accents,** the 3,500 distinctive music boxes in **Die Musik Box,** and the Christmas crafts at **Kris Kringl.** Check out the **Nussknacker Haus** and the **Leavenworth Nutcracker Museum** (735 Front Street, 2B, P.O. Box 129, Leavenworth, WA 98826; 509–548–4708), upstairs from it. The Nutcracker Museum is open afternoons daily from May through October and on weekends only November through April. The U.S. Forest Service Information Center in downtown Leavenworth has maps that direct you to mountain trails and wildflower displays.

Don't miss a walk along the Wenatchee River in tranquil **Waterfront Park,** off Commercial Street. Just a block and a half from the busy shopping area, the park is a quiet spot with benches, trees, and views of the river and the steep peaks around Icicle Canyon. The Wenatchee River is one of the state's most popular rafting rivers.

DINNER: Autumn Pond Bed and Breakfast, 10388 Titus Road; (800) 222–9661. Rests on three quiet country acres, surrounded by panoramic views of the majestic Cascades. Guests can relax on a wooden swing by the private pond or in an outdoor hot tub. Six guest rooms, each with a private bath, queen bed, and country ranch decor. Common room has comfortable seating, games, and plenty of interesting reading material.

LODGING: Run of the River, 9308 East Leavenworth Road, P.O. Box 285, Leavenworth, WA 98826; (509) 548–7171 or (800) 288–6491. Bed-and-breakfast in a log lodge on the river a mile from downtown. Six comfortable rooms, warm hospitality, deck with hot tub.

Day 2 / Morning

BREAKFAST: A bountiful country breakfast is served in the open dining room at Run of the River.

Continue on Route 2 to **Cashmere,** passing miles of apple orchards that bloom white and pink in spring and are laden with fruit in fall. Apples are big business in Washington; seven billion are grown annually, 60 percent of the nation's apple production.

In Cashmere, at Liberty Acres, just off Route 2, the home of the **Aplets and Cotlets** manufacturing plant, 117 Mission Street (509–782–4088), take the brief tour and watch the making of the famous fruit-and-nut confections.

Bob's Apple Barrel, on Route 2, sells cider, apple butter, and jam and has a large selection of Washington wines.

Not to be missed is **Chelan County Historical Museum and Pioneer Village,** 600 Cottage Avenue (509–782–3230), where you step from the highway into the past. On the museum grounds, a typical pioneer village, complete with blacksmith shop, mission, assay office, saloon, dentist's office, hotel, millinery shop, and jail house, is open to the public.

From Cashmere, drive on to **Wenatchee,** the apple capital, where the Wenatchee and Columbia Rivers meet. The **Wenatchee Valley Museum and Cultural Center,** 127 South Mission Street (509–664–3340), in downtown Wenatchee, features out-of-the-ordinary displays. A coin-operated 1892 railroad diorama, aviation exhibits showing the historic 1931 transpacific crossing, a nine-rank Wurlitzer theater organ, and Native American artifacts are part of the disparate collection.

A side trip north on U.S. Route 97 Alt., on the west bank of the river, leads you to the **Washington Apple Commission Visitor Center,** 2900 Euclid Avenue (509–662–9600). It's open daily from May through December 23 and on weekdays the rest of the year. The gift shop is open Monday through Friday year-round. You'll get an in-depth look at the apple industry at the center, which offers souvenirs, an eighteen-minute video, pies, and free samples of Washington's famous apples. Continue north on Route 97 Alt. to nationally known **Ohme Gardens,** 3327 Ohme Road (509–662–5785), where you can look down on the junction of the Wenatchee and Columbia Rivers. Drive on another few miles to **Rocky Reach Dam** (509–663–7522; www.chelanpud.org), a 5,000-foot-long structure with a 1,700-foot-long fish ladder and 10,000 years of history in the Gallery of the Columbia; open March 1 through mid-November.

Afternoon

Drive south on Route 97, leaving the orchards to head into the forests of the Wenatchee Mountains, and descend from there into cowboy country. The climate here is hot and dry in summer, while winters are harsh, with far more snowfall than occurs west of the Cascade Range.

The scenic route, over the old Blewett Pass Road, is narrow and winding and closed in winter. It is a shortcut that leaves, then rejoins, Route 97, which is open all year.

When you reach **Ellensburg,** stop at the chamber of commerce on Sprague Street for a walking-tour map of the historic downtown. It's full of interesting architecture, with redbrick buildings dating from the late 1800s, an Art Deco theater, and modern structures on the Central Washington University campus. Antiques shops abound, along with stores selling the famous Ellensburg Blue agate (found only in this region).

In the **Clymer Gallery** view the paintings of John Clymer, a noted western artist; in the **Kittitas County Historic Museum** (114 East Third Street, P.O. Box

265, Ellensburg, WA 98926; 509–925–3778), see what frontier life was like. Tour the **Thorp Grist Mill** (509–964–9640), built back in 1883 when Ellensburg (having changed its name from Robbers' Roost) was booming; to get there, take Interstate 90 north to exit 101.

Southeast of town, off I–90, is **Olmstead Place State Park,** 921 North Ferguson Road (509–925–1943), where you can step into one of the first farms in Kittitas Valley. There's a log cabin, built in 1875, and several buildings, including a barn and schoolhouse, open for tours in summer.

DINNER: Valley Cafe, 105 West Third, Ellensburg; (509) 925–3050. Art Deco surroundings, good European dishes.

LODGING: Rose Hill Farm, 16161 North Thorp Highway, Thorp; (509) 964–2427 or (866) 279–0546. Located on a working farm situated along the Yakima River, the main house has four bedrooms, two of which have soaking tubs. Also on the premises are a small studio and tiny cottage.

Day 3 / Morning

BREAKFAST: Rose Hill Farm Bed and Breakfast delivers a basket of fresh muffins, plus tea or coffee, to your room, and then at 9:00 A.M. brings a full breakfast consisting of homemade granola, yogurt, fruit, and assorted cereals, followed by a hot entree.

Take a **horseback ride** through the hills behind the ranch, in the **L. T. Murray Wildlife Recreation Area.** It offers 100,000 acres of wilderness, honeycombed with walking and riding trails. If you're not enthused about horses, go hiking, relax at the ranch, or go to Ellensburg to see what you missed the day before.

You might choose a **rafting trip** on the Yakima River instead, or travel 25 miles east to Vantage, on the Columbia River. This section of the river is a dam-created lake, **Wanapum Lake.** The views are spectacular, overlooking the river and surrounding dry, brushy hills. Nearby is **Ginkgo Petrified Forest State Park,** where you can see prehistoric petrified woods of many species. In the park there are petroglyphs, an interpretive center, walking trails, wildlife, and picnic areas.

LUNCH: The Circle H provides a saddlebag lunch; eat at the ranch or take it with you for a picnic in Ginkgo Petrified Forest State Park.

Afternoon

After lunch, take I–90 northwest (or a byway, State Route 10) to **Cle Elum.** Once a coal-mining and railroad town, it's now a gateway to mountain and lake outdoor recreation. Stop at the **Cle Elum Bakery** (509–674–2233) for caramel-nut rolls and coffee; closed Sunday. Also check out **Glondo's Sausage Company** (509–674–5755) for Yugoslav sausage and Polish kielbasa. Almost every town has its special museum; Cle Elum preserves phone history in the **Cle Elum Historical**

Telephone Museum (221 East First Street, P.O. Box 43, Cle Elum, WA 98922; 509–674–5702). Another interesting spot is the **Carpenter Museum,** 302 West Third Street (509–674–5702), a stately mansion that now houses exhibits from life in an earlier day in the region. Both museums have limited hours; be sure to call first.

Continue west to **Roslyn,** a quiet, pleasant little community with a couple of good cafes and one of the oldest operating saloons in Washington state, **The Brick.** Roslyn is famous for its dozens of ethnic cemeteries, where miners are buried among their own cultural groups, banded together on a hillside west of town.

Proceeding northwest on I–90, you'll come to **Kachess Lake,** a recreation area with beautiful old trees, walking paths, and a pretty lake where you can swim, boat, and fish.

Continue on I–90 through thick forests and mountain terrain over Snoqualmie Pass and on to **Snoqualmie Falls** (for more information on the Snoqualmie Falls area, see Seattle Escape Three).

On your way back to Seattle, if there's time, stop in **Issaquah** for coffee or tea and a look around the shops of Gilman Village. While you're so close, you might as well pick up a sample from **Boehm's Candies,** 255 Northwest Gillman Boulevard (425–392–6652), for a sweet touch to end your trip.

There's More

Animal Lovers, reserve March–November for a Saturday or Sunday Chimposium at the Chimpanzee and Human Communication Institute, Central Washington University, Ellensburg; (509) 963–2244. Watch chimps "talk" in sign language.

Bicycling. Bicycle routes for all abilities surround the Leavenworth area. Rent bicycles at Der Sportsman (509–548–5623) or Das Rad Haus (509–548–5615).

Golf. Leavenworth Golf Club, 9101 Icicle Road; (509) 548–7267. Eighteen holes.

Rock Island Golf Course, 314 Saunders Road, Rock Island, east of Wenatchee; (509) 884–2806. Eighteen holes.

Rafting. Raft the white water of the Wenatchee River with Leavenworth Outfitters and Outdoor Center, 21588 State Highway 207, Leavenworth; (509) 763–3733 or (800) 347–7934. Scenic float trips also available.

Osprey Rafting Company, 9342 Icicle Road, Leavenworth (800–743–6269), is another outfitting option.

Skiing. Leavenworth: Cross-country ski trails are numerous in the Leavenworth/ Wenatchee area. Icicle River Trail and Lake Wenatchee are popular, and so are the golf course and city park in Leavenworth (509–548–6977).

Leavenworth Winter Sports Club, P.O. Box 573, Leavenworth, WA 98826; (509) 548–5477.

Stevens Pass: Open November to mid-April. Downhill: Six double chair lifts, two triples, longest run 6,047 feet; (206) 812–4510.

Wenatchee: Mission Ridge has four chair lifts and runs up to 5 miles long; (509) 663–6543.

Special Events

Late April/early May. Washington State Apple Blossom Festival, Wenatchee. Parades, carnival, arts-and-crafts fair.

Mid–May. Maifest, Leavenworth. Maypole dance, bandstand entertainment, hand-bell ringers, outdoor breakfast, flea market, antiques bazaar, street dancing, flowers.

Early June. Founders Day, Cashmere. Celebrate the historic figures who first settled the Northwest's apple country.

June. Leavenworth International Accordian Celebration, Leavenworth. Old World architecture, flowering gardens, and artisans provide the backdrop for this musical celebration.

Early September (Labor Day weekend). Chelan County Fair, Cashmere.

Ellensburg Rodeo. One of the major U.S. rodeos. Four-day event, with cowhands competing for cash prizes. Also carnival rides, produce and craft displays, home-made pies, and music.

Late September/early October. Autumn Leaf Festival, Leavenworth. Grand parade, accordion and oompah music in bandstand, art displays, street dance, food booths, pancake breakfast.

Mid–October. Cashmere Apple Days, Cashmere. Pie-baking contest, races, music, dancing, pioneer entertainment. Fund-raiser for Chelan County Museum.

Late November. Christkindlmarkt, Leavenworth. A German-style Christmas village with booths filled with holiday foods and gift items. Christmas music and an Olde World Puppet Theatre for children.

Early December. Christmas Lighting, Leavenworth. Snowman contest, sledding, food booths, concerts, lighting of village.

Other Recommended Restaurants and Lodgings

Cle Elum

Hidden Valley Guest Ranch, 3942 Hidden Valley Road; (509) 857–2344 or (800) 526–9269. Wilderness ranch with cabins, horses, swimming pool, hiking trails, cross-country skiing, hot tub. Gold panning also available. All meals included.

Iron Horse Inn B&B, 526 Marie Avenue, P.O. Box 629, South Cle Elum, WA 98943; (509) 674–5939 or (800) 22–TWAIN. A former bunkhouse for railroad workers, restored as an attractive bed-and-breakfast with a railroad theme. Four genuine caboose cars have been lovingly renovated. All cars feature private baths, TV/VCRs, microwaves, refrigerators, and outside sun decks. Full breakfast.

Ellensburg

The Inn at Goose Creek, 1720 Canyon Road; (509) 962–8030 or (800) 533–0822. Ten rooms, some with Jacuzzi tubs. All with goose-down comforters and refrigerators. Filling continental breakfast bar, plus late-night snacks for the room.

The Pub Minglewood, 402 North Pearl; (509) 962–2260. Lamb and seafood, pasta, light meals at tables with linens and candlelight. Dinner only.

The Wren's Nest Bed & Breakfast, 300 East Manitoba Avenue; (509) 925–9061. Antiques-furnished guest rooms. Easy walk to Central Washington University campus and historic downtown Ellensburg. Full gourmet breakfast with egg and meat dishes, waffles, Swedish pancakes, and fresh-baked bread.

Yellow Church Café, 111 South Pearl; (509) 933–2233. This former little church, which was built for German Lutherans in 1923, serves breakfast, lunch, and dinner. Traditional breakfasts include eggs and pancakes; also available for breakfast are wraps and a berry granola cobbler. Lunch menu offers salads, soups, quiches, and sandwiches. Dinner fare includes steaks, chicken, pastas, and vegetarian dishes.

Leavenworth

All Seasons River Inn, 8751 Icicle Road; (509) 548–1425 or (800) 254–0555. Adults only. Bed-and-breakfast with six spacious rooms. All but one room have whirlpool tubs. Private decks, river views, antiques, hearty breakfast.

Anna Hotel Pension, 926 Commercial; (509) 548–6273 or (800) 509–ANNA. Fifteen units in a Bavarian-style inn. Traditional European breakfast included.

Enzian Motor Inn, 590 U.S. Highway 2; (509) 548–5269 or (800) 223–8511. Hotel combining Old World atmosphere with contemporary comfort. Heated pool, hot tub, 104 rooms, some fireplaces. Full European buffet breakfast included.

Homefires Bakery, 13013 Bayne Road; (509) 548–7362. Freshly made whole grain breads, European and specialty breads, pies, cinnamon rolls, and cookies, baked in a wood-fired masonry oven.

J. J. Hills Restaurant, 505 U.S. Highway 2; (509) 548–8000. Old photos and a model railroad capture Leavenworth's beginnings as a railroad town. Barbecued ribs, steaks, Bavarian sausages, and other German entrees leave all diners satisfied.

Mountain Home Lodge, 8201 Mountain Home Road, P.O. Box 687, 98826; (509) 548–7077 or (800) 414–2378. Intimate getaway in roomy stone-and-wood lodge with pool. In the hills, 3 miles from town. Full breakfast included. All meals served during winter months.

Sleeping Lady Conference Retreat, 2½ miles from town at 7375 Icicle Road; (800) 574–2123. A sixty-seven-acre conference retreat center with guest rooms, gourmet meals, and music concerts in a natural setting dedicated to preserving the environment. Ideal for larger groups. Individuals must stay two nights and reserve within sixty days of arrival.

Wenatchee

Apple Country Bed and Breakfast, 524 Okanogan Avenue; (509) 664–0400. Featherbeds with goose-down comforters. Warm poached pears, pecan sticky buns, rhubarb sour cream coffee cake, and apple strata satisfy the most discriminating palates.

Warms Springs Inn Bed and Breakfast, 1611 Love Lane; (509) 662–8365 or (800) 543–3645. Situated on ten acres along the Wenatchee River. Six guest rooms in a 1917 mansion with spectacular grounds. Voted "Best Breakfast in the Northwest."

For More Information

Cashmere Chamber of Commerce, P.O. Box 834, Cashmere, WA 98815; (509) 782–7404; www.cashmerechamber.com.

Cle Elum–Roslyn Chamber of Commerce, 401 West First Street, Cle Elum, WA 98922; (509) 674–5958.

Ellensburg Chamber of Commerce, 609 North Main Street, Ellensburg, WA 98926; (509) 925–3138 or (888) 925–2204; www.ellensburg-chamber.com.

Leavenworth Chamber of Commerce, P.O. Box 327, Leavenworth, WA 98826; (509) 548–5807; www.leavenworth.org.

Monroe Chamber of Commerce, 118 North Lewis Street, Suite 112, Monroe, WA 98272; (360) 794–5488.

Sultan Chamber of Commerce, P.O. Box 46, Sultan, WA 98294; (360) 793–0983.

Wenatchee Valley Chamber of Commerce, 300 Columbia, Wenatchee, WA 98807; (509) 662–2116; www.wenatchee.org.

SEATTLE ESCAPE FIVE

North Cascades

Untamed Wilderness / 2 Nights

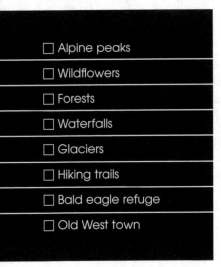

- ☐ Alpine peaks
- ☐ Wildflowers
- ☐ Forests
- ☐ Waterfalls
- ☐ Glaciers
- ☐ Hiking trails
- ☐ Bald eagle refuge
- ☐ Old West town

Because of their jagged peaks, immense glaciers, and high meadows splashed with summer wildflowers, the North Cascades are often called the American Alps. The wilderness around them, a 505,000-acre national park bisected by only one road, provides a remarkable retreat from crowded streets into natural beauty.

Along the route through North Cascades National Park, and on the occasional side roads that extend from it, you'll encounter numerous opportunities for outdoor adventure. This three-day trip suggests a few. It's a summer excursion, as much of the road is closed in winter. To reach the skiing areas mentioned during the ski season, you have to take a different route, approaching from the south.

Day 1 / Morning

Travel north from Seattle on State Route 9 to **Snohomish,** about 30 miles. The river town, founded in 1859 on the banks of the Snohomish and Pilchuck Rivers, is one of Washington's oldest communities. It's thus fitting that Snohomish not only has examples of Victorian architecture but is also known as the antiques capital of the Northwest. Dozens of shops, many within a 4-block radius, sell antiques of all kinds.

But before you begin browsing, give yourself a jump-start at **The Maltby Cafe,** just outside of Snohomish at 8809 Maltby Road (425–483–3123). Voted "Best Breakfast in Western Washington," this plain-looking cafe is located in the basement of a former schoolhouse. Customers come from miles around; you can expect a long wait on the weekend. The scrambles, the country potatoes, and the fresh orange juice are favorites. Tender homemade cinnamon rolls are enormous.

The three-level **Star Center Antique Mall,** 829 Second Street (360–568–2131), houses 150 dealers who sell everything from native artifacts to art nouveau. The mall is open every day. **First Bank Antiques,** 1015 First Street (360–568–7609), carries oak and mahogany furniture and country primitives; **Snohomish**

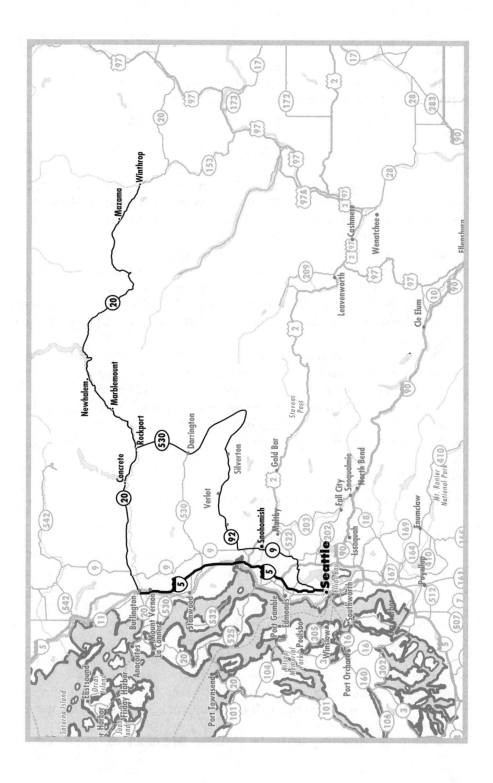

Antique Station, 1108 First Street (360–568–4913), represents twenty dealers offering glassware, furniture, china, and collectibles.

At the **Old Snohomish Village Museum,** on Second and Pine Streets, and at **Blackman House Museum,** 118 Avenue B (360–568–5235), you can see how many of these antiques were once used in daily life. Both museums are open daily for tours in summer.

Now head north toward **Lake Stevens,** curving to State Route 92 toward Granite Falls.

On this scenic route, known as the **Mount Loop Highway** (part of it is closed in winter), you'll follow the **South Fork of the Stillaguamish River** and pass through the evergreen forests of **Boulder River Wilderness,** eventually turning north toward Darrington and the North Cascades Highway.

From **Granite Falls,** follow Route 92 east 11 miles to Verlot. The ranger station, across the road from 5,324-foot Mount Pilchuck, will provide maps and suggestions. The 7-mile road leading to the trail up the mountain is east of Verlot. From the trailhead, the hike up Mount Pilchuck is 2½ miles, leading to **Mount Pilchuck Lookout.** From here you gain one of the finest viewing points in the state for scenic splendor.

The forest fire observation tower was built in 1918 on the western edge of the Cascade Range, near Boulder River Wilderness. From the lookout you can see for miles, a view encompassing White Horse and Three Fingers Mountains.

As you enter the **Mount Baker–Snoqualmie National Forest,** edging the Stillaguamish shore, you'll drive for 14 miles, through Silverton to the turnoff for the **Big Four Mountain.** At the base of the immense escarpment, which soars 6,120 feet, a popular inn once stood. It was destroyed by fire long ago, but the site is a good picnic spot.

LUNCH: Picnic at **Mount Pilchuck** or Big Four Mountain.

Afternoon

Follow the trail to the **Big Four Ice Caves,** which some say is the lowest-lying glacier in the contiguous United States. The ¼-mile-long ice field is fed from a snow cone on Big Four.

Continue now over **Barlow Pass** (elevation 2,600 feet), turning north to travel beside the tumultuous **South Fork of the Sauk River** for 19 miles to Darrington. The road is unpaved, but it's well graded.

The slate-blue Sauk is a favorite with white-water rafters and kayakers because of its swift rapids. Through the trees on this narrow, winding road you'll glimpse mountain peaks—Sloan, Pugh, and White Chuck—and the Monte Cristo Range in **Henry M. Jackson Wilderness.** The Monte Cristo area was once the site of gold, copper, and silver mines.

When you reach **Rockport,** you'll see **Rockport State Park** on the bank of

Glaciers and snowfields abound on the slopes of the rugged North Cascades.

the **Skagit River.** The attractive park has campsites and a network of trails, partially accessible to wheelchairs.

On the western border of the park, a 7-mile road winds up Sauk Mountain, leading to **Sauk Mountain Trail.** This trail, a one-and-a-half-hour walk, is considered by many hikers to be one of the most beautiful walks in the North Cascades, with wildflowers and panoramic views from the mountain. You may see hang gliders here.

After your hike, drive west 12 miles on State Route 20 to your night's lodging.

DINNER: North Cascade Inn, 44628 Highway 20, Concrete; (360) 826–8870. Standard, dependable American fare.

LODGING: Cascade Mountain Inn Bed and Breakfast, 40418 Pioneer Lane, Concrete; (360) 826–4333 or (888) 652–8127. European-style inn with five rooms and a suite on ten acres of grounds. Down comforters, friendly hosts. View of Sauk Mountain.

Day 2 / Morning

BREAKFAST: Enjoy expansive views and a full breakfast in the dining room or on the patio of Cascade Mountain Inn Bed and Breakfast.

Take the picnic lunch the innkeepers have packed for you (request this in advance), and drive east on Route 20, the North Cascades Highway. Considered the most scenic mountain drive in Washington, this route is closed in winter.

Again keep an eye out for eagles, especially between **Rockport State Park** and **Marblemount.** In Marblemount you can pick up maps and backcountry permits (and gasoline—this is the last gas stop for 75 miles).

If you didn't bring a picnic, check out the buffalo menu at **Buffalo Run Restaurant,** 60084 State Route 20 (360–873–2461). Sandwiches, soups, and salads, as well as elk, venison, and vegetarian entrees, are available in a casual atmosphere.

Route 20 and the Skagit River flowing beside it divide the northern portion of North Cascades National Park from its southern part. There are almost no other roads in the national park, a wonderland of high mountains, jagged ridges, countless waterfalls, and glacially sculpted valleys. There are 318 glaciers, more than half of all the glaciers in the contiguous United States. On off-road trails, you'll hear crashing icefalls and see broad snowfields and flower-dotted slopes.

Two short walks are located near the manicured village of **Newhalem. Trail of the Cedars** is a nature walk, wheelchair accessible, with interpretive signs that explain the forest's growth. The **Ladder Creek Rock Garden** walk winds up a hillside, passing fountains and landscaped plantings to reach Ladder Creek Falls.

LUNCH: Picnic in Newhalem or along the trail, or eat at Buffalo Run Restaurant in Marblemount.

Afternoon

Continue in leisurely fashion on Route 20, stopping at the numerous turnouts to admire particularly striking views of ridges and green valleys. At **Diablo Lake Trail,** enjoy a panoramic vista of the smooth blue lake, Sourdough Mountain, Davis Peak, Colonial Peak, Pyramid Peak, and the Skagit River.

Beyond Diablo is **Ross Lake,** its blue-green glacial waters extending far north into the wilderness, across the Canadian border. The only access to the lake is by boat or trail.

Ross Lake is named after James Ross, the engineer who designed dams on the Skagit River. Another Ross, Alexander, explored the southern section of the present park in 1814. After him came more explorers, then miners (mining efforts were abandoned because of the arduous terrain) and a few homesteaders. The dams were built by Seattle City Light to generate electricity.

Fall is especially beautiful in the North Cascades. An example of the leaf color you can see, flaming red and orange against the hillsides, is at **Ruby Creek,** 20 miles past Newhalem.

Rainy Pass has an elevation of 4,860 feet. It's crossed by the Pacific Crest National Scenic Trail. Near the Rainy Lake rest stop is the **Rainy Lake National Recreation Trail,** a 1-mile paved path, wheelchair accessible, that leads to **Rainy Lake.** There's a memorable view here of the subalpine lake and waterfall streaming in from snowfields.

Whistler Basin Viewpoint provides an opportunity for a close look at the wildflowers that grow in alpine meadows. In July and August these fragile, open spaces are full of color.

For the most splendid close-up view of the Cascades, don't miss the **Washington Pass Overlook** (elevation 5,400 feet). **Liberty Bell Mountain** soars 7,808 feet above the valley. Next to it, almost as high, are the **Early Winter Spires; Silver Star Mountain** rises a steep 8,875 feet on the east. Against the dark ridges and snow-filled ravines, the leaves of Lyall larch glow a brilliant yellow.

Now, as the road descends east of the Cascades into Washington's dry side, the scenery changes. There are no dense rain forests, thick with ferns and mosses; the vegetation thins, and firs give way to widely spaced pines. To the north lie the mountains and forests of the rugged, roadless **Pasayten Wilderness.** In recent years wolves have been found living deep in the wild—a welcome comeback, since they were thought to have disappeared.

Twelve miles from Washington Pass you'll come to **Mazama,** a popular ski center.

DINNER: Mazama Country Inn, 15 Country Road, (509) 996–2681; within Washington, (800) 843–7951. Pasta, chicken, and barbecued ribs are favorites here. Light suppers of soup, salad, and bread available.

LODGING: Mazama Country Inn. Spacious cedar lodge, eighteen simple but immaculate rooms. No phones, no TVs—no interruptions. Stone fireplace in living/dining area, windows on three sides offering views of forest. Two separate cabins and ranch house with full kitchens available. Bicycle rentals and horseback rides.

Day 3 / Morning

BREAKFAST: Mazama Country Inn. The lodge serves three meals a day (included in the American Plan rates in winter only).

Drive eastward on Route 20 into the lovely **Methow Valley,** carved by glaciers 11,000 years ago. Farmers' fields, punctuated with rocky outcroppings, extend from the meandering **Methow River,** while its banks are outlined by poplar and ponderosa pines.

Drive 13 miles from Mazama, and you'll arrive in **Winthrop,** a town nestled in the upper Methow Valley, almost surrounded by national forestland. Here migrant Native American tribes once camped along the river, digging for camas root and fishing for salmon. White settlers and miners arrived after 1883.

When you visit Winthrop, you might think the townsfolk never left the late 1800s. The entire town has a frontier motif, with boardwalks, Old West storefronts, and saloon replicas.

Guy Waring and his wife and two children were among the early settlers. They came from Massachusetts and named the town after the governor of that state, John

Winthrop. The Warings' home, built in 1897 after most of the town was destroyed by fire, is now the **Shafer Museum,** 285 Castle Avenue (509–996–2712). It contains historical artifacts, wagons, and a stagecoach. Open Thursday through Monday, 10:00 A.M. to 5:00 P.M., Memorial Day weekend through September.

With 300 days of sunshine a year and an abundance of lakes, forests, mountainous terrain, and clean country air, the Methow Valley offers virtually limitless outdoor recreation. Fishing, photography, boating, river rafting, and skiing are among the most popular activities.

LUNCH: Duck Brand Hotel and Cantina, 248 Riverside Avenue; (509) 996–2192. Tasty Mexican dishes, as well as sandwiches, steaks, pies, and chocolate cake.

Afternoon

Turn west on Route 20 for the return trip, stopping at the overlooks and trails you missed on the way out, continuing this abundant feast for the senses.

In Marblemount, stop at Buffalo Run Restaurant for a coffee break; then continue westward toward Sedro Woolley. At Burlington, join Interstate 5 for the forty-five-minute drive south to Seattle.

There's More

Boating. Ross Lake provides superb high-country canoeing in the wilderness. From Ross Dam parking lot, portage your canoe down a ¾-mile trail. You can choose to paddle to Ross Dam from Diablo Lake; for a fee, Ross Lake Resort will haul you up to the lake. Call Ross Lake Resort in Rockport; (206) 386–4437.

Diablo Lake Trail birding and hiking. North side of Diablo Lake. To reach Diablo Dam Trail, turn off at Milepost 126 for Diablo, cross Stetattle Creek, turn right at the fork in the road, and continue past the Diablo Powerhouse, community hall, and incline railway office to the signed trailhead (about 1½ miles from Route 20). The richly diverse Diablo Lake Trail is 7.6 miles round-trip and has an elevation gain of 1,500 feet. About 2 miles from the trailhead, a small trail turns right and leads to a dramatic view of Diablo Lake and surrounding peaks. This area is a pleasant lunch spot and a great place to look for bald eagles, red-tailed Cooper's, and sharp-shinned hawks. The longer hike offers a gentle climb through rich and varied habitats, including mature fir forests, mixed deciduous growth, and rocky outcroppings touching the open sky. For more information, contact the North Cascades National Park at Wilderness Information Center; (360) 873–4500.

Fishing. In streams and lakes, fish for brook, Dolly Varden, golden, and rainbow trout.

Horseback riding. Horse Country Farm, 8507 Highway 92, P.O. Box 2, Granite

Falls, WA 98252; (360) 691–7509. Trail rides in the Cascade foothills, along the Pilchuck River. Just forty-five minutes from downtown Seattle. Ponies, lessons, family trail rides, and spring and summer camps are also available.

Skiing. Methow Valley Ski Touring Association, Box 147, Winthrop, WA 98862; (509) 996–3287. Provides information and maps on Nordic ski trails in Sun Mountain, Rendezvous, and Mazama areas. Methow Valley Sport Trails Association gives recorded updates on trail conditions. The Methow Valley, with 100-odd miles of cross-country ski trails, is known as one of the best Nordic skiing centers in the world.

Special Events

July. Bluegrass Festival, Darrington.

Late September. Historic Home Tour, Snohomish.

Early October. Granite Falls Railroad Days, Granite Falls.

October. Festival of Pumpkins, Snohomish. Juried art show; Pumpkin River Race.

Other Recommended Restaurants and Lodgings

Winthrop

Sun Mountain Lodge, P.O. Box 1000, 98862; (509) 996–2211 within Washington, (800) 572–0493 outside Washington. Rustic, log-beamed lodge in the Methow Valley. Rock fireplace, swimming pool, tennis, beautiful mountain setting. Dining room serves breakfast, lunch, and dinner. Wolf Creek Bar and Grill offers lighter fare.

For More Information

Concrete Chamber of Commerce, P.O. Box 743, Concrete, WA 98237; (360) 853–7042; www.concrete-wa.com/chamberofcommerce.

North Cascade Chamber of Commerce, 59831 Star Route 20, P.O. Box 175, Marblemount, WA 98267-0175; (360) 873–2106 or (800) 875–2448; www.marble mount.com.

Sedro-Woolley Chamber of Commerce, 714-B Metcalf, Sedro-Woolley, WA 98284; (360) 855–1841; www.sedro-woolley.com.

Snohomish County Visitor Information Center, 19921 Poplar Way, Lynnwood, 98290; (425) 776–3977.

Winthrop Chamber of Commerce, 202 Highway 20, Winthrop, WA 98862; (509) 996–2125 or (888) 463–8469; www.winthropwashington.com.

Mount Rainier Loop

Cascades Grandeur / 1 Night

The highest mountain in the Cascade Range can be seen for 200 miles when the weather is clear. Mount Rainier's snowy bulk rises 14,411 feet, enticing climbers, hikers, and other lovers of the wilderness. Twenty-six massive glaciers hold an icy grip on the tallest volcanic mountain in the contiguous United States.

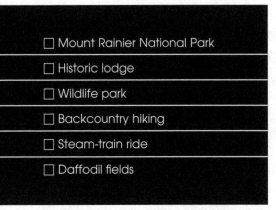

☐ Mount Rainier National Park

☐ Historic lodge

☐ Wildlife park

☐ Backcountry hiking

☐ Steam-train ride

☐ Daffodil fields

Old-growth forests encircle the mountain. Douglas fir, red cedar, and western hemlock soar 200 feet above the moss-covered valley floors. Through those trees, more than 300 miles of trails meander, leading to wildflower-spangled meadows and clear ponds. Glacier-fed streams rush through every valley.

Rainier is moody, and its weather unpredictable. Rain and snow may suddenly appear on a mild day and retreat as quickly. Glimpsed through the clouds, the mountain is beautiful. Under sunny skies, when Rainier appears in all its dazzling glory, it is magnificent.

Much of the route outlined here is open only in summer; check with the visitor information centers for road conditions.

Day 1 / Morning

From Seattle, take Interstate 90 east to Interstate 405 south to State Route 167 south to Highway 410. At Greenwater, the road turns south and within a few miles enters **Mount Rainier National Park.** You're on the Mather Memorial Parkway, paralleling the White River in the shadow of Sunrise Ridge. At the Sunrise/White River road, turn right and drive 17 miles to the 6,400-foot ridge top. Trails lead from the visitor center through the fragile, subalpine vegetation to ever-higher and more breathtaking views of glaciers and rocky crags.

From **Sunrise Point,** the summit's crater rim and **Emmons Glacier,** 4½ miles long, are clearly visible. Mount Adams lies to the south, and Mount Baker rests on the northern horizon.

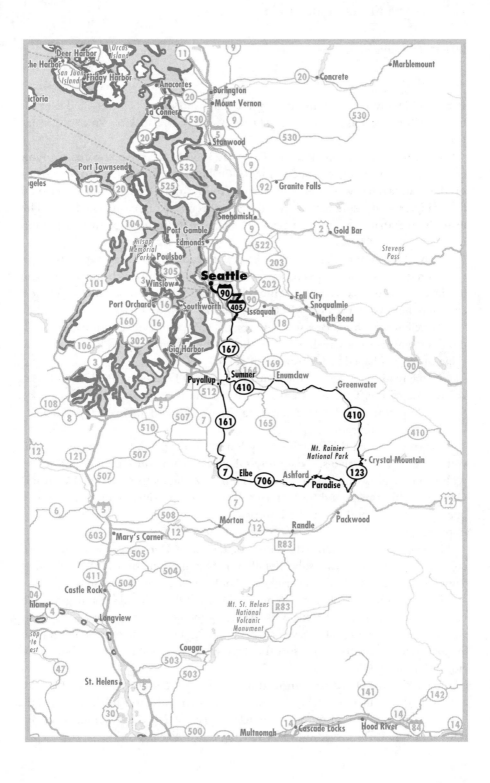

LUNCH: Picnic at Sunrise.

Afternoon

Return to Highway 410, continue south to **Cayuse Pass** (4,694 feet), and veer left toward **Chinook Pass** (5,430 feet). Drive 3 miles for a striking view of Mount Rainier's east side.

Return to Cayuse Pass and take Route 123 south. Near the **Stevens Canyon** entrance, at the southeastern end of the national park, watch for signs to the **Grove of the Patriarchs.** Walk the 1-mile trail, crossing the Ohanapecosh River on a footbridge, to an island where you'll be in the midst of an ancient forest. The princely trees that grow on the island—Douglas fir, western red cedar, and western hemlock—are 1,000 years old.

Drive the Stevens Canyon road west to **Paradise.** The road angles through thick forest, across rivers and creeks, rounding the bend at **Backbone Ridge** and heading north to **Box Canyon.** Through this narrow canyon, scoured by glaciers and carved by water, runs the Muddy Fork of the Cowlitz River.

Traveling west from Box Canyon, you'll see Stevens Ridge looming high on the right, with Stevens Creek below. In the fall the vine maples on the slopes of the ridge in this U-shaped valley blaze with color.

As the road twists toward the southern shores of Louise and Reflection Lakes, at the base of the **Tatoosh Peaks** you'll see the three most prominent peaks, Stevens, Unicorn, and Pinnacle, thrusting sharply skyward, dramatically punctuating the rugged landscape.

When you reach the Paradise Valley Road, turn right and climb upward until you arrive at last in Paradise. **Nisqually Glacier** and **Wilson Glacier** hang above, with Rainier's peak capping the view. At **Henry M. Jackson Memorial Visitors' Center,** pick up maps and trail information. The center offers slide and film programs on Rainier and the park's history, as well as 360-degree views of the awe-inspiring surroundings.

During July and August the slopes of **Paradise Park** become tapestries of color and beauty, as delicate subalpine flowers bloom by the thousands. Trails wind through the meadows and over trickling brooks, luring you to explore.

Head out on your own, or join one of the naturalist-led walks that begin at the visitor center. An easy one-hour walk exploring the flower fields starts at 2:00 P.M. Another undemanding hike leaves the center at 2:30 P.M. and concentrates on the geology, glaciers, and fine views of the dirty snout and pristine, almost-blue interior of Nisqually Glacier.

Take **Skyline Trail** to **Panorama Point** for a comfortable, half-day hike replete with grand vistas. Marmots whistle and streams sing in the crisp, clear mountain air. A side trail crosses snowfields to end at Ice Caves, remnants of the once-immense caves carved by water flowing under glaciers.

DINNER: Paradise Inn Dining Room, Mount Rainier National Park; (360) 569–2275. Grilled salmon, steak, and chicken, served in the dining room of a grand old lodge.

At 7:30 P.M., meet a park naturalist in the lobby for a one-hour evening stroll in the valley. It's an excellent opportunity for taking photographs and for observing wildlife.

At 9:00 P.M., interpreters give slide-illustrated talks in the lodge lobby. Topics vary: Meadow ecology, volcanic geology, human effects on the mountain, and Native American views are a few.

LODGING: Paradise Inn, Mount Rainier National Park. Open May through October. Imposing, 118-room lodge of Alaskan cedar. Simple rooms; some share baths. The views are incomparable. For reservations (a must), contact Mount Rainier Guest Services, 55106 Kemahan Road East, P.O. Box 108, Ashford, WA 98304; (360) 569–2275; (360) 569–2400 for reservations only.

Day 2 / Morning

Rise at dawn for an early hike, if the weather is clear. There are few sights more exhilarating than Rainier's rosy-hued glaciers under the first rays of the morning sun.

BREAKFAST: Paradise Inn. Standard breakfast menu, lavish Sunday brunch.

Head south from Paradise Park to the small community of **Longmire,** and stop for a tour of the second-oldest national park museum in the country. Open daily, from 9:00 A.M. to 4:00 P.M., the small museum offers exhibits that cover Rainier's geology, wildlife, and history.

As you drive west toward the Nisqually entrance, 6.2 miles from Longmire, you're surrounded by trees 600 to 800 years old. Their high branches create a green canopy above the road.

From the park's entrance, continue west on Route 706, along the banks of the **Nisqually River.** At Elbe, follow the signs to **Mount Rainier Scenic Railroad** (Box 921, Elbe, WA 98330; 360–569–2588). The old-fashioned train operates daily mid-June through September, weekends in winter, on a 14-mile ride. Behind a vintage steam engine, open cars chug, steam, and whistle across high bridges and through deep forest to Mineral Lake. The train ride takes ninety minutes. The dinner train ride on Sunday lasts four hours.

From Elbe, take Route 7 and Route 161 to **Eatonville** and **Northwest Trek Wildlife Park,** 11610 Trek Drive East (360–832–6117), a 715-acre wildlife park. Here the visitors are enclosed in a bus for a fifty-five-minute tour, and the animals roam freely in their natural habitat. Bison, moose, bighorn sheep, and caribou move undisturbed through the woodlands and open meadows. Cougar, wolves, eagles, and owls are kept in spacious, enclosed areas. Spring is a good time to see the newborns.

Northwest Trek has 5 miles of nature trails; one is accessible to wheelchairs.

LUNCH: Northwest Trek snack bar. Sandwiches, soups, and hamburgers. Eat indoors or take your lunch to the picnic meadow, where tame deer may wish to share your meal.

Afternoon

Continue on Route 161 north to **Puyallup,** home of the daffodil and once the bulb basket of the world. Valley farmers shipped worldwide a generation ago, and tourists flocked in to admire the acres of fragrant flowers and watch the street parade held in spring in their honor.

That was before urban development covered many fields and before fresh-cut flowers became a lucrative business; now most of the daffodils are cut and shipped while they're unopened buds. But you can still see a few fields in bloom—glorious yellow carpets, with Mount Rainier an immense white backdrop. The April festival and parade remain a major annual event in both Puyallup and Tacoma.

In Puyallup, tour **Meeker Mansion,** 312 Spring Street (253–848–1770), a seventeen-room home of the 1890s. Among its ornate splendors are six fireplaces with carved ceramic tiles, Victorian furnishings, and floral painted ceilings. Well worth a visit, the mansion is open afternoons, Wednesday through Sunday, March through December.

Another restored home, this one in neighboring **Sumner,** is **Ryan House,** 1228 Main Street (253–863–8936), built in 1875 by the town's first mayor. He was a hops farmer and lumberman.

To return to Seattle, drive north on Route 167 or take Route 161 to Interstate 5 for the final 15 miles.

There's More

Farmers' Market at Pioneer Park, Second and Meridian, Puyallup; (253) 840–2631. Fresh fruit and produce from local farms on summer Saturdays. Open May through October.

Hiking. Naches Loop Trail, near Chinook Pass and Tipsoo Lake (off Route 410, on the eastern border of the national park), is enchanting, with its subalpine firs and mountain hemlock trees, wooden bridge, and summer wildflowers. The trail connects with the Pacific Crest Trail, which extends from Mexico to Canada.

Silver Falls Trail, above Laughingwater Creek on the Ohanapecosh River, is a 3-mile loop trip from Ohanapecosh Campground, 2 miles south of the Stevens Canyon junction on Route 123. The trail leads to an 80-foot cascade of water so clear it has a silver cast. The vibrant green of the ferns and mosses in the Silver Falls gorge is stunning on a cloudy day.

Trail of the Shadows is a ½-mile trail through a meadow with bubbling mineral springs; you may see a beaver family. The trail begins across the road from Longmire Museum.

Mountain climbing. Climbing Rainier demands skill and experience. One-day seminars and equipment rentals are available from Rainier Mountaineering Inc., in Ashford; (888) 892–5462 (summer only). They have exclusive rights to conduct guided climbs of the mountains. Winter address: P.O. Box Q, Ashford, WA 98304.

Skiing. Camp Muir snowfield. Gentle slope, snow covered all year, on Mount Rainier's south side. No lifts. Hike up and ski down.

Crystal Mountain, one of the state's major ski areas; at 7,000 feet, it's Washington's highest. Commercial resort with ski lifts.

Reflection Lakes. Safe cross-country trail skiing, easy access, and scenic grandeur. Camping allowed when snowpack is 3 feet deep. Park at Narada Falls, near Paradise.

Van Lierop Bulb Farm, 13407 Eightieth Street East, Puyallup; (253) 848–7272 or (888) 666–8377. Stroll brick walkways in a small garden with flowering trees and a gazebo. Buy bulbs and plants in the gift shop. Put your name on the mailing list for a lovely catalog.

Special Events

Mid–April. Daffodil Festival, Puyallup and Tacoma. Elaborate parade, flower show, bake sale, dog show, barbecues, auction, dances.

Late June. Meeker Days, Puyallup. Honors an early Puyallup pioneer. Arts-and-crafts fair, fun run, pancake breakfast, family track meet, chicken barbecue, and ice-cream social.

September. Western Washington Fair, Puyallup. One of the state's major fairs and the sixth-largest state fair in the United States, with livestock exhibitions, races, carnival rides, food booths, handicrafts, and big-name entertainers.

Other Recommended Restaurants and Lodgings

Ashford

Alexander's Country Inn, just outside Mount Rainier Park, 37515 Highway 706 East; (360) 569–2300; within Washington, (800) 654–7615. Landmark country restaurant and inn with twelve rooms. Fresh fish entrees and memorable blackberry pie.

Rainier Overland Restaurant and Lodge, 31811 Highway 706 East; (360) 569–0851 or (800) 582–8984. Located 1 mile east of Ashford on Route 706 and 5 miles west of the southwest Nisqually entrance of Mount Rainier National Park. The motel and cabins are available year-round, with rooms for up to four people and cabins for up to eight people. The restaurant menu features poultry and seafood entrees, salads, and sandwiches. Open daily Memorial Day through Labor Day. Breakfast and lunch are also available.

Crystal Mountain

Crystal Mountain Hotels, 33818 Crystal Mountain Boulevard; (360) 663–2262 or (888) SKI–6400. Crystal Mountain Hotels offers full-service mountain lodge facilities in two separate buildings: The Alpine Inn is traditional Bavarian-style; the Village Inn is more contemporary.

Longmire

National Park Inn. Historic cedar lodge, remodeled 1989–1990. Rustic and woodsy, with twenty-five rooms (two are wheelchair accessible) and a view across Longmire Meadow to mountain's peak. The only lodge in the park open all year. Reservations: Mount Rainier Guest Services, P.O. Box 108, Ashford, 98304-0108; (360) 569–2275.

Packwood

Inn of Packwood, 3032 Highway 12; (877) 496–6666. Thirty-four older but very clean rooms. Nice views of Mount Rainier from window.

Puyallup

Casa Mia, 505 North Meridian Street; (253) 770–0400. New York–style Italian food. Serving pasta, soups, salads, pizza, and other Italian specialties in generous portions. Open for lunch and dinner. All-you-can-eat pasta Sunday through Thursday.

Hungry Goose Bistro & Boutique, 1618 East Main; (253) 845–5747. Inventive pasta dishes, plus a nice variety of beef and seafood entrees.

Sumner

Gast House Bakery, 1012 Main Street; (253) 863–4433. Serves up pork and schnitzel sandwiches, and knockwurst and bratwurst with hot potato salad. Strudel or apple cake is a perfect ending to your meal.

Manfred Vierthaler Winery and Restaurant, 17136 Highway 410 East; (253) 863–1633. Unusual dining room on a hill, offering view of valley and vineyards. German-style wines in the tasting room, steak and Bavarian dishes on the menu.

For More Information

The Chamber of Eastern Pierce County, 417 East Pioneer, Puyallup, WA 98371; (253) 845–6755; www.puyallupchamber.com.

Enumclaw Chamber of Commerce, 1421 Cole Street, Enumclaw, WA 98022; (360) 825–7666; www.enumclawchamber.com.

Mount Rainier National Park, Tahoma Woods, Star Route, Ashford, WA 98304; (360) 569–2211; www.nps.gov/mora.

SEATTLE ESCAPE SEVEN

North Kitsap Peninsula

A Northwest Heritage / 1 Night

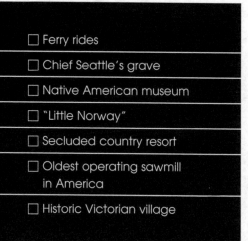

☐ Ferry rides

☐ Chief Seattle's grave

☐ Native American museum

☐ "Little Norway"

☐ Secluded country resort

☐ Oldest operating sawmill in America

☐ Historic Victorian village

There's a lot of diversity within a comparatively small area on the northern Kitsap Peninsula. You can drive from a Scandinavian-style village to a New England mill town in less than half an hour, with time out for sightseeing, or you can watch Suquamish Indians carve a dugout canoe a few miles from fine dining opportunities on a country estate.

Day 1 / Morning

Kitsap Peninsula lies west of Seattle, across Puget Sound. Board the Winslow ferry at Elliott Bay for the thirty-five-minute crossing to **Winslow,** on **Bainbridge Island.** Have breakfast here at the **Streamliner Diner,** 397 Winslow Way (206–842–8595), or drive Route 305 north toward Agate Passage and the bridge to the peninsula.

Take an immediate right on Suquamish Way, and follow the signs to the grave of **Chief Seattle** (or Sealth). The grave of the famous Salish Indian leader, who died in 1866 and for whom Seattle is named, lies in a hilltop cemetery beside a small church. Marked by a cross and framed with traditional dugout canoes, the great chief's resting place overlooks the waters of the sound. On the horizon rise the tall buildings of Seattle's skyline.

After paying homage to the man who sought peace between his people and the white settlers, the man who said that "the very dust under your feet . . . is the ashes of our ancestors," visit nearby **Old Man House State Park** (signs clearly mark the way). This shady hillside park above the bay was the site of a native communal home, the "Old Man House," built of cedar and 900 feet long. The dwelling is typical of construction used by the Kitsap Indians.

Learn more about the culture of these Native Americans at the **Suquamish Museum,** 15838 Sandy Hook Road, Suquamish (360–598–3311), named by the Smithsonian as the best Native American museum in the Northwest. Follow Route

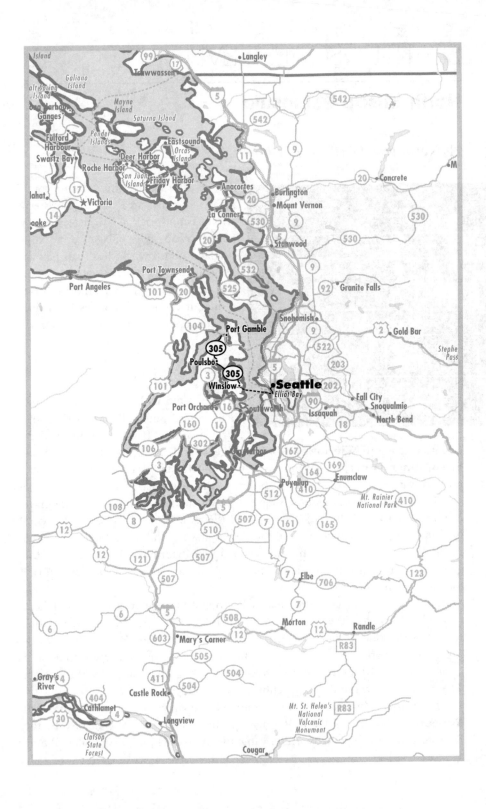

Chief Seattle's grave lies under a frame of dugout canoes in Suquamish.

305 west; the museum is just off the highway on the **Port Madison Indian Reservation,** home to the Suquamish people, 15838 Sandy Hook Road, Poulsbo (360–598–3311). Near the entrance, under a shelter, you may see carvers patiently forming a long, dugout canoe from a huge log of cedar. The excellent, sometimes poignant museum artifacts and photographs depict native life as it was for thousands of years before white settlement and the results after it.

Continue west on Route 305 as it curves up toward Liberty Bay and **Poulsbo.** Turn left on Lincoln Road, which ends at the waterfront. When you see painted murals on downtown buildings and signs reading VELKOMMEN TIL POULSBO, you know you're deep into Scandinavian country.

The little town was settled in the late 1880s by fishers, loggers, and farmers, many of them from Norway; *Poulsbo* means "Paul's Place" in Norwegian. Liberty Bay, then called Dogfish Bay, and its inlets reminded the settlers of the fjords of their native land. The town's tie to the water remains strong today, with three marinas on the bay's waterfront. The people of Poulsbo take pride in their rich heritage. They hold several traditional festivals to honor their roots, and numerous shops sell Scandinavian handicrafts, jewelry, and foods.

LUNCH: Tizley's Europub, 18928 Front Street; (360) 394–0080. Schnitzel sandwiches, garlic rosemary chicken sandwiches, and classic Reubens are among the many selections here. Specials might be a sausage plate or a Scandinavian platter. Down the street is **The Bayside Broiler,** 18779 Front Street; (360) 779–9076. This waterfront restaurant offers seafood, soups, salads, steaks, and chops, along with views of the Olympic Mountains.

Afternoon

Visit **Verksted Gallery,** 18937 Front Street Northeast (360–697–4470), an artist co-op stocked with wood carvings, leather work, handpainted shirts, chocolate sculpture, and cribbage boards made from elk horn.

Stroll **Liberty Bay Park,** which is connected by a wooden causeway over the water to American Legion Park, to soak up the maritime flavor of this engaging town. Pennants snap in the wind on fishing and pleasure boats as they come and go in the busy harbor. Liberty Bay has a picnic area and a covered pavilion used during the summer for dancing, concerts, and arts festivals. At the **Poulsbo Marine Science Center,** 18743 Front Street Northeast (360–779–5549), on Liberty Bay, you can examine sea life under microscopes, touch anemones, see ghost shrimp, and watch videos and documentaries.

Raab Park, at Caldart Avenue off Hostmark Street, is Poulsbo's largest park. On its fourteen acres are grassy slopes, covered picnic facilities, barbecue grills, a playground, horseshoe pits, a sand volleyball court, and an outdoor stage.

Browse the shops along **Front Street** for unusual souvenirs, such as the brass and nautical items in Cargo Hold and merchandise imported from Norway at Five Swans. The fragrance wafting from Sluy's Bakery (360–697–2253) will draw you to this famous shop, where fresh-baked breads and toothsome pastries are sold.

Leaving Poulsbo, take Bond Road west to Big Valley Road and turn left. Drive 4 miles through idyllic countryside, where forested hills back green fields, to the **Manor Farm Inn.** If you arrive by 3:30 P.M., you'll be in time for tea, a regular ritual at this country estate.

After tea, stroll around the farm and reacquaint yourself with tranquillity. In this setting, right from *All Creatures Great and Small,* Manor Farm Inn offers an opportunity to experience a slower pace. Horses and dairy cows graze in the pastures, and lambs gambol in the fields. Walk to the trout-stocked pond in back, or sit on the veranda and admire the flower-filled courtyard.

DINNER: **Molly Ward Gardens,** 27462 Big Valley Road Northeast; (360) 779–4471. Near your night's lodging. Reserve a table in this small restaurant, where you are surrounded by dried flowers and fine food.

LODGING: The Manor Farm Inn, 26069 Big Valley Road Northeast; (360) 779–4628. French country–style farmhouse with seven rooms in two wings. Masses of flowers, luxurious rooms, enthusiastic hospitality. Full breakfast every day for guests; breakfast available to public on weekends.

Day 2 / Morning

BREAKFAST: The Manor Farm Inn. Hot scones and juice in your room begin the day. Then comes breakfast in the dining hall. Full country breakfast at 9:00 A.M. is included in your room cost.

Spend the morning at the farm petting the animals or reading on the veranda, or borrow a bicycle and explore the winding country roads.

Kitsap State Memorial Park is less than 2 miles from the inn.

LUNCH: After the morning's bountiful meal, most guests prefer to skip lunch or snack at the restored 1853 trading post in Port Gamble.

Afternoon

Follow Big Valley Road to State Route 3, and turn north toward **Port Gamble.** This historic, picturesque village, which lies across an inlet from the eastern, and northernmost, tip of Kitsap Peninsula, is one of the last company towns still in existence. Port Gamble is owned by Pope and Talbot, one of the world's major timber companies.

The founders of Port Gamble came from New England in the mid-nineteenth century and built the new town to resemble the one they'd left—East Machias, Maine. Today Port Gamble has been restored to its early-twentieth-century appearance, with neat Victorian homes, a steepled church, and a general store.

The 1856 **Port Gamble Cemetery,** burial site of the first U.S. Navy man killed in action in the Pacific Northwest, draws a lot of people to this town.

Main Street is lined with elm trees brought around Cape Horn from Maine in 1872. The entire town is on the National Register of Historic Places. The **Port Gamble Historic Museum,** 1 Rainier Avenue (360–297–8074), explains the area's history. In the same building, the **Museum of Shells and Natural History,** Rainier and Vista Streets (360–297–7636), holds a collection of more than 14,000 species of shells and marine life.

Visitors are surprised that such a tiny town would have such a good bookstore. **The Dauntless** (360–297–4043) sells new and secondhand books in a historic mill house. Kids can curl up with Harry Potter books in a cozy cubbyhole under the stairs, while their parents browse for special-interest books or literary works.

Prepare yourself for the drive back to Seattle with a pot of tea at **LaLa Land Chocolates and Tea Room** (360–297–4291), or, better yet, go for high tea, and feast on cucumber and salmon sandwiches, scones, cakes, and chocolate fondue. For the road, select a few handmade truffles, or a cup of Mayan hot chocolate, spiced up with habanero chili.

From Port Gamble turn south on State Route 104, along the wooded bluff above Port Gamble inlet to Port Gamble–Suquamish Road. You're headed back to the village of Suquamish.

Take Suquamish Way to Route 305 and recross Agate Passage. Drive again through the woodlands and pastoral countryside of Bainbridge Island, and at Winslow catch the ferry back to Seattle.

There's More

Clearwater Casino and Bingo, 15347 Suquamish Way (800–375–6073), has been a big hit since it opened on the Port Madison Reservation in Suquamish in 1990. Gaming tables, no slot machines. Entertainment lounge and cafe featuring Northwest food.

Old Schoolhouse, Northeast Main Street, on the three-acre Kola-Kole Park, 2 miles west of Kingston.

Point No Point Lighthouse. White, square tower in Hansville, at the tip of Kitsap Peninsula. Lighthouse established in 1879; present structure built in 1900.

Special Events

Mid-May. Viking Fest, Poulsbo. Three-day event in honor of Norway's Independence Day, with a Sons of Norway luncheon, pancake breakfast, arts-and-crafts show, fun run, carnival, food booth, parade.

June. Skandia Midsommarfest, Poulsbo. Skandia Folk Dance Society performs in costume. Midsummer pole raising and dance.

Mid-August. Chief Seattle Days, Suquamish. Native American dancing, canoe races, food stands, softball games.

September. Trawler-Fest, Poulsbo. Three-day event featuring classic yacht show, food booths, wine tasting, beer garden, live music. Live animals and a petting zoo for the little ones.

December. Yule Fest, Poulsbo. Scandinavian legends and storytelling, lighting of the Yule Log, Sons of Norway bazaar, Lucia Bride, strolling musicians.

Other Recommended Restaurants and Lodgings

Seabeck

Willcox House, 2390 Tekiu Road Northwest; (360) 830–4492 or (800) 725–9477. Bed-and-breakfast inn in former private waterside mansion. Five rooms, marble fireplaces, pool, view of Hood Canal, Olympic Mountains. Full breakfast served; dinner, available by reservation, is not included in price of guest room.

For More Information

Greater Poulsbo Chamber of Commerce, 19131 Eighth Avenue Northeast, Poulsbo, WA 98370; (360) 779–4999; www.poulsbochamber.com.

Silverdale Chamber of Commerce, 3100 Bucklin Hill Road, Suite 100, Silverdale, WA 98383; (360) 692–6800 or (800) 416–5615; www.silverdalechamber.com.

Port Madison Indian Reservation, 15838 Sandy Hook Road, Suquamish, WA 98392; (360) 598–3311.

Washington State Ferries, 2901 Third Avenue, Suite 500, Seattle, WA 98121–3014; (206) 464–6400 or (888) 808–7977; www.wsdot.wa.gov/ferries. All ferries depart from Pier 52.

SEATTLE ESCAPE EIGHT

Skagit County

Spring Flowers by the Sea / 1 Night

Here's a two-day sojourn into the country, a brief escape that's full of color and activity. Have fun with this one—maybe do your gift shopping for the year in La Conner's myriad shops, where you may find unexpected treasures.

The route suggested allows time to stroll La Conner's busy downtown area (packed with tourists on summer weekends and during the tulip festival), but it takes you to quiet byways, too, where you can observe wildlife, smell the flowers, and revel in rural serenity.

☐ Fields of spring flowers

☐ Quaint waterfront

☐ Boutiques

☐ Art galleries

☐ Historical museum

☐ Wildlife refuge

☐ Antiques shops

Day 1 / Morning

Drive north on Interstate 5, past Mount Vernon and over the **Skagit River** to State Route 20 (about 60 miles), and turn west. When you see the EDISON-BOW sign, where Best Road turns left, turn right; it may be unsigned, but you are on Farm to Market Road. Follow signs left down Josh Wilson Road and right down Bayview-Edison Road to **Padilla Bay National Estuarine Research Reserve,** 10441 Bayview-Edison Road, Mt. Vernon (360–428–1558), which offers hands-on learning about the adjacent estuary. Bayview-Edison Road edges the shore of **Padilla Bay,** a body of water well protected by a circling group of islands: Fidalgo, Guemes, and Samish.

The reserve is one in a nationwide system that teaches visitors about estuaries—mixes of salt and fresh water—that teem with life. Walk the uplands nature trail, view aquatic displays and Padilla Bay, and, if you're still curious, learn more in the center's research library. Hours vary seasonally.

Retrace your steps and cross Route 20. You are now on Best Road, in the heart of the tulip, iris, and daffodil fields of the **Skagit Valley,** where great swaths of springtime color draw hordes of admirers. The world's greatest volume of tulips comes from the fertile farmlands of Skagit County.

In other seasons the valley is equally beautiful, if not as brightly colored, with its tawny summer fields and autumn mists and leaf and harvest fragrances. **Mount Baker** stands on the far horizon, a high, snow-mantled cone.

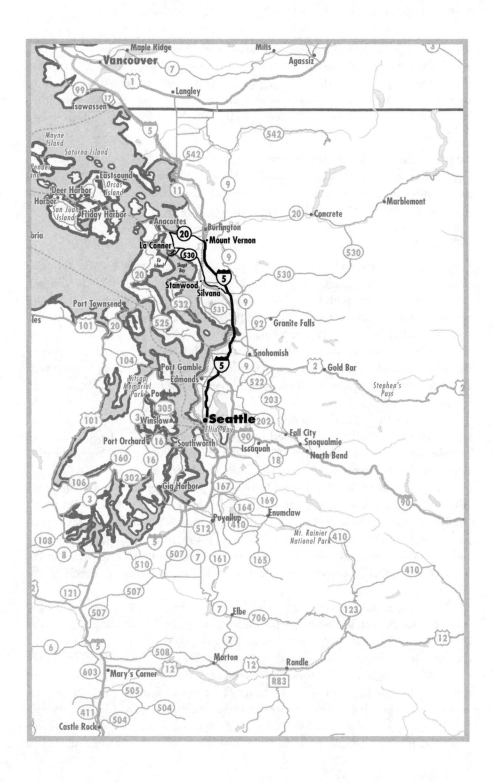

When you come to **La Conner Flats Rhododendron Garden,** 15920 Best Road (360–466–3190), stop for a tour of this English country garden. Eleven acres bloom with color March through October, from the daffodils and rhododendrons of March to June's roses, August's dahlias, and the brilliant foliage of fall. In addition to the array of flowers are savory-scented herb gardens and vegetable and berry gardens.

LUNCH: Kerstin's, 505 South First Street; (360) 466–9111. Open for lunch and dinner. The creative menu here includes wild salmon with lime butter sauce and local Samish Bay oysters, baked on the half shell. Lamb shanks prepared in a variety of ways also show up on the menu regularly.

Afternoon

Continue on Best Road to Chilberg Road, and turn west toward **La Conner** proper. The historic, picturesque little town had its beginnings in 1867 as a trading post. A few years later, John Conner, from Olympia, bought the store and town and seventy additional acres for the sum of $500. In 1872 he named the settlement after his wife, Louisa Ann Conner, using her initials.

La Conner, perched on the edge of **Swinomish Channel,** which lies between the mainland and Fidalgo Island, grew into an active port and fishing community. But when the Great Depression brought business to a standstill, La Conner began to fade.

In the 1970s energetic townsfolk decided to make some changes to encourage tourism. Their efforts succeeded beyond all expectation. La Conner has not only been discovered; it has gained fame for its charming waterfront and early-twentieth-century architecture, and its numerous shops and art galleries.

On your way to the downtown district, stop at **Tillinghast Seed Company, Inc.,** 623 Morris Street (360–466–3329 or 800–466–3329). The wooden porch overflows with flowers at this old-fashioned store, the oldest mail-order seed company in the Northwest. Inside you'll find seeds, plants, kitchen tools, country gifts, and spicy scents; upstairs there's a Christmas shop, and out in back a nursery in the shade of a tree that's a century and a half old—the largest European beech on the West Coast.

First and Second Streets, above the harbor, are lined with **antiques shops, boutiques,** and **art galleries.** A sampling: Earthenworks, showing top-quality Northwest ceramics, fabrics, watercolors, and photographs; La Conner Gallery, a channelside showroom with crystal and jewelry; The Wood Merchant, for finely carved sculptures and tools; Homespun Market, where European laces, handwoven throws, and homespun fabrics are sold; and The Scott Collection, with Northwest pottery and porcelains, jewelry, bronze and brass sculpture, and soapstone carvings.

As you explore the town, you'll see, just off Second Street, one of La Conner's oldest landmarks—a bank built in 1886, now the city hall, a triangular-shaped building. Near it is the **Magnus Anderson Cabin,** a pioneer home constructed in 1869 by a Swedish immigrant.

The **Gaches Mansion,** 703 South Second Street, is a twenty-two-room structure that dates from 1891. Once used as a hospital, the mansion has been restored and is open for tours on weekend afternoons. **La Conner Quilt Museum** (360–466–4288), housed in the Gaches Mansion, is said to be the only quilt museum in the United States.

The **Museum of Northwest Art,** 121 South First Street (360–466–4446), is in a striking contemporary building, showcasing past and present arts of the Pacific Northwest and one of the few devoted solely to Northwest artists.

Skagit County Historical Museum (501 Fourth Street, P.O. Box 818, La Conner, WA 98257; 360–466–3365) features exhibits showing life as it was in a previous century, and its windows frame views of the valley's fields with Mount Baker behind them.

DINNER: Nell Thorn's Restaurant and Pub, 205 East Washington Street; (360) 466–4261. The town's consistently best restaurant, serving Northwest and French cuisine; perfect for a special occasion. Fresh local seafoods, pastas, wines. Tables upstairs, cozy booths in the downstairs pub.

LODGING: The Channel Lodge, 205 North First Street, P.O. Box 573, La Conner, WA 98257; (360) 466–1500 or (888) 466–4113. Stylish inn with country-contemporary decor. Forty rooms, all with fireplaces, most with harbor views.

Day 2 / Morning

BREAKFAST: The Channel Lodge.

You might rent a bicycle and take a ride in the country, passing fields green or ablaze with color; perhaps you'll see swans gliding through the marshes in the morning mist.

Alternatively, check the shops you missed yesterday. If you're interested in antiques, La Conner has plenty to offer. Cameo Antiques showcases Victorian and American primitives in oak and pine, Creighton's Quilts is known for its Amish quilts, and Morris Street Antique Mall carries a wide range of furniture, glassware, toys, and books. Nasty Jack's has a large selection of oak furniture.

LUNCH: Conner Fruit and Produce Market, 116 South First Street; (360) 466–3018. Not just fresh produce, but soups, salads, sandwiches, and baked goods, right on the waterfront.

Afternoon

Leaving La Conner, take Chilberg Road south to Fir Island. Less than a mile after you cross the bridge, the toasty scent of freshly baked waffles will draw you to **Snow Goose Produce,** 15170 Fir Island Road (360–445–6908). The open market sells produce, flowers, fresh seafood, and, most important, huge and delicious ice cream cones. The hot waffle cones are baked as you watch.

The Fir Island coast, along Skagit Bay, is ragged with islands and waterways, as the Skagit flows into the bay in a dozen places. Take exit 221 west to Fir Island Road, 1½ miles west of Conway. Meander through the new **Hayton/Fir Island Farms Reserve,** and view the teeming wildlife at the mouth of Brown Slough. The Hayton grain fields are cut in November to provide food for the snow geese that arrive in late fall and stay through April, while trumpeter and tundra swans and more than 70,000 ducks arrive each winter. Bald eagles, peregrine falcons, red-tailed hawks, and short-eared owls also feed and rest here. Paved parking and a ramp are available for universal access.

Take a peek at the tiny **Fir-Conway Lutheran Church,** which houses a lovely sanctuary and a fine pipe organ. The congregation has roots dating back to 1888, when it first conducted services in a schoolhouse on Fir Island. In 1896 the congregation erected this small church building—just 24 by 42 feet and only 14 feet high. By 1916 the congregation had grown, and another church was built. In the following year the Conway Norwegian Evangelical Lutheran Church united with the Fir church and became the Fir-Conway Lutheran Church.

Some say a visit to this area isn't complete without a stop at the friendly **Conway Pub and Eatery** in downtown Conway, 18611 Main Street (360–445–4733), for a half-pound bacon cheeseburger. Wash it down with a brew or beverage that suits your fancy.

Back on Fir Island Road, head east across the Skagit to Route 530 and turn south. It's a few miles down the road to **Stanwood,** a small farming community. Stanwood was settled between 1870 and 1890. Called Centerville at the time, the community was the first Norwegian settlement in what is now Washington State. Stanwood's local museum of history, the **D. O. Pearson (Pioneer) House and Museum,** 27108 102nd Avenue Northwest (360–629–6110), provides a comprehensive perspective of the region's development.

Also worth the visitor's time is an easy but informative walk, best taken with the historical walking-tour guide published by the Stanwood Historical Society.

The 43.6-acre Heritage Park, with several ball fields and a skateboard park, is a friendly spot for families with young children to stop and stretch.

From Stanwood, drive to **Silvana** on State Route 531. The pastoral valley is far more picturesque and relaxing than the freeway ride, and it doesn't add much time. You'll pass sprawling green fields and tidy plots, a red barn half-submerged in ivy, and a gray one with a moss-covered roof. A flag flies from the porch of an old-fashioned farmhouse, behind the lilacs.

About a half mile from Stanwood, you'll see a small white church on a hill. **Peace Lutheran Church,** built in 1884, is now a historic site, still in use and a favored location for weddings.

Blink as you enter the village of Silvana, on your way to join I–5, and you may miss it. You left the Fir Island turnoff just 23 miles ago.

Drive south on I–5 for the return to Seattle.

There's More

Cruises. *Victoria Clipper,* 2701 Alaska Way, Pier 69, Seattle; (206) 448–5000 or (800) 888–2535. Provides transportation, tours, and accommodation packages to Victoria and the San Juan Islands.

RoozenGaarde, 15867 Beaver Marsh Road, Mount Vernon; (360) 424–8531. Display garden and gift shop, open daily. Main blooming season is late February to late July.

Skagit Display Gardens, 16650 Memorial Highway, Mount Vernon; (360) 428–4270. Open daily for self-guided tours.

Skagit Valley Gardens, 18923 Johnson Road, Mount Vernon; (360) 424–6760 or (800) 732–3266. One of the oldest public display gardens in Skagit County. Year-round botanical garden: thousands of tulips, crocuses, daffodils in spring; brilliant annuals in August; poinsettias in November; Christmas display. Visitors welcome; bring a lunch to the gazebo and picnic table.

Skagit Valley Bulb Farms, 15002 Bradshaw Road, Mount Vernon; (206) 424–8152. Picnic facilities; walk in fields of flowers.

West Shore Acres Bulb Farm and Display Garden, 956 Downey Road, Mount Vernon; (360) 466–3158. A one-and-a-half-acre flowering bulb display garden surrounding an 1896 Victorian farmhouse.

Special Events

Early April to end of May. Skagit Valley Tulip Festival, Mount Vernon. Major Northwest festival, with parades, flower shows, street fair, pancake breakfast, salmon barbecues, dances, pick-your-own and display flower fields, food fair, sports events (gymnastics, Slug Run). Park and ride to avoid traffic congestion. Go early, preferably on a Tuesday or Wednesday.

Other Recommended Restaurants and Lodgings

La Conner

Calico Cupboard, 720 South First Street; (360) 466–4451. Cafe that's famous for cinnamon rolls, muffins, breads, biscuits. Eat here, or take pastry to go and eat by the water. Coffee drinks, too. (Crowded in the busy season.)

The Heron Inn, 117 Maple Avenue; (360) 466–4626 or (877) 883–8899. Victorian-style inn with twelve units. Waterfront guesthouse available also. Pamper yourself at the on-site Watergrass Day Spa. Full breakfast included.

Hotel Planter, 715 South First Street; (360) 466–4710 or (800) 488–5409. Twelve guest rooms in renovated building. Inexpensive. Private hot tub in garden.

La Conner Country Inn, 107 South Second Street; (360) 466–3101 or (888) 466–4113. Attractive, twenty-eight-room inn with theme of a country guesthouse. In the heart of town. Continental breakfast.

Ridgeway Farm Bed-and-Breakfast, 14914 McLean Road, P.O. Box 475, 98257; (360) 428–8068 or (800) 428–8068. Dutch colonial farm home on two acres. Tulip fields, six guest rooms, homemade desserts, full breakfast.

Wild Iris Inn, 121 Maple Avenue; (360) 466–1400 or (800) 477–1400. Nineteen-room, two-story hotel in Victorian style. Guest and public dining Sunday through Wednesday. Full guest breakfast served daily.

For More Information

La Conner Chamber of Commerce, 413 Morris, P.O. Box 1610, La Conner, WA 98257; (360) 466–4778 or (888) 642–9284; www.laconner.net.

Mount Vernon Chamber of Commerce, 105 East Kinkaid Street, Mount Vernon, WA 98273; (360) 428–8547; www.mountvernonchamber.com.

VANCOUVER
ESCAPES

VANCOUVER ESCAPE ONE

Explore the Fraser Valley

Farm and Garden Route between the Mountains / 2 Nights

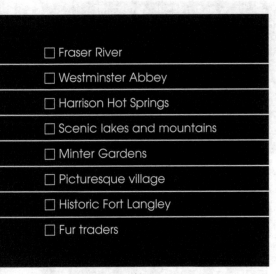

- ☐ Fraser River
- ☐ Westminster Abbey
- ☐ Harrison Hot Springs
- ☐ Scenic lakes and mountains
- ☐ Minter Gardens
- ☐ Picturesque village
- ☐ Historic Fort Langley
- ☐ Fur traders

Fur trader Simon Fraser explored the 850-mile-long Fraser River from its source in the Rocky Mountains to the Fraser Canyon, then down the fertile Fraser Valley to the delta where the city of Vancouver now stands. He built fur-trading posts for the Hudson's Bay Company along the way.

When prospectors struck gold in the Fraser Valley in 1858, the traffic came from the opposite direction, with hordes of would-be miners going up the Fraser in search of their fortunes. The Colony of British Columbia was proclaimed from Fort Langley, on the Fraser. The river city of New Westminster is still called the Royal City because Queen Victoria named it the first provincial capital.

All of those "treasures," except the gold strikes, are still there in the 80-mile-long Fraser Valley, whose fruit and vegetable farms have fed city folk for generations. The glorious lakes and mountains are still the backdrop to every valley scene, as they were in the days of the fur traders. Living history sites tell the old stories. Fruit farms, show gardens, and hot springs tempt you to stop along the way.

This escape follows the north side of the Fraser River to the glorious lake-and-mountain setting of Harrison Hot Springs and comes back down the south side, past Minter Gardens and Historic Fort Langley to the Royal City of New Westminster.

Day 1 / Morning

Follow Highway 7A east as Hastings Street becomes Inlet Drive and then Barnet Road. Turn left at **Port Moody,** and find yourself on Highway 7, known to all and sundry as the Lougheed Highway. Several miles of roadside commerce lead you over the Pitt River into **Pitt Meadows** and **Maple Ridge,** where our tour begins.

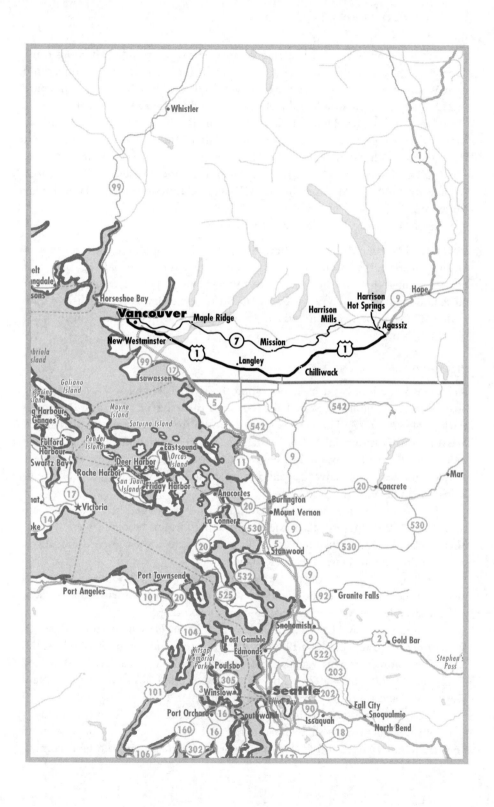

This was a lively riverboat town a century ago when people and goods came downriver, picking up produce and other freight for the cities of Vancouver and New Westminster. Pick up a **Heritage River Walk** brochure from the InfoCentre at 22238 Lougheed, and follow directions downhill to the **Fraser River.**

The restored Port Haney buildings are on River Road. The old Bank of Montreal building is now the popular **Billy Miner Pub.** Walk out on the rebuilt **Port Haney Wharf;** then join the Haney bypass road to see **Haney House,** 11612 224th Street (604–463–1377), the **Maple Ridge Museum,** 22520 116th Avenue (604–463–5311), and the old **CP Rail Caboose** (in the Maple Ridge Museum).

Rejoin Highway 7 and head for **Mission.**

LUNCH: The **Blackberry Kitchen** (604–826–0210), located in the Fraser River Heritage Park, serves homemade soups and sandwiches in an old log cabin and offers stunning views of the Fraser River Valley. Open May 1 through September 30. A good year-round choice is **Fogg 'n' Suds** at the Best Western Mission City Lodge, 32281 Lougheed Highway (640–820–5500), which features an international lunch menu.

Afternoon

Railway Avenue loops you back east along the river to Highway 7, and the signboard directs you uphill on Stave Lake Road to **Fraser River Heritage Regional Park** (604–826–0277). The park is located on the former grounds of **St. Mary's Mission and Residential School,** established in 1861 and founded by a Catholic order from France that wanted to educate the poor, particularly the First Nations people who were being adversely affected by the influx of white settlers coming to British Columbia for the gold rush.

St. Mary's began as a center for educating First Nations children and was operational until 1961. In 1965 all of the deteriorating mission buildings were demolished. Today the only remaining traces of St. Mary's are a few cement foundations scattered throughout Fraser River Heritage Park.

While here, be sure to walk through the several lovely gardens in the park, including the Marcellus Rhododendron Walk, the Ernest Jacobsen Rose Garden, and the lavender garden, a memorial to honor loved ones.

Continue up Stave Lake Road and turn right on Dewdney Trunk Road to **Westminster Abbey,** part of a Benedictine monastery and Seminary of Christ the King. The complex crowns a grassy hill with spectacular views at 34224 Dewdney Trunk Road (604–826–8975). The abbey was named after the city of New Westminster and is not related to the famous abbey in London, England.

The slender columns of the contemporary abbey create a beautiful modern echo of the ancient cross-shaped cathedrals of Europe. Tour buses bring visitors from the United States and Canada to enjoy the sanctuary and the light coming through the stained-glass windows. Services are open to visitors, and the monastery is used as a retreat.

Follow Dewdney Trunk Road downhill, and take Highway 7 east across the bridge at Hatzic; then turn immediately left into the **XA:YTEM** (pronounced "hay-tem") **Longhouse Interpretive Centre,** 35087 Lougheed Highway (604–820–9725). The Sto:lo Nation honors a large rock on an ancient river terrace, sacred site of their ancestors. Closed December and January.

You will pass general stores at Dewdney and Deroche and waterfront cottages at Lake Errock before following the shore of Harrison Bay into **Harrison Mills,** where lumber mills once thrived on the timber floated down Harrison Lake.

The family of Charles Pretty owned large tracts here. His sons created a hunting lodge and a home that now offer unusual lodging choices to those who turn left up Morris Valley Road and follow signs to historic, rustic **Fenn Lodge** or the elegant **Rowena's Inn on the River.**

When Highway 7 crosses the Harrison River, follow signs right to **Kilby Historic Store and Farm,** a 1920s living history site taken over by the Province of British Columbia to preserve the old general store, post office, milk house, log cabin, and tearoom in farm country near the Harrison River.

It is about a fifteen-minute drive from there on Highways 7 and 9 to **Harrison Hot Springs.** When the road dead-ends at the lake, turn left and check in at the Harrison Hot Springs Resort and Spa.

DINNER: Dine and dance in the elegant Copper Room, or watch the view from the Lakeside Cafe in the **Harrison Hot Springs Resort and Spa.**

LODGING: Harrison Hot Springs Resort and Spa, 100 Esplanade Avenue, Harrison Hot Springs, B.C.; (604) 796–2244 or (800) 663–2266. This resort complex has always dominated the center of town, overlooking Harrison Lake and its surrounding mountains. Take one of the nicely restored rooms in the historic original building, or stay in the 1950s addition on one side or the new brick high-rise on the other side.

Day 2 / *Morning*

BREAKFAST: Lakeside Cafe, Harrison Hot Springs Resort and Spa.

From your breakfast terrace you can enjoy the mountains that embrace Harrison Hot Springs on every side, the lake that shimmers away to **Echo Island,** and the distant **Breckinridge Mountains.** Below you, people walk the esplanade to the left, along the shore to the original hot springs, or to the right, past the boat docks and the grassy playgrounds, to the enclosed lagoon. The town stretches only a few blocks along the lake and is only a few blocks wide.

The hot springs were known to the Coast Salish people for centuries. According to legend, three 1850s gold-rush miners discovered the springs when one miner fell in the water and discovered it was warm. The St. Alice Hotel was famous on this spot after 1885, and the water rights to the hot springs are still held by its successor, the Harrison Hot Springs Resort and Spa. The springs are piped straight into the hotel pools; nonguests can use the public pool at Hot Springs Road and Esplanade.

Spend your morning exploring the pools and the town. Rock hounds explore for jade, garnets, agates, fossils, and even gold in the surrounding hills. Or join the search for the legendary apelike Sasquatch, twice the size of a man. His huge foot-prints are supposed to have been sighted for years here in Sasquatch country.

LUNCH: Picnic on the sand beach at Harrison Hot Springs.

Afternoon

Buy tickets at the hotel and cruise 40-mile-long **Harrison Lake** with Shoreline Tours and Charters (604–819–3418). You'll wind among the beautiful islands and between the mountains that soar out of the lake.

If you feel ambitious, drive Highway 7 east for 22 scenic miles along the north side of the Fraser River to the town of **Hope,** where a Hudson's Bay fort once stood at the entrance to the Fraser Canyon.

Walk through the **Othello Quintette** tunnels once used by the Kettle Valley Railway. Ten miles east of Hope on Highway 3, you can see the results of the 1965 **Hope Slide,** 45-meter-deep rock rubble created by the collapse of one side of Johnson Peak. Return on Highway 7 or along the south side of the river on Highway 1, and follow the signs to Harrison Hot Springs.

DINNER: The Copper Room, 310 Hot Springs Road; (604) 796–8422. Fine dining in a cavernous room with a large dance floor and bandstand.

LODGING: Harrison Hot Springs Resort and Spa.

Day 3 / Morning

BREAKFAST: Lakeview Restaurant, 150 Esplanade; (604) 796–9888. Great view.

Follow Highway 9 through **Agassiz** and across the Rosedale Bridge to **Minter Gardens,** 52892 Bunker Road, Rosedale, B.C. (604–794–7191; toll-free in Canada, 800–661–3919 or 888–646–8377). You will find thirty-two acres of showcase gardens set against the Coast Range at the foot of Mount Cheam. Paved wheelchair-accessible paths wind through eleven themed garden settings that change with the season.

Allow at least an hour, especially during tour-bus season, to salute the flowered flag, photograph the flowered peacock, and say hello to the bush ladies, their skirts covered with flowers grown on moss, who peek out under the trees in their sum-mer hats.

Continue south on Highway 9 across Highway 1 (the Trans-Canada Highway) and follow the signs to **Bridal Veil Falls.** You can picnic in **Bridal Falls Provincial Park,** but you must park and climb fifteen minutes uphill to see the falls tumbling down 7,000-foot-high Mount Cheam.

If you have children in the backseat, they may not let you go past the two kid-popular attractions on Bridal Falls Road: **Dinotown** and the better-known **Trans-Canada Water Slides**, both of which are open during the summer months.

Join Highway 1, the Trans-Canada Highway, going west. Divert to the commercial services available in **Chilliwack,** the main town of the Fraser Valley, or continue west to exit 73 and turn south a few blocks on 264th Street to another popular family attraction: the **Greater Vancouver Zoological Centre,** 5048 264th Street, Aldergrove, B.C. (604–856–6825). This 200-acre game farm takes you on foot and onboard a small red train around large paddocks that are home to rhinoceroses, giraffes, llamas, tigers, and other species. Open daily year-round.

Continue on Highway 1 to exit 66, and follow signs to the picturesque and historic village of **Fort Langley.**

LUNCH: Lamplighter Garden Cafe, 9213 Glover Road, Fort Langley, B.C.; (604) 888–6464. Locals fill the tables noon to 1:00 P.M., but after that you can sit inside or out in a cozy setting on the main street of town. Ask about the well-known chicken-and-everything sandwich, known as "The Clucker."

Afternoon

The village is only a few streets wide and a few streets long, so plan to walk the picturesque streets, explore the shops, and visit the historic sites. Located on the banks of the Fraser River, **Historic Fort Langley** is known as the birthplace of British Columbia, because the province was proclaimed a colony in the fort's "Big House." Start your tour by picking up a walking map at the Info Centre, located in the old green-and-white railway station at the corner of Glover and Mavis.

Two blocks down Mavis you'll find the rebuilt fort that was born as a fur-trading post and became famous as the place where Governor James Douglas proclaimed the creation of the Colony of British Columbia.

Watch the short film and walk through the palisaded walls into the old fort, where "fur traders" still live and work every day as part of the fort's living history program. During its many special events, "fur traders" at the **Fort Langley National Historic Site,** 23433 Mavis Avenue (604–513–4777), paddle the old *canoes du nord,* bundle skins for their journey east, and put on social events in the Big House.

This part of British Columbia is known for its horse ranches, so ask about any special events or horseback pleasures available at the moment. For example, **Campbell Valley Regional Park** may be offering Pub Rides: You ride to the pub, tie up for a burger and brew, and ride back.

You can follow Glover Road until it dead-ends a few blocks from town at the ferry terminal. A tiny car ferry crosses the Fraser River to Maple Ridge and the north shore. It carries only a few cars at a time, so prepare to wait during busy periods.

From Fort Langley it is only a forty-five-minute drive back to Vancouver. Consider diverting to **Westminster Quay** in the Royal City of **New Westminster.** Buy fish, fruit, vegetables, and flowers in the market. Follow the river walk. Dine upstairs or down while the boats struggle upriver and coast down.

There's More

Golden Ears Provincial Park. Turn north off Highway 7, 2 miles east of Maple Ridge, for a day trip, a one-hour diversion into scenic lake and mountain country, or a camping adventure. With 353 well-spaced vehicle and tent campsites at two locations, Golden Ears (604–924–2200) contains one of the largest campgrounds in the province. Tall stands of hemlock and fir obscure drive-in sites and provide shelter during the summer rain that sometimes appears as respite from heat waves. Campers can watch meteor showers in early August on the open beach.

The *West Coast Express,* 601 West Cordova Street, Vancouver, B.C., a commuter train, runs several times a day between Vancouver and the communities on the north side of the Fraser River to Mission. Call (604) 488–8906 or (800) 570–7245 to speak to a service representative, or visit www.westcoastexpress.com.

Special Events

May. Dixieland Jazz Festival, Chilliwack.

Late May. Seabird Island First Nations Festival. Ball hockey and war canoe races. Music and cultural exhibits.

Early July. Mission Pow Wow.

July. Festival of the Arts, Harrison Hot Springs. A celebration of music, theater, and visual arts.

Late July. Mission Folk Music Festival. Located in the Fraser River Heritage Regional Park. Offerings range from ancient to contemporary folk music.

Early August. Fur Brigade Days and Fort Festival, Fort Langley National Historic Site, Fort Langley.

September. Agassiz Fall Fair and Corn Festival.

World Championship Sand Sculpture Competition, a well-known event at Harrison Hot Springs.

Annual Chilliwack Bluegrass Festival. Featuring bands from all over North America and Europe.

Other Recommended Restaurants and Lodging

Fort Langley

Marr House, 9090 Glover Road; (604) 888–6455. Highly recommended for its food; a historic house setting. Lunch, dinner. Afternoon tea is available from 3:00 to 5:00 P.M.

Harrison Hot Springs

The Black Forest Steak & Schnitzel House, 180 Esplanade; (604) 796–9343. German specialties in a fine setting inside or on a terrace overlooking Lake Harrison in summer.

Conca D'Oro, 234 Esplanade; (604) 796–2695. Pasta and a terrace view on the lakefront.

Executive Hotel Harrison Hot Springs, 190 Lillooet Avenue. This establishment is a good choice as one of the town's few midrange business hotels. It's part of Choice Hotels Canada. Call (888) 265–1155 for reservations or (604) 796–5555 for general hotel information.

Harrison Heritage House & Kottages, 312 Lillooet Avenue; (604) 796–9552 or (800) 331–8099. Just steps away from Harrison Lake, this establishment contains bed-and-breakfast rooms, cottages, and a cabin, all nestled in a tranquil setting along the peaceful banks of the Miami River. The rooms have private entrances and private bathrooms, sitting areas, refrigerators, and down duvets for winter warmth. Breakfast is delivered to guest rooms.

Little House on the Lake Bed and Breakfast, 6305 Rockwell Drive; (800) 939–1116. Beautiful contemporary log house on a bluff overlooking Lake Harrison. Deck, hot tub, dock. Five minutes from town.

Old Settler Pub, 222 Cedar Avenue; (604) 796–9722. This is where locals go for a casual dinner and a drink in a comfortable setting.

Harrison Mills

Historic Fenn Lodge, 15500 Morris Valley Road; (604) 796–9798 or (888) 990–3399. Former hunting lodge of wealthy pioneer Charles Fenn Pretty. Located on ninety acres of woods, wetland, mountain, and meadow, with a ½-mile private riverfront. Eagles, hummingbirds, and trumpeter swans make this space home. Guests have access to a 60-foot saltwater pool and a labyrinth, a spiral path used for meditation.

Rowena's Inn on the River, 14282 Morris Valley Road; (604) 796–0234 or (800) 661–5108. An elegant, large home on a sweep of grass between cedar groves and the Harrison River. Three large, beautiful guest rooms and public dining room in the house; luxurious cabins nearby. Sandpiper Golf Club on premises.

For More Information

Fort Langley Visitor Info Centre, 23245 Marvis Avenue, Fort Langley, B.C. V1M 2R5; (604) 888–1477; www.pc.gc.ca/lhn-nhs/bc/langley.

Harrison Hot Springs Visitor Info Centre, 499 Hot Springs Road, Harrison Hot Springs, B.C. V0M 1K0; (604) 796–5581.

Hello BC, 300–1803 Douglas Street, Victoria, B.C. V8T 5C3; (800) HELLO-BC; www.hellobc.com.

Maple Ridge and Pitt Meadows Chamber of Commerce, 22238 Lougheed Highway, Maple Ridge, B.C. V2X 2T2; (604) 463–3366.

Mission Visitor Info Centre, 34033 Lougheed Highway, Mission, B.C. V2V 4J5; (604) 826–6914.

VANCOUVER ESCAPE TWO

Mountain/Canyon Circle

High Country and the Gold Rush / 2 Nights

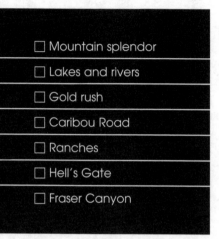

- ☐ Mountain splendor
- ☐ Lakes and rivers
- ☐ Gold rush
- ☐ Caribou Road
- ☐ Ranches
- ☐ Hell's Gate
- ☐ Fraser Canyon

There are often more European than Canadian travelers on this circular mountain route, which winds through the high ranch country of the Pemberton Valley and down the mighty Fraser River to the terror of Hell's Canyon.

They come to see glacier-green lakes and roaring rivers amid uninhabited mountain splendor. They come to relive legends about fur traders and gold prospectors and especially the Caribou Trail. They come to raft wild rivers, hike mountain trails, and ride horses into glorious places that have never seen roads.

This escape is for you if you like long stretches of scenic open road between funky little towns, where you bed down in bed-and-breakfast accommodations, roadside motels, or small historic hotels.

Day 1 / Morning

Pack a picnic lunch and follow Highway 99 to Horseshoe Bay and up Howe Sound toward Whistler. If you start early, you will have time to stop at the **British Columbia Museum of Mining** (P.O. Box 188, Britannia Beach, B.C. V0N 1J0; 800–896–4044) at **Britannia Beach, Shannon Falls Provincial Park** near Squamish, and the entrance to **Garibaldi Provincial Park.** The museum, located on Sea to Ski Highway 99 North, is closed December and January.

Commercialism ends where our route begins, just beyond Whistler. We leave condominiums behind and drive toward snowcapped mountains silhouetted against a blue sky to the east. Turn into **Nairn Falls Provincial Park.** You will hear the roar of the **Green River** when you open your car door. Follow the path cut like a ledge against the side of a forested hill high above the river, and clamber over smooth rocks to a fenced view of the 196-foot falls. About a mile round-trip.

LUNCH: Picnic at Nairn Falls Provincial Park.

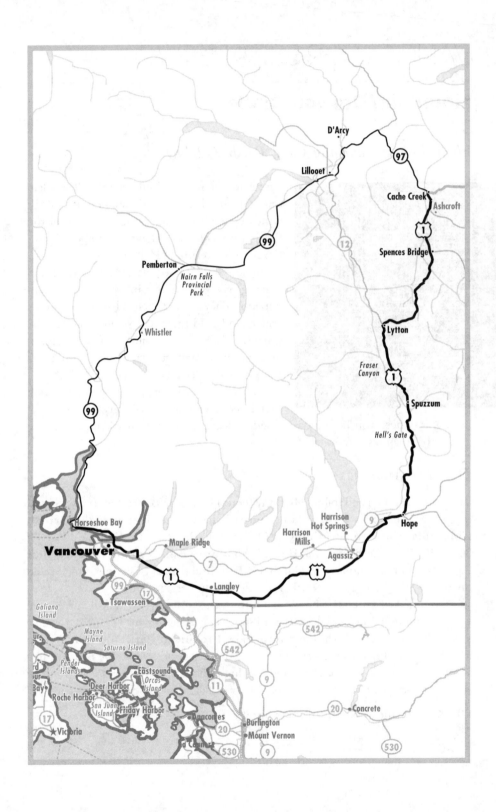

Afternoon

Highway 99 bursts out of the mountains into the **Pemberton Valley,** a plateau of ranches and farmland where the Lillooet River rushes into Lake Lillooet. The valley is surrounded by tree-covered mountains, stony ridges, and ice-capped peaks. The black rock ridge of Mount Currie rises above **Pemberton Village.**

A path and boardwalk encircle **One-Mile Lake** at the entrance to the village. Turn right at the stop sign and right again into **Pemberton Adventure Ranch** (604–894–5200), at the foot of majestic Mount Currie and perched alongside the glacial waters of the Lillooet River. Here, friendly staff lead horseback rides and jet-boating and white-water rafting excursions. After an adventure, guests can unwind beside the swimming pool or in the country gardens.

There are three other Pemberton attractions on this side road: **Big Sky Golf and Country Club** (800–668–7900), a community course called **Pemberton Valley Golf and Country Club** (800–390–GOLF), and the terminal building that opened in 1996 at **Pemberton Airport. Prime Air** serves travelers from Seattle, Vancouver, and Whistler.

Turn left out of this airport road into the village of 1,000 people, and check into your bed-and-breakfast.

You might consider the scenic 20-mile drive northeast to **D'Arcy,** at the south end of Anderson Lake, with a side trip to the canoeing and fishing pleasures of Birkenhead Lake; a drive along the Lillooet River to **Meager Creek Hot Springs;** or a trip along a gravel road to the old gold-mining towns of **Bralorne** and **Gold Bridge.** Check road conditions, as some require four-wheel drive.

It is only a five-minute walk from anywhere in Pemberton Village to the heritage log buildings of **Pemberton District Museum and Archives Society,** Prospect Street (604–894–5504). The museum houses artifacts from the Lillooet and Pemberton Valleys and Anderson Lake.

DINNER: Big Smoke Mountain BBQ Restaurant, 2021 Portage Road, Mount Currie (just outside Pemberton on Highway 99); (604) 902–4227. This restaurant is housed inside a bright red refurbished barn. Local art adorns the walls, and a large patio offers views of Mount Currie. Succulent barbecued meats are the big draw, but southern specialties such as gumbo and dirty rice also are popular.

LODGING: Country Meadows Bed and Breakfast, 1431 Collins Road, Pemberton; (604) 894–6605. A three-room, European–style home on six acres with a spectacular view of mountains, meadows, and a vineyard.

Day 2 / Morning

BREAKFAST: Country Meadows Bed and Breakfast serves generous country breakfasts including farm-fresh eggs and fresh fruit.

Cross the Lillooet River to the village of **Mount Currie,** in the Mount Currie Indian Reserve. Stop at the **Spirit Circle,** a cafe and crafts shop that schedules produce and crafts fairs on summer Saturdays. There are no gas stations or other commercial buildings between here and Lillooet.

When you pass the north end of Lake Lillooet, there is nothing to indicate what this historic waterway meant during the gold rush of the 1860s. While the Royal Engineers were chipping their way inch by inch through the Fraser Canyon to provide access to the gold camps in the north, other enterprising explorers found a water passage north from Harrison Lake to Lillooet Lake and on through Anderson and Seton Lakes to Lillooet. Port Pemberton existed briefly where Highway 99 passes Lake Lillooet.

From there, Highway 99 climbs steeply up the mountain. Watch for the B.C. PARKS sign to **Joffre Lake.** Park and walk five minutes down a groomed trail to a tiny jewel of a lake and a full-face view of **Joffre Glacier.**

The highway swings in wide loops uphill and down, with the silver gleam of **Duffy Lake** visible between the mountains ahead. **Duffy Lake Road** was a gravel road used only by the locals and a few intrepid drivers until it was paved in the mid-1990s. It follows the rushing green-and-white waters of **Cayoosh Creek** past gleaming white waterfalls as the treed mountains of the valley give way to drier slopes around Lillooet.

Turn left at the B.C. HYDRO sign, and park in the recreation area above **Seton Lake.** Photograph the glorious green lake spreading away between mountains to the horizon and read the interpretive signs. Steamships carried prospectors north via a chain of lakes from Harrison Lake to the landing spot below on the Harrison-Lillooet Trail. You can turn left to picnic and swim in the kid-friendly shallows at **Second Beach,** or go right to **First Beach,** on Sta'atl'imc Nation land, where the water drops off sharply and boat tours are available from the dock.

Stop at the **spawning channel,** especially during September in odd-numbered years, when the great run of salmon comes upstream. There are three single-lane bridges between Seton Lake and Lillooet. Stop at the second one and watch for mountain goats on the bluff ahead.

Lillooet is where the chain of lakes meets the **Fraser River.** Turn right on Main Street and park where the street turns right again. You are at the Lillooet Info Centre, the **Lillooet Museum,** 790 Main Street (250–256–0043 or 250–256–4308), and the **Mile 0 Cairn.** The Caribou Trail, which led north to places like 100 Mile House, measured all distances from this spot.

Lillooet was the biggest little boomtown in the territory until the lake-and-river route was made obsolete by the Caribou Wagon Road through Fraser Canyon. Main Street is wide enough to turn around a double-freight wagon hauled by ten yoke-spans of oxen; that's what was needed to pull twenty tons over 5,000-foot Pavilion Mountain on the trail ahead.

Pick up a walking-tour booklet and see the sights, including the 1890s **Miyazaki Heritage House** on Russell Street and the nearby **Hangman's Tree,** an old ponderosa pine used by Matthew Begbie, who is said to have used the tree as a gallows for more than eight thieves.

Swimmers and boaters have replaced steamships full of gold prospectors on Seton Lake.

LUNCH: Elaine's Coffee Garden, 842 Main Street (250–256–4633), where you can enjoy espresso or tea with sandwiches and baked goods, inside or out.

Afternoon

There are two routes south from here. Highway 12 follows the river 40 miles along the Fraser River directly to Lytton. We will stay on Highway 99 and travel just over 100 miles via Cache Creek and Spences Bridge to Lytton. Either way you leave Lillooet across the **Bridge of the 23 Camels,** which commemorates camels brought in during the gold rush and then abandoned.

Highway 99 circles north and east from here, passing through **Marble Canyon Park** and past three lakes: **Pavilion, Crown,** and **Turquoise.** Just before reaching Highway 97, which goes north into Caribou country and the gold-mining town of Barkerville, follow the signs to **Historic Hat Creek Ranch,** 7 miles north of Cache Creek (800–782–0922). Tour the property in a stagecoach or wagon, and visit the working blacksmith shop. The 326-acre site also houses a miners' camp serving authentic roadhouse meals. The ranch is a privately managed British Columbia park attraction with an admission fee and is open to the public May through October.

There is still a piece of the **Caribou Wagon Road** in front of the old hotel on the ranch, where passengers and mining supplies stopped on their way to the goldfields. Stop at the Reception Centre, with its gift shop, tearoom, and video.

Teamster Fred Paige will help you onboard the old freight wagon for a tour of the grounds. Walk over to the **Native Interpretive Site,** where a member of the Shuswap Nation will lead you into a Kekuli, a circular pit house.

Take a guided tour of **Hat Creek House** (Box 878, Cache Creek, B.C. V0K 1H0), one of the stagecoach stops on the Caribou Wagon Road between Yale and Barkerville. (For reservations call 800–782–0922.)

It is 7 miles south to the town of **Cache Creek.** Rock hounds should check out **Caribou Jade and Gifts,** where owner Ben Roy will tell you how Chinese railway workers recognized the value of British Columbia jade and sent shiploads of it home as "ballast" before North Americans caught on.

This is the junction of Highway 97 and Highway 1 (the Trans-Canada Highway). Less than twenty minutes away from Cache Creek on Highway 97C is the historic community of **Ashcroft,** cozily situated amid rolling hills. Like Cache Creek, Ashcroft enjoys a surprisingly arid climate. Fishing opportunities at Loon Lake—abundant in rainbow trout, kokanee, and steelhead—draw many visitors. Ashcroft is known as "The Heart of Gold Country," yet it cherishes an even earlier history from Aboriginal and Chinese communities; artifacts of all these cultures are on exhibit in the Ashcroft Museum. A self-guided walking tour of the village might include the Historic Ashcroft Fire Hall (rebuilt after the Great Fire of 1916), the Chinese Cemetery, the Ashcroft Cemetery, and the Masonic Hall. An interpretive trail in Millennium Park offers additional insights into the region's development.

Follow Highway 1 through dry sagebrush-covered mountains to Spences Bridge, where a toll bridge was built across the **Thompson River** to hasten supplies to the goldfields. In this narrow section of the Thompson Valley, where the river bends briefly east-west, there is just room between two barren mountains for the wide, strong river bracketed on either side by a road, a railroad, and a strip of houses.

DINNER: The Inn at Spences Bridge, 3649 Merr-Spences Bridge Highway; (250) 458–2311 or (877) 354–1997. Serves lunch and dinner. On its dinner menu, this vegetarian restaurant features homemade lasagna, ravioli, burritos, samosas, and stir fries. Closed in January and February, the restaurant reopens in March and serves dinner from 5:00 to 8:00 P.M.

LODGING: The Inn at Spences Bridge. Historic inn on the Thompson River. Twelve attractively decorated rooms, some with river views. Private and shared bathrooms. Spectacular wildlife viewing. Continental breakfast.

Day 3 / Morning

BREAKFAST: Sit at a window at The Inn at Spences Bridge's small, popular dining room and watch the action on the river.

The Ryans have been leading class 3 white-water rafting trips down the Thompson to the Fraser River for more than ten years from a grassy campsite on the river below the hotel. Several years ago, they bought the inn as a logical accompaniment. Rafters often camp overnight on the grassy bank before launching into the strong current of the river.

The Thompson River is 50 to 100 yards wide and beginning to white-water as you follow it downstream. Campers sit on a ledge of grass beside the river in **Skihist Provincial Park.** It is 23 miles downriver to **Lytton,** where the Thompson flows into the mighty Fraser at the north end of **Fraser Canyon.** Native fishers once harvested tons of salmon from this junction of two big rivers. Their trail became the supply trail for the gold rush and is now Highway 12. Several white-water rafting companies begin or end their rafting trips here, prompting the name "Rafting Capital of Canada." The area has also been called the "hot spot of Canada" because of high summer temperatures.

Cross the bridge above the river junction, and take the first left, Ferry Street, downhill to the Fraser River. You can ride the tiny orange-and-white ferry free across the river and back. It is called a "reaction ferry": Two men spin the wheel furiously at takeoff to change the direction of underwater paddles that use the power of the river current to move the ferry to the other side. There is no schedule. The ferry moves to pick up whatever automotive or foot passengers are waiting for it.

Join Highway 1 high above the river, and begin your journey south through Fraser Canyon, which runs from Lytton for about 60 miles south to Yale. This canyon was the setting for one of the most difficult road-building jobs in the world.

The interior of British Columbia was untouched except for native villages and fur brigades when the 1858 cry of "Gold!" lured 25,000 prospectors into impassable mountains and terrifying canyons on their trek north to the Caribou goldfields.

James Douglas, who had ruled the Hudson's Bay Company from Vancouver Island, brought the uninhabited mainland into what is now British Columbia. He ordered the impossible: Chip a trail, then a mule track, and finally a wagon road into cliffs high above the Fraser River to supply the gold camps. Most of the towns on our route exist today because of the gold rush and the Caribou Trail.

The most difficult part of the canyon is between Boston Bar and Yale. Boston Bar is just a scattering of houses today. Seven miles south you see a red line above the river far below, which means you are approaching **Hell's Gate.**

Turn right into the parking lot. You can hike down the steep hill, cross the bridge free, and make the steep climb back, but most people pay to ride the **Hell's Gate Airtram,** 43111 Trans-Canada Highway (P.O. Box 129, Hope, B.C. V0X 1L0; 604–867–9277). You can ride one way and hike the other if you like.

The original wagon road is just below the deck where the tram begins its 502-foot descent toward the roaring waters. The river is only 110 feet wide here, but the water is 150 feet deep in spring. Two million salmon swim up through the

Hell's Gate Fishways every year. See the video, the fishery exhibits, and the gift shop on the landing below. Two river-rafting companies actually bring their motorized rafts through that boil of water (see "There's More").

LUNCH: Salmon House, at the base of the air tram. Try the salmon chowder.

Afternoon

Drive south on Highway 1 a very short distance to the provincial park at **Alexandra Bridge.** The first bridge across the raging river was built here to access the Caribou Road. It was washed away, but you can walk across a second bridge preserved intact within the park.

Highway 1 crosses a newer bridge to **Spuzzum,** two gas stations and a restaurant at the spot where men and mules were once ferried across the river.

When you drive into **Yale** today, you see a small, typical Canadian town, with only a little brown church and a few other historic mementos of the days when fur brigades, gold miners, and settlers made this strategic spot, at the foot of the canyon, the jumping-off place for destinations north. The Caribou Wagon Road began here, as did every attempt to tame the canyon as a transportation route. Visit the **Anglican Church of St. John the Divine,** built in 1863, the oldest church in mainland British Columbia.

It is only a short drive from here—past **Emory Creek Provincial Park,** where prospectors once struck gold on **Emory's Bar**—to **Hope,** where the Fraser turns west toward the Pacific Ocean. Stop for a cup of coffee at the **Euro Cafe,** 243 Commission Street, and enjoy this small town at the eastern end of the Fraser Valley.

Hope calls itself the "Chainsaw Carving Capitol." You can see the work of wood-carver Jack Ryan in **Memorial Park,** behind the District Hall, where families picnic and play in the block between Park and Wallace Streets.

The **Othello Tunnels** are west of town; they were built for the old Kettle Valley Railroad and are now part of a scenic walking tour. You can park and walk half an hour or do the full circle, which has steep parts, in an hour. Carry a flashlight for the tunnels.

It is almost 100 miles back to Vancouver; the trip takes less than two hours along the Trans-Canada Highway, Highway 1. The gold miners came up the Fraser River, through this lush valley, to the end of navigation at Yale. Imagine the relief of settlers who later came downstream out of Fraser Canyon into this wide green valley, with mountains rising on either side only as scenery.

There's More

Fishing. British Columbia Fisher-Guided Fishing Charters; (604) 795–0493. Half-day, full-day, or overnight charters, May through September.

Gliding. Pemberton Soaring Centre Ltd., Pemberton Airport, 1860 Airport Road, Pemberton, B.C. V0N 1L0; (604) 894–5727 or (800) 831–2611. The Pembertown Valley, surrounded by mountains, creates thermals that are excellent for gliding.

Rafting. Fraser River Raft Expeditions, Box 10, Yale, B.C. V0K 2S0, 0.6 mile south of Yale on Highway 1; (877) 325–7770. Offers paddling and motorized tours on the Fraser (including Hell's Gate), the Thompson, and other places. Also eight-day float trips, and half-hour and one-hour Zodiac (a twelve-person, rigid-hull rubber craft) rides.

Kumsheen Raft Adventures Ltd., 281 Main Street, P.O. Box 30, Lytton, B.C. V0K 1Z0; (250) 455–2296 or (800) 663–6667. Offers half-day to three-day rafting trips on the Thompson and Fraser Rivers, combined with climbing and mountain-biking tours on request. Motorized raft tours through Hell's Gate.

Special Events

July. Lytton River Festival. Three-day festival with a powwow, fiddlers, games, and gold panning.

August. Feast of Fields. A festival of foods, celebrating regional cooking and harvests.

Early November. Remembrance Day Powwow, Lytton. A festival of dance and music to recognize Native Canadians who fought in the Canadian armed forces.

Other Recommended Restaurants and Lodging

Cache Creek

Cache Creek Bed and Breakfast, 1387 Quartz Road; (250) 457–6570 or (250) 574–2703. A perfect spot for enjoying nine holes of golf or catching trout in a nearby lake. In the winter, groomed cross-country trails are the main attraction. In the summer, a cool swim in the indoor pool is a perfect way to begin the day.

Lytton

Totem Motel, 320 Fraser Street, Box 580, Lytton, V0K 1Z0; (250) 455–2321. Nicely decorated rooms in an old two-story house or in red-and-white cabins, with kitchens, overlooking the Fraser River.

Pemberton

Log House Bed and Breakfast Inn, 1357 Elmwood; (604) 894–6000 or (800) 894–6002. Seven rooms open onto a balcony overlooking a spacious sitting room; views of Mount Currie, outdoor hot tub.

For More Information

Gold Country, 301 Brink Street, P.O. Box 1239, Ashcroft, B.C. V0R 1H0; (877) 453–9467; www.exploregoldcountry.com.

Hello BC, 300–1803 Douglas Street, Victoria, B.C. V8T 5C3; (800) HELLO–BC; www.hellobc.com.

Lillooet Chamber of Commerce, P.O. Box 650, Lillooet, B.C. V0K 1V0; (800) 217–3847; www.lillooetchamberofcommerce.com.

Lytton Visitor Info Centre, 400 Fraser Street, Box 460, Lytton, B.C. V0K 1Z0; (250) 455–2523.

Okanagan Connector Regional Visitor Info Centre, Highway 97C, Box 26042, Westbank, B.C. V4T 2G3; (250) 767–6677; www.okanaganbritishcolumbia.com.

Vancouver Island: West Shore

The Wild Pacific Coast / 2 Nights

The western coast of Vancouver Island holds some of the world's most dramatic wilderness scenery. In this temperate, wet climate, where rainfall is 160 inches a year, vegetation grows in lush profusion; dense jungles of ferns, mosses, and shrubbery grow under the tall evergreen trees. This is logging country, but some of the wilderness is almost untouched, allowing visitors to gain a sense of the primeval forests that once covered the entire island.

- ☐ Spectacular waterfalls
- ☐ Pristine wilderness
- ☐ Ancient forests
- ☐ Native art
- ☐ Whale watching
- ☐ Beaches
- ☐ Boat rides
- ☐ Scenic hikes

An abundance of water makes for lush, verdant growth, and Vancouver Island has plenty of both. The coast is fringed with fjordlike inlets, bays, and coves, while dozens of lakes and rivers are scattered throughout the inland regions. It's a recreational wonderland, waiting to be explored.

Day 1 / Morning

Pack a picnic lunch and take the ferry from Horseshoe Bay west on its two-hour run across the Georgia Strait to Nanaimo, on **Vancouver Island.** Drive north 21 miles on Route 19 to Parksville.

When you reach the Route 4 junction, turn west and travel 3 miles to Errington Road. Head south to **Errington,** a small farming community. On Errington Road you'll pass the general store, a log complex with a cafe, post office, Laundromat, and video store. Across the street is the **Farmers' Market.** Stop here for fresh fruits and produce in season, on Saturday mornings, May through September.

From the highway it's 5 miles to **Englishman River Falls Provincial Park.** The road travels through rolling rural countryside dotted with horse ranches and enormous old barns before entering the cool, dense forest of the park.

Tall cedars, firs, and hemlocks form green canopies over fern-filled hollows and mossy boulders in this scenic retreat. Walk the easy trail to **Englishman Falls,**

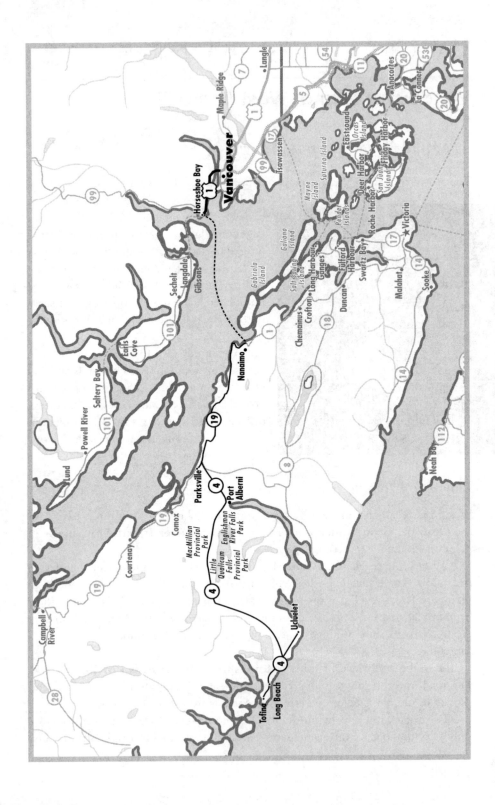

a roaring torrent of water that pours into a narrow chasm between two wide rock ledges. The park contains picnic tables, a shelter, fireplaces, firewood, drinking water, and campsites.

LUNCH: Picnic at Englishman River Falls.

Afternoon

Continue west on Highway 4, with a possible stop at the gift and craft shops in Coombs, to **MacMillan Provincial Park** and **Cathedral Grove.** In this awe-inspiring ancient forest, giant hemlock trees and Douglas firs stand in silent, shadowed splendor. Some of the oldest trees in British Columbia, they've been living for up to 800 years. Trails wind through the virgin grove, crossing weathered wooden bridges and logs with chinked steps. Interpretive signs explain the trees' long cycle of growth and decay.

Continue to **Port Alberni,** a logging community at the tip of a long fjord. The port is named after a Spanish explorer, Don Pedro Alberni, whose expedition came to the West Coast in 1791. The area's first sawmill was built here in 1860; now the MacMillan-Bloedel Company maintains a large complex that includes two sawmills and a pulp-and-paper mill.

Fishing is another significant industry, with 320 commercial vessels operating from Port Alberni's harbor. Recreational fishers are lured to the area during the peak salmon runs of August and September. The famous MV *Lady Rose* (800–663–7192), a stout packet freighter and passenger ferry, leaves from the Harbour Quay, steaming down the scenic fjord to the **Broken Group Islands** and the coast, 30 miles west, Monday, Wednesday, and Friday. It cruises to Ucluelet, a picturesque fishing village, on Monday, Wednesday, and Friday, too. On Tuesday, Thursday, and Saturday, the freighter heads out to Bamfield, a tiny hamlet on the Barkley Sound.

From Port Alberni, Highway 4 winds along the Taylor and Kennedy Rivers, passing thickly forested ridges and logged-off slopes, on its way to the ocean shore. **Pacific Rim National Park,** established in 1970, borders this untamed coast, stretching along the shoreline from **Tofino** to Port Renfrew. The park has three divisions: the rugged **West Coast Trail** to the south; Broken Group Islands, one hundred picturesque islands dotting Barkley Sound; and **Long Beach,** a 7-mile stretch of surf-washed sand and rocky headlands north of Ucluelet.

At Long Beach, 2 miles off Route 4, is **Wickaninnish Interpretive Centre** (250–726–7721), just above the beach. Tour the center to learn about marine life and wave action, enter a replica of the *Explorer 10* submersible, see a native whaling canoe, and watch a presentation on humpback whales.

After a brisk walk in the briny air of Long Beach, return to the highway and drive on to the **Shorepine Bog Trail.** A boardwalk trail rests upon the surface of this fascinating, soggy forest of stunted trees and sphagnum moss. Pick up a

Long Beach, on Vancouver Island's west shore, is part of Pacific Rim National Park.

pamphlet from the box at the trail entrance for an explanation of the delicate, colorful ecosystem.

Continue on Highway 4 to check in at **Pacific Sands Beach Resort.** Drive 4 miles more to Tofino for a stroll around town before dinner. Surrounded on three sides by water, this quaint village at the end of the road has unparalleled views of **Clayoquot Sound,** the moody ocean, and the thick forests of fir, pine, cedar, and hemlock that rise from the shore.

Cafes, shops, and galleries line the main street, quiet in the off-season and jammed in summer. The population of 1,000 swells when visitors flock to the cool coast for recreation and natural beauty.

DINNER: The Blue Heron, at Weigh West Marine Resort, 634 Campbell Street; (250) 725–3277. Attractive restaurant above a busy marina; views of Clayoquot Sound and Strawberry Island. Steak, chicken, and seafood; the fresh crab is best. Another possibility is the **RainCoast Café,** 120 Fourth Street, No. 1 (250–725–2215), a cozy bistro near downtown and the harbor. Offers creative Pacific Rim cuisine with fresh regional ingredients. Upbeat ambience. Open daily for dinner; reservations recommended.

LODGING: Pacific Sands Beach Resort, 1421 Pacific Rim Highway, P.O. Box 237, Tofino, B.C. V0R 2Z0; (800) 565–2322 from 9:00 A.M. to 8:00 P.M. Sixty-five ocean-facing rooms on lovely Cox Bay. Lodge rooms, suites with full kitchens, and villas. Spacious and clean, with balconies and some fireplaces.

Day 2 / *Morning*

BREAKFAST: If your accommodation has a kitchen, you can prepare your own morning repast; or drive into Tofino and enjoy a healthful breakfast at **Common Loaf Bakery,** 180 First Street (250–725–3915). The cozy, offbeat cafe serves good home-baked breads and pastries and will stoke you up for the morning's adventure. Soups, sandwiches, and salads are available for lunch.

After breakfast, go to **Jamie's Whaling Station** for your whale-watching trip (Box 129, 606 Campbell Street; 250–725–3919 or 800–667–9913 for reservations). Tour the Clayoquot Sound, taking you past the feeding bays of the gray whales, and visit Hot Springs Cove at Maquinna Provincial Park. The springs are perched right at the water's edge overlooking the open ocean and are accessible only by boat or float plane. **Remote Passages** will supply you with boots, a hat, and a full-length, waterproof flotation outfit. At a nearby wharf you'll board a 24-foot Zodiac (a twelve-person, rigid-hull rubber craft) and ride twenty-five minutes to the feeding grounds of the gray whales.

An experienced skipper will provide commentary on the sights, as well as a safe, exhilarating journey through flying, salty spray. High mountains and glaciers are the backdrop as the zippy Zodiac winds through Clayoquot Sound, passing native villages, sea lion rookeries, and a reserve where tufted puffins reside. Seals, otters, and occasionally orca whales may be seen.

On a two-and-a-half-hour expedition, you'll watch the 50-foot grays spout and dive, and maybe, if you're lucky, see one of these magnificent, gentle mammals breach or "spy-hop."

On the return trip your skipper may run the boat past **Strawberry Island** for a close view of *Weeping Cedar Woman,* a figure carved in 1984 as a protest against logging the virgin forests of **Meares Island.** This issue is still unresolved; Tofino residents are fighting to preserve some of the last of the old-growth forests.

Meares is a place of legends and ancient tradition. Rootlets from the towering spruce were once used by the Clayoquot Indians to make stout ropes, the yew made harpoon shafts, and cedar was the material of daily goods: clothing, utensils, homes, baskets. Salal berries and herbs were gathered for food and medicinal uses.

An interesting feature on little Strawberry is the ferry that perches on dry land like a wide brown ark. The boat was used as transportation in Vancouver before the Lion's Gate Bridge was constructed over Burrard Inlet. Now it's a private home.

On land again, return your borrowed gear and head over to **Breakers Deli.**

LUNCH: Breakers Deli, 430 Campbell Street; (250) 725–2558. Serves hearty foods all day long, beginning with breakfast burritos and wraps and continuing with whole-wheat crust pizza, sandwiches, and salads. Homemade desserts and organic coffees, plus a full deli selection of meats and cheeses.

Afternoon

One of Tofino's greatest attractions is its collection of art galleries showing native works. Not to be missed is the **Eagle Aerie Gallery** (350 Campbell Street, Box 10, Tofino, B.C. I0R 2Z0; 250–725–3235), where Roy Vickers's paintings and books are strikingly displayed.

Himwitsa Native Art Gallery, 300 Main Street (250–725–2017), sells limited-edition prints, silver jewelry, weavings, carvings, and pottery.

Stop in at **Pasticceria Conradi,** 311 Neil Street (250–725–3799), for thin-crust pizza, salads, and fabulous pastries.

At the **Crab Bar,** 601 Campbell Street (250–725–3733), buy a batch of fresh crab and a bottle of white wine and return to Pacific Sands Resort. Spend the rest of the afternoon relaxing on the beach at Cox Bay or exploring the long stretches of driftwood-covered sand beaches for which this coast is famous, especially **Combers Beach** and Long Beach. Photograph the great view from the top of **Radar Hill.** The best places to spot whales from land are in Grice Bay, where whales sometimes move in for the summer, or from the beach at Florencia Bay at the south end of the park.

DINNER: Pick up a boxed deli meal at **Breakers Deli** (250–725–2558), and picnic at the Cox Bay Beach or on your balcony as you watch the sunset.

LODGING: Pacific Sands Beach Resort.

Day 3 / Morning

BREAKFAST AND LUNCH: For a light breakfast, dine at the **Wickaninnish Inn's Driftwood Coffee Lounge.** Or, take a long walk along the beach. Some 250 birds live in the area, and you're likely to see blue herons, bald eagles, osprey, cormorants, tufted puffins, and swans, plus several varieties of gulls.

Refreshed by your walk, you may be mesmerized by the 240-degree view of the Pacific Ocean at the Pointe Restaurant (250–725–3100), also at the Wickannish Inn, which offers hearty breakfasts and Canadian-inspired lunches.

Drive south to the village of Ucluelet and the lighthouse that sits on a headland where the road ends. Walk the wooden boardwalk just south of the lighthouse at He Tin Kush Park. Return to walk the picturesque streets of the village, which looks across a scenic inlet to the mountains.

Afternoon

Before leaving town, satisfy that afternoon sweet craving at **Chocolate Tofino** (250–725–2526), and watch chocolatier Gordon Austin create handcrafted chocolates, homemade ice cream, gelato, and sorbet. That accomplished, drive north back to Route 4. Follow the road as it turns east. You'll pass the steep slopes of the heavily logged MacKenzie Range on your way back toward Port Alberni and the island's east coast. Nearing **Parksville,** stop at **Little Qualicum Falls,** where white cascades foam into the rushing green **Little Qualicum River.** Woodsy trails wind through the park, leading to overlooks.

About ½ mile west of Coombs is **Butterfly World,** 1080 Winchester Road (250–248–7026). In this unusual, tropical greenhouse garden, a thousand butterflies live and fly freely. It's a unique opportunity to photograph exotic species and see the colorful creatures at close hand. Wheelchair accessible, Butterfly World is open from 10:00 A.M. to 5:00 P.M., mid-March through October.

Coombs is known for its **Old Country Market** (250–248–6272). The picturesque landmark has a turf roof; many a visitor has halted in surprise at the sight of goats placidly walking on the roof and nibbling the grass.

At Parksville, turn south on Route 19.

DINNER: The Mahle House Restaurant, 2104 Hemer Road, Nanaimo; (250) 722–3621. Closed Monday and Tuesday. Country-home-turned-restaurant serving excellent Northwest cuisine. Fresh seafood and produce, pastas, homemade desserts, daily specials.

From Nanaimo, catch the ferry east to Horseshoe Bay and Vancouver.

There's More

Amphitrite Point, Ucluelet. Rhododendrons, ferns, and coastal pines grow profusely near paved paths leading to the coast guard station and lighthouse. Watch the surf crash against jagged rocks.

Diving. Barkley Sound's clear, quiet waters make it a popular divers' destination. It has rich marine life, reefs, and 200-year-old shipwrecks to explore.

Fishing. Jay's Clayoquot Ventures Inc., Tofino; (250) 725–2700. Boat rentals, guided charters at marina.

Canadian Princess Resort, Ucluelet; (250) 598–3366. Fishing and sightseeing charters.

Golf. Long Beach Golf Course, Tofino; (250) 725–3332. Nine-hole scenic course, narrow and challenging.

Hiking. The Central Westcoast Forest Society, Clayoquot Sound (250–726–2424), has completed three nature trails that highlight spectacular old-growth trees and rain forests. The Wild Pacific Trail offers fantastic views of the open ocean as well as access to beautiful beaches and rain forests. The Hot Springs Trail and the Norm Godfrey Nature Trail lead visitors into the region's old-growth forests.

Hot Springs Cove. A natural geothermal hot springs lies in a sheltered inlet north of Tofino, inaccessible by road. Its steaming pools, sea caves, and abundant marine life and wildlife make it an appealing side trip. (Bring sneakers; there are sharp rocks.)

Kayaking. Tofino Sea Kayaking Company, 320 Main Street, P.O. Box 620, Tofino, B.C. V0R 2Z0; (250) 725–4222 or (800) 863–4664. Kayak rentals and guided trips around Clayoquot Sound offer some of the best sea kayaking in the Pacific Northwest. In the same building, you can browse in a well-stocked retail store filled with kayaking supplies. A large bookstore offers more pleasant distraction, and the adjoining Paddlers Inn provides overnight accommodations to individuals and groups.

Petroglyph Provincial Park, located 2.5 miles south of Nanaimo (250–474–1336), boasts numerous rock carvings of mystical wolflike creatures and fish and human figures, created by the First Nations community. Interpretive boards provide details of the area's history and help to decipher the petroglyphs. A sandstone gallery of petroglyphs, located on a hill overlooking Nanaimo Harbor, is just a short distance from the interpretive area.

Special Events

Mid-March. Pacific Rim Whale Festival, Tofino and Ucluelet. Films, displays, exhibits, whale-watching excursions, and hikes.

July. Nanaimo Marine Festival, Nanaimo. With a food fair, entertainment, and activities for children.

Early August. Filbert festival of arts and crafts, Comox.

Early September. Salmon Festival, Port Alberni. Fishing competition with cash prizes up to $20,000. Other events: children's bullhead derby, horse rides, bed race, entertainment, boat raffle, fireworks, salmon barbecue.

Other Recommended Restaurants and Lodgings

Tofino

Middle Beach Lodge, 400 MacKenzie Beach Road, P.O. Box 100, V0R 2Z0, (250) 725–2900. Two lodges with thirty-two rooms, and twenty rustic self-contained cabins, situated on forty acres of secluded West Coast oceanfront. Guests can beachcomb on a mile of private beach.

Tofino Motel, 542 Campbell Street; (250) 725–2055. Completely refurbished in 2004, this establishment has spacious rooms, all with balconies overlooking

Clayoquot Sound. Kitchen suites available. Very reasonably priced and centrally located.

Wickaninnish Inn, in Wickaninnish Centre, Osprey Lane at Chesterman Beach, P.O. Box 250, V04 2Z0; (250) 725–3100 or (800) 333–4604. Seaside location. Custom-made armoires, desks, and chairs in every room. The inn's Pointe Restaurant serves breakfast, lunch, and dinner.

Ucluelet

Canadian Princess Resort, 1943 Peninsula Road, P.O. Box 939, V0R 3A0; (250) 726–7771 or (800) 663–7090. Moored survey ship with lodgings and nautical restaurant and lounge. Small berths on board, larger units in modern hotel section on shore. Open March through September.

Little Beach Resort, 1187 Peninsula Road, (250) 726–4202. White, 1930s-style duplex cottages overlooking a small, protected cove where newer accommodations have been built. Good view, moderate prices, great for families.

Matterson Tea House, 1682 Peninsula Road; (250) 726–2200. Historic house, fresh bread, good lunch or dinner.

For More Information

Alberni Valley Chamber of Commerce, 2533 Port Alberni Highway, Port Alberni, B.C. V9Y 8P2; (250) 724–6535.

BC Ferries, 1112 Fort Street, Victoria, B.C. V8V 4V2; Vancouver (888) 223–3779; www.bcferries.com.

Hello BC, 300–1803 Douglas Street, Victoria, B.C. V8T 5C3; (800) HELLO–BC; www.hellobc.com.

Pacific Rim National Park Reserve, Box 280, Ucluelet, B.C. V0R 3A0; (250) 726–7721.

Tofino Chamber of Commerce, 331 Campbell Street, Box 249, Tofino, B.C. V0R 2Z0; (250) 725–3414; www.tourismtofino.com.

Ucluelet Chamber of Commerce, 100 Main Street, P.O. Box 428, Ucluelet, B.C. V0R 3A0; (250) 726–4641.

VANCOUVER ESCAPE FOUR

South Vancouver Island

High Tea and High Seas / 1 or 2 Nights

- ☐ Ferry rides
- ☐ Scenic water views
- ☐ World-renowned museums
- ☐ Provincial capital
- ☐ Antiques shopping
- ☐ Native crafts
- ☐ Heritage sites
- ☐ Beaches
- ☐ Fine cuisine

The southern end of Vancouver Island is rich with contrast and beauty. It has pastoral farmlands and rugged wilderness, clear streams and ocean whitecaps, quiet villages and a city known for its shopping and dining. This itinerary will give you a taste of them all, as you curve from east to west, sampling some of the best a lovely land has to offer.

Day 1 / Morning

Board the ferry at Tsawassen, crossing the **Strait of Georgia** to **Swartz Bay,** on Vancouver Island. The scenic ride across the strait's blue waters takes about ninety minutes.

From here it's 13 miles south to **Victoria,** the province's capital city, where British traditions and Canadian breeziness meet on the Pacific shore.

If you've never visited Victoria, start with a stroll around the lively **Inner Harbour** to soak in the atmosphere. Sailboats bob on the water, and ferries nose against the wharves; bagpipers play on the corners under hanging baskets of flowers, while tourists climb into double-decker buses. The venerable **Empress Hotel,** the **Parliament Buildings,** the wax museum, the undersea garden, and the **Royal British Columbia Museum,** 675 Belleville Street (250–356–7226 or 888–447–7977), cluster around these harbor streets. The museum contains an IMAX National Geographic Theatre (250–953–IMAX). The atmosphere around the Inner Harbour is vibrant and festive.

LUNCH: The Empress Hotel, 721 Government Street; (250) 384–8111; reservations recommended. Sandwiches, tea, and scones in a historic landmark. Tea is served from noon through the afternoon. The grand old ivy-covered hotel, facing the harbor, has been renovated with style. If you want a heartier lunch in the Victorian mode, try the curry special in the Empress Bengal Lounge.

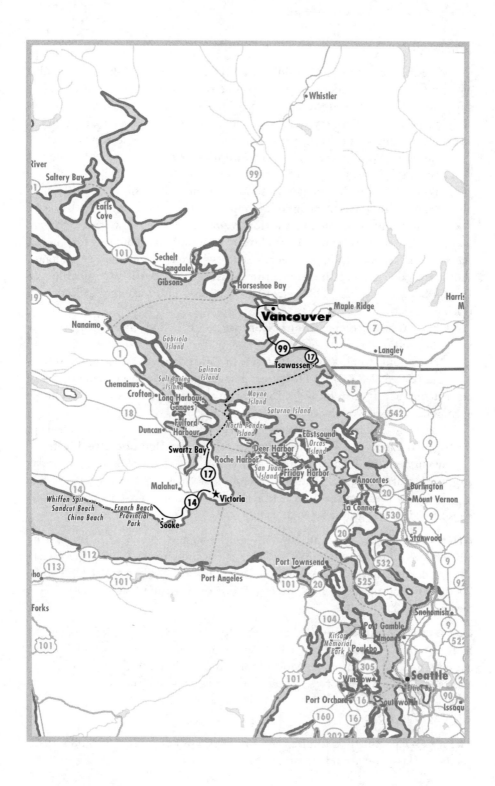

Afternoon

Cross the street to one of the world's great museums, the Royal British Columbia Museum, which has undergone a major renovation. It traces Vancouver Island's story from the Ice Age to the present day. Indian totems and masks, the lives of early trappers and settlers, explorers' ships, homes of the early twentieth century— all these and more are brilliantly presented to allow visitors a sense of participation.

Outside, totem poles are grouped in **Thunderbird Park,** eloquent reminders of a rich past and a living form of expression.

Poking about in the intriguing shops is a must for visitors to downtown Victoria. You'll find dozens of antiques shops and specialty stores selling woolens, tweeds, china, and chocolates. In **Bastion Square** you'll see how the city began. James Douglas, a British explorer, established a Hudson's Bay Company fort on this site in 1843. The complex of nineteenth-century buildings now houses restaurants, shops, art galleries, and the **Maritime Museum of British Columbia,** 28 Bastion Square (250–385–4222, ext. 102), which has an outstanding collection of marine artifacts.

Check **Eaton's Department Store** for the best finds in inexpensive souvenirs of good quality.

Drive about ½ mile from downtown to **Craigdarroch Castle,** 1050 Joan Crescent (250–592–5323), off Fort Street. The baronial stone manor, built by a coal magnate in 1887, is open for tours. Lavishly furnished, the thirty-nine-room home exemplifies Victorian opulence.

Travel east to **Oak Bay,** a bayside district of gracious homes and well-kept gardens, and check in at your hotel, the **Amethyst Inn Bed and Breakfast.**

Sealand of the Pacific is nearby, on Marine Drive (250–598–3373). Canada's largest oceanarium, Sealand offers a close look at Pacific Northwest marine life. Watch orca whales and sea lions perform, and see octopus grottoes and wolf-eel dens in underwater galleries. Open daily.

DINNER: On Fort Street are several good restaurants to choose from, offering scrumptious entrees ranging from steaks to curry and teriyaki. Among them: Café Brio, 994 Fort Street (250–383–0009); India House, 506 Fort Street (250–361–9000); Koto Japanese, 510 Fort Street (250–382–1514); and Siam Thai, 512 Fort Street (250–383–9911).

LODGING: Amethyst Inn Bed and Breakfast, 501 Fort Street; (888) 265–6499. Sixteen rooms in a fully restored 1885 Victorian mansion, with 13-foot ceilings, antiques, and period furniture. Most rooms have fireplaces, and many have sitting areas and double hydrotherapy spa tubs. Near museums and galleries.

Day 2 / Morning

BREAKFAST: Amethyst Inn Bed and Breakfast, 718 Fort Street; (250) 385–1012. Serves breakfast, lunch, and afternoon tea.

Cross the **Johnson Street Bridge** to **Esquimault.** On Lampson Street you'll find a bit of England that predates the Victorian era by 400 years. Cyril Lane, owner of the **Olde England Inn,** has painstakingly built a replica of **Anne Hathaway's Cottage,** a reproduction of William Shakespeare's wife's home and an authentic example of a sixteenth-century residence. The guided tours are well informed and interesting.

From here, join Route 1A (Island Highway) traveling west to Ocean Boulevard. Follow the signs to **Fort Rodd Hill National Historic Park.** On its peaceful, grassy grounds are bunkers and gun batteries erected between 1878 and 1956.

Cross the Causeway to tour **Fisgard Lighthouse,** the first lighthouse on Canada's west coast. It has been restored to its 1859 condition. Looking east from the lighthouse, your view is of the Victoria skyline across Esquimault Harbour.

Continue on Route 1A to **Mill Hill Park** in Langford for a short walk to the summit observation point or a hike in **Galloping Goose Regional Park.** The park, opened in 1988, follows an old railbed for 26 miles.

Take Route 14 west, and when you reach **Sooke** (46 miles from Victoria), stop at the **Sooke Region Museum and Visitor Infocentre,** 2070 Phillips Road (250–642–6351). It's a treasure of a find, with handsome displays of pioneer and native artifacts. On the property is a pioneer homestead that shows how life was lived here a century ago.

Sooke, the home of Salish Indians for centuries, has a comparatively mild climate and bountiful supplies of fish, fowl, berries, and produce.

If this is a one-night trip, turn back on Route 14 toward Victoria. Join Route 17 for the drive north to Swartz Bay; from there a ferry will take you back to the Tsawassen terminal near Vancouver.

If you are continuing your travels, drive to **Sooke Harbour.** Board a charter boat that will take you out to sea for some of the best salmon fishing on the coast. (Whale-watching cruises are available, too, March through October.) As you sail past the rugged cliffs and green forests of the island and head for deeper waters, you may see bald eagles, whales, and sea lions.

For a fishing cruise, contact **Sooke Charter Boat Association,** 8760 West Coast Road, Sooke (250–642–7783). Tackle and bait are supplied. Boats are 17 to 30 feet long.

Afternoon

DINNER: Sooke Harbour House; (250) 642–3421. One of the finest restaurants in British Columbia, with innovative cuisine featuring local fresh seafood (probably caught that morning by the owner). Herbs, vegetables, and edible flowers are grown in gardens on the premises. Incomparable setting and atmosphere.

LODGING: Sooke Harbour House, 1528 Whiffen Spit Road; (250) 642–3421 or (800) 889–9688. Exquisite inn on two waterfront acres. Beautifully furnished rooms with views of well-tended gardens and the sea.

Day 3 / Morning

BREAKFAST: Sooke Harbour House. Breakfast included in room rate.

From the inn, drive northwest on Route 14 to surf-washed shores. Waves toss high, and spindrift streams in the wind on blustery days. The coast has seen storms so wild, and has had so many shipwrecks, that sailors call it the graveyard of the Pacific. On mild days, however, the coast is benign, and you may see divers and surfers catching the waves.

A majestic rain forest grows in green splendor on the east. In this forest stands the largest Douglas fir tree, 41 feet around, and the tallest Sitka spruce, 310 feet, in Canada. Environmental controversy rages around the spruce and its tall companions.

Stop at **French Beach Provincial Park** to watch for birds and orca and gray whales.

Ten miles past Point No Point, a fifteen-minute walk through the forest will lead you to **China Beach,** a lovely, protected cove of white sand. You might see black bears in this park.

Another pretty spot on the coast is **Sandcut Beach.** A short trail provides access to the beach, which has small waterfalls and sandstone formations.

Revel in the expansive ocean views; then head back toward Sooke.

LUNCH: Included in your room rate at Sooke Harbour House.

Afternoon

Stroll through the inn's gardens, with their forty varieties of geraniums and 300 types of herbs; then hike out to **Whiffen Spit** for a last view of the far southwest corner of Canada and the Strait of Juan de Fuca.

Take Route 14 to Victoria and Route 17 north to Swartz Bay and the Tsawassen ferry.

There's More

Beacon Hill Park, Victoria (866–810–6645), a 200-acre park officially established in 1882, is lovingly landscaped with bridges, lakes and ponds, and alpine and rock gardens. It is home to numerous species of ducks, birds, and other wildlife.

Golf. The Greater Victoria area has numerous eighteen-hole golf courses, most of them open all year. One such course:

Cordova Bay Golf Course, 5333 Cordova Bay Road, Victoria; (250) 658–4444.

Historic Home. Emily Carr House, 207 Government Street, Victoria; (250) 383–5843. Home to Canada's most revered artist and author, Emily Carr, who was born in Victoria in 1871. The charming home is filled with her memorabilia and furnishings.

Sooke Potholes Provincial Park, Sooke. Off Sooke River Road, a forested park with waterfalls, hiking trails, swimming in river.

Victoria Bobby Walking Adventures, 414–874 Fleming Street, Victoria; (250) 995–0233. One-hour guided walks through old town Victoria. A quick and entertaining way to learn about the city's history.

West Coast Trail. This rugged wilderness path, originally constructed to assist shipwrecked sailors, begins at Port Renfrew, 50 miles west of Sooke. Hikers take a water taxi across the inlet to the southern end of the trail, which extends 48 miles north. It's part of Pacific Rim National Park and has been overcrowded, so you must make reservations; (250) 726–4212 mid-March to October; (250) 726–7721 year-round.

Special Events

May. Victoria Harbour Festival, Victoria. World-class regatta.

Late May. Victoria Day, huge parade, teacup races, and the launch of the Victoria Exhibition on the birthday of city's namesake, Queen Victoria.

June. Jazz Festival International, Victoria.

Third Saturday of July. All Sooke Day, Sooke. Grilled salmon, barbecued beef feast, loggers' sports.

July. Bard on the Beach, Victoria. Shakespeare Festival with four evenings of fireworks, buffet dinners, and Bard Theater.

December. Christmastime at Buchart's, Victoria. Ice skating, caroling, and holiday music.

Other Recommended Restaurants and Lodgings

Sooke

Point-No-Point Resort, 10829 West Coast Road; (250) 646–2020. Rustic cabins in an expansive, spectacular cliff-top setting in the woods, above the island's western shore. The restaurant is renowned for its lunches, dinners, and traditional English afternoon tea.

Markus' Wharfside Restaurant, 1831 Maple Avenue South; (250) 642–3596. Carefully prepared Mediterranean classics, such as Tuscan-style seafood soup, risotto, and home-smoked Sooke trout.

Whiffin Spit Lodge Bed and Breakfast, 7031 West Coast Road; (250) 640–3041 or (800) 720–1322. A 1918 home surrounded by lush gardens. Two guest rooms, a suite, and a renovated cottage with a Jacuzzi and fully equipped kitchen.

Victoria

Brasserie L'école, 1715 Government Street; (250) 475–6260. Dinner only. French country cooking served in a historic room that was once a schoolhouse for the Chinese community. The chef purchases local, seasonal, organic ingredients to create menus that change daily and might include such fare as duck confit, steak frites, and mountain trout.

Café Brio, 994 Fort Street; (250) 383–0009. Regional cuisine with a menu that changes daily. For dinner only. Appetizers might include local mussels with saffron and olive tapenade, or a luscious risotto with wild mushrooms and white truffles. Main dishes could be braised halibut, Cowichan Bay duck breast, or wild spring salmon with hazelnut gnocchi. Handmade pastas made daily.

Camille's, 45 Bastion Square; (250) 381–3433. Dinner only. Fresh local products such as lamb, duck, and seafood, and regional exotica that might include game and ostrich. Romantic setting in a historic building in Bastion Square. A 300-item wine list is one of the best on the island.

Dashwood Manor Bed and Breakfast, 1 Cook Street; (250) 385–5517 or (800) 667–5517. Bed-and-breakfast mansion near Beacon Hill Park, overlooking the water. Suites have fireplaces and kitchens.

Helms Inn at Beacon Hill Park, 600 Douglas Street; (250) 385–5767 or (800) 665–4356. Forty-two rooms in three buildings. Ideally nestled between Victoria's Inner Harbor and Beacon Hill Park, and adjacent to the Royal British Columbia Museum and IMAX National Geographic Theatre.

Olde England Inn, 429 Lampson Street; (250) 388–4353. Antiques-furnished rooms and restaurant in British manor house and village. Colorful gardens.

Paprika Bistro, 2524 Estevan Avenue; (250) 592–7424. Small Hungarian restaurant serving perfectly prepared classic dishes with a few innovations.

Royal Scot Suite Hotel, 425 Quebec Street; (800) 663–7515. Surrounded by lavish landscaped gardens are 178 guest rooms, a swimming pool, an exercise room, and a billiards room. All within walking distance of Inner Harbor, the legislative buildings, the Royal British Columbia Museum, and downtown shopping.

Shamrock Suites on the Park, 675 Superior Street; (250) 385–8768 or (800) 294–5544. Sixteen newly renovated suites; full kitchens. Footsteps from the Royal British Columbia Museum, Inner Harbor, and Parliament buildings.

The Victoria Regent Hotel, 1234 Wharf Street; (250) 386–2211 or (800) 663–7472. Downtown waterfront property offering rooms, suites, and penthouses overlooking Victoria's Inner Harbor. Balconies with views of the bustling quay and marina. Walking distance to Victoria's shops, theaters, museums, and galleries.

For More Information

BC Ferries, 1112 Fort Street, Victoria, B.C. V8V 4V2; (888) 223–3779; www.bc ferries.com.

Hello BC, 300–1803 Douglas Street, Victoria, B.C. V8T 5C3; (800) HELLO–BC; www.hellobc.com.

Sooke Visitor Information Centre, 2070 Phillips Road, Sooke, B.C. V0S 1N0; (250) 642–6351.

Tourism of Vancouver Island, No. 203-335 Wesley, Nanaimo, B.C. V9R 2T5; (250) 754–3500; www.bcadventure.com.

Tourism Victoria Visitor Info Centre, 812 Wharf Street, Victoria, B.C. V8W 1T3. Information, (250) 953–2033; reservations, (800) 663–3883; www.tourism victoria.com.

Vancouver Island Tourist Services Ltd., 666 Sumas Street, Victoria, B.C. V8T 4S6; (250) 382–4207.

West Shore Visitor Info Centre, 2830 Aldwynd Road, Victoria, B.C. V9B 3S7; (250) 478–1130.

VANCOUVER ESCAPE FIVE

The Gulf Islands

Island Hopping in the Georgia Strait / 3 Nights

- ☐ Picturesque landscapes
- ☐ Ocean views
- ☐ Mild climate
- ☐ Wildlife
- ☐ Whale watching
- ☐ Tranquil setting
- ☐ Evergreen forests
- ☐ Hiking trails
- ☐ Secluded beaches
- ☐ Fine dining

Between British Columbia's mainland and Vancouver Island lies the Strait of Georgia, its waters sprinkled with lumpy green hummocks called the Gulf Islands. Some are tiny and uninhabited, but several are populated year-round and draw tourists for their outdoor recreation, natural beauty, and pebble-strewn beaches.

This itinerary will introduce you to three islands: Galiano, North and South Pender, and Mayne. Each has a distinct character and much to offer the curious traveler.

A note about riding the ferries: You can reserve space on Canadian ferries from Tsawassen to the Gulf Islands and back, and it will be held for you until thirty minutes before departure. This is a boon to line-weary travelers, especially on busy summer weekends when long waits are common. Fares to the Gulf Islands are the same as to Victoria, while traveling interisland costs much less.

There are many routes and schedules you can follow in touring the islands. This itinerary is just one example, designed for a Friday-through-Monday getaway and based on current ferry schedules for those days. Those schedules may change without notice; be sure to consult an up-to-date one.

Day 1 / *Morning*

From the Tsawassen docks, south of Vancouver off Route 17, board the ferry to the **Pender Islands.** With a mighty blast of its whistle, the great white behemoth will ease into the channel and plow its way past densely forested islands. Seabirds wheel and call, clouds scud across the sky, and your tensions begin to slip away.

After a stop at **Mayne Island,** the ferry continues to **North Pender,** arriving at **Otter Bay.** North and South Pender are divided by a channel and connected by a narrow bridge. A rock isthmus once joined them, but it was blasted out in 1903 to allow boats through. The little bridge was built in 1950.

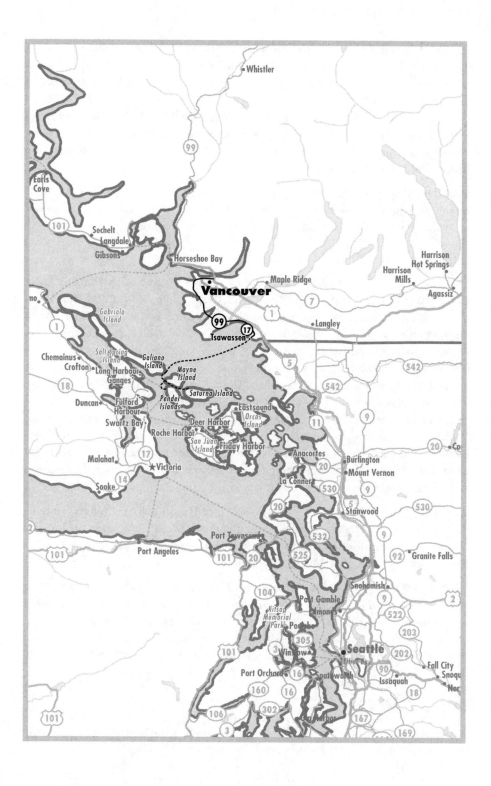

While housing development has increased rapidly in recent years, the Penders have retained much of their wild charm. There are several coves, lakes, and parks where you can enjoy the natural surroundings, and country roads that are fine for bicycling.

From Otter Bay, head south on Otter Bay and Bedwell Harbour Roads toward **Port Browning.** The sheltered harbor bustles with action in summer, as boats enter and depart the marina. Walk the rocky beach here, watch the sailboats, and bask in the islanders' friendly welcome.

LUNCH: Pistou Grill, in the Driftwood Centre, North Pender; (250) 629–3131. Lunch and dinner bistro fare. Just stopping by at lunchtime for a bowl of savory soup and a hunk of fresh bread is well worth the traveler's time.

Afternoon

Heading south, take Canal Road and cross the bridge to **South Pender.** Take Canal Road and Spalding to Gowlland Point Road, and proceed to the end. From the unmarked beach here, you have a good chance of observing orca whales. Perch on the boulders and watch the water's surface for spouts and the distinctive flukes of the great black-and-white mammals. You may see them swimming in pods of fifteen or so, an awesome sight. Another good whale-watching site is the cove at the end of Higgs Road, also off Gowlland Point Road. You'll hear the steady moan of offshore buoys and the shrieks of seabirds as you search for whales.

A private path at the end of Higgs Road allows access to the beach and cove. Visitors are permitted to use it, as is often the case on the islands. Local residents know which landowners have granted permission for their trails to be used, and most will be happy to tell you where those trails are. After you've sighted the orcas and relaxed in the sun, retrace your route to the bridge and North Pender.

DINNER: Aurora Restaurant at the Poet's Cove Resort and Spa. Offers contemporary regional cuisine using locally raised lamb, duck, and seafood in an inspired setting overlooking Bedwell Harbor. Ingenious fare uses local produce and ingredients. Open for breakfast, lunch, and dinner.

LODGING: Poet's Cove Resort and Spa, 9801 Spalding Road; (888) 512–7638. Hidden in a secluded bay on Pender Island. Twenty-two well-appointed waterfront rooms with fireplaces and balconies that face west for sunset views. Cottages nestled among the trees, with living and dining rooms, kitchens, and two or three bedrooms. All with private decks or patios. Several plush villas also available.

Day 2 / Morning

Rise early, and you may see the river otter that nests at the bottom of the cliff, the shorebirds of dawn, and the bald eagles that frequent the area.

BREAKFAST: The Aurora Restaurant serves a continental breakfast.

This is a morning for relaxing in your island hideaway. You can rent a boat or mountain bike at Bromley's Otter Bay marina, take a whale and wildlife tour, picnic at Penny's private ten-acre "Sahhalla," or watch her feed the eagles.

Leave Poet's Corner Resort and Spa for Otter Bay (2 miles) in time to catch the ferry bound for Sturdies Bay on **Galiano Island.**

Galiano's distinctive feature is its very dense greenery. The island is 75 percent forest-zoned land, so it has both logged-off areas and miles of Douglas fir forest. With 950 permanent residents, it's less developed and less pastoral than Pender.

LUNCH: The **Hummingbird,** 47 Sturdies Bay Road; (250) 539–5472. A friendly, open pub with windows overlooking a grassy picnic area. Good soups and salads, several kinds of beer. Dartboards and a casual atmosphere.

Afternoon

There is currently only water access to the driftwood-strewn beaches of Dionisio Point Provincial Park and Porlier Pass Channel, which separates Galiano and Valdes Islands.

Landlubbers follow Porlier Pass Road north from the ferry for about 10 miles and turn right on Cottage Way, which ends at Bodega Ridge Provincial Park. You can walk for several miles on a park footpath that follows a cliff 800 feet above the sea.

Go south again on Porlier Road to Clanton Road and turn right to **Montague Harbour Provincial Marine Park** (250–391–2300). You can make campground reservations with British Columbia Provincial Parks (800–689–9025). Montague offers boat rentals, groceries, fishing and camping equipment, and an espresso–ice cream cafe.

DINNER: Wisteria dining room at **Woodstone Country Inn.** Fine dining in a small hotel restaurant.

LODGING: Woodstone Country Inn, 743 Georgeson Bay Road; (250) 539–2022 or (888) 339–2022. Twelve light, airy guest rooms furnished with wicker and antiques. Some fireplaces. Scenic setting.

Day 3 / Morning

BREAKFAST: A hearty breakfast is included in the room rate at Woodstone Country Inn.

Drive to Sturdies Bay in time to board the ferry to **Village Bay, Mayne Island.**

Mayne, 4 miles across, is the smallest of the islands on your brief tour, and it's the sweetest. Less developed than Pender, less forested than Galiano, its tone is softly pastoral. Open green fields and gardens surrounded with high wire fences (to keep the numerous deer out) characterize much of Mayne's landscape. Along the road-

Galiano Island has numerous driftwood-strewn, secluded beaches.

sides, Scotch broom bursts a brilliant yellow in spring, followed by summer's fox-glove and lupine. As on the other islands, you'll see groves of madrona trees, with their distinctive, peeling red bark, along with towering firs.

Take Village Bay Road to **Miners Bay,** the local gathering spot and the island's commercial center. The picturesque bay was named after the many miners who stopped here in the mid-1800s on their way to the Fraser River/Caribou gold rush.

Pick up picnic foods at the grocery store in Mayne Mall or at **Miner's Bay Trading Post.** Hike up Mount Parke, in the center of the island, for a spectacular view of sea and islands.

LUNCH: Picnic at Mount Parke.

Afternoon

Hike back down the mountain and head southwest to Dinner Road. You'll be just in time for tea and check-in at **Oceanwood Country Inn.**

Williams Place is a short street off Dinner Road, ending in eleven-acre **Dinner Bay Community Park** and beach. After tea you might like to visit the sandy beach to search for shells, watch for bald eagles, and breathe the fresh, briny air.

DINNER: Oceanwood Country Inn. Prix fixe menu of continental dishes, specializing in fresh seafood and local ingredients imaginatively prepared. British Columbia house wines.

LODGING: Oceanwood Country Inn, 630 Dinner Bay Road; (250) 539–5074. Spacious, renovated Tudor-style inn overlooking a small bay. Gracious host Jonathan Chilvers welcomes guests to rooms furnished with verve and style. Three have fireplaces and whirlpool tubs.

Day 4 / Morning

BREAKFAST: Jonathan Chilvers serves a full breakfast—fruit, eggs, bacon, coffee, juice—in the pink stucco dining room at Oceanwood Country Inn.

Head for Miners Bay and gather picnic supplies. You might stop at **Mayne Street Mall** and go to the Manna Bakery Cafe, where sandwiches, soups, and baked goods are offered, as well as espresso and cappuccino.

From Fernhill Road, turn northeast on Campbell Bay Road. As the road curves toward **Campbell Bay,** you'll see a grassy meadow and just beyond it a parking turnout. An unmarked trail borders the meadow. Walk this trail about ¼ mile, and you'll come to a wide, serene, protected beach, just right for sunbathing, beachcombing, and exploring the sandstone shelves that shelter brilliantly colored starfish.

Mayne Island has many attractive beaches, but Campbell Bay, with its deep, fjordlike bay, is one of the most appealing. It's the most popular swimming area on the island and a good, safe place to bring children.

LUNCH: Picnic on the beach at Campbell Bay.

Afternoon

Take Campbell Bay Road to Waugh Road and follow it to Georgina Point Road, headed toward **Oyster Bay.** At the tip of **Georgina Point,** on a grassy field with gnarled apple trees, is a lighthouse that is open to the public daily from 1:00 to 3:00 P.M. Originally built in 1885, **Active Pass Light Station** was replaced by the present structure in 1940, with a new tower opened in 1969.

After your lighthouse tour, take Georgina Point Road back toward Miners Bay. On the way you'll pass little **St. Mary Magdalene Church,** a historic structure built about 1898, and several early-twentieth-century homes.

In "downtown Mayne," see **Plumper Pass Lockup,** a minuscule jail that was built in 1896 to accommodate rowdy miners. (The story goes that it housed only one inmate—and he escaped.) Now it's a museum.

Overlooking the waterfront at the bottom of the hill is **Springwater Lodge,** 400 Fernhill Road (250–539–5521). Built in the 1890s, it's the oldest continuously operating hotel in British Columbia. The pub is a favorite local hangout, but the place to be on a sunny afternoon is the hillside deck. From your umbrella-shaded table, watch the boats and tourists go by as you quench your thirst.

After a few days of relaxing on "island time," your watch may seem irrelevant. But don't miss the late-afternoon ferry back to Tsawassen. The 10-mile ride will get you to the mainland in about an hour and a half.

There's More

Afternoon Sailing Cruises. (800) 970–7464. Cruise the islands on a 43-foot classic sloop. Departs from Montague Marina.

Archaeology dig. On North Pender, a Salish Indian dig dating back 10,000 years. Occasionally open for summer tours.

Arts and crafts. Artery Studio, Oyster Bay, Mayne Island; (250) 539–2835. Paintings and prints by Frances Faminow and other artists. Open afternoons.

Charterhouse, Charter Road near Bennett Bay, Mayne Island; (250) 539–2028. Heather Maxey's home studio. Quilts, fine woolens, and enamels-on-copper. Open afternoons in summer, weekends in winter.

Red Tree Gallery, Pender Islands Artisan Cooperative. An artist-operated co-op showcasing a variety of crafts that include painting, photography, printmaking, collage, handpainted glassware, and wearable art.

Beaches and picnic sites. Montague Harbour Provincial Park, R.R. 6 on Trans-Canada Highway, Galiano Island. Waterside park; site of ancient tribal village. Sandy beach, picnic and camping sites.

Bluff Park, Galiano Island, 650 feet above Active Pass. Grand view of Gulf and San Juan Islands. Good spot for sighting eagles and orca whales.

Magic Lake Walk, southern end of North Pender Island. Loop path leading from Shingle Bay to Buck Lake and pretty Magic Lake.

Boating. Galiano Gulf Islands Kayaking, 637 Southwind Road, Galiano Island; (250) 539–2442. Guided sea-kayak trips available. No experience necessary. Office at ferry landing.

Mayne Island Kayak and Canoe Rentals; (250) 539–5599. Ferry landing pickup and dropoff. Camping and showers available.

Diving. Galiano Island Diving Services; (250) 539–3109.

Farmers' market. Driftwood Centre, North Pender Island. Fresh local produce sold every summer weekend.

Fishing. Mel-n-I Fishing Charters, Galiano Island; (250) 539–3171.

Golf. Galiano Golf and Country Club, 24 St. Andrews, Galiano Island; (604) 539–5533. PGA-rated nine-hole course in quiet, wooded setting. (Tennis also available; rent rackets at clubhouse.)

Horseback riding. Bodega Resort, Galiano Island; (250) 539–2677. Experienced guides at the farm/resort offer one- and two-hour horseback rides on trails and logging roads. The well-trained horses carry you through sun-dappled valleys and along ridge tops that afford magnificent views of Georgia Strait and Trincomali Channel.

Special Events

May. Pender Harbor Blues Festival, Pender Islands.

June. Galiano Weavers Exhibit and Sale, Galiano Island.

July. Salmon barbecue and fish derby, Pender Islands.

Canada Day Jamboree. Parade, games, food booths, and exhibits, Galiano Island.

Artists Guild Exhibition and Sale, Galiano Island.

Early August. Music Festival, Mayne Island.

August. Art Show and Fall Fair, Pender Islands.

Mid–August. Fall Fair, Mayne Island. Arts, crafts, photography, needlework, baking, canning, flowers, honey, wine, and produce exhibited in booths near the Agricultural Hall.

Early September. Lions Club Salmon Barbeque, Mayne Island.

September. Pender Harbor Jazz Festival, Pender Island. Indoor and outdoor venues.

November. Christmas Craft Fair, Mayne Island.

December. Christmas Eve Bonfire, Mayne Island.

Other Recommended Restaurants and Lodgings

Galiano Island

Bodega Resort, 120 Manastee Road, Box 115, V0N 1P0; (250) 539–2677. Log cottages with kitchens on twenty-five pastoral acres of meadows and trees. Horses, sheep, hiking trails.

Galiano Golf and Country Club, 24 St. Andrews; (250) 539–5533. Home-style cooking in a cafe setting; fixed menu of three-course dinners.

Island Time Bed and Breakfast, 952 Sticks Allison Road; (250) 539–3506 or (877) 588–3506. Waterfront location and the only five-star accommodation on Galiano Island, complete with hot tubs and tennis courts. Overlooks the Georgia Strait. Panoramic vistas of Mount Baker and the Vancouver coastline, stretching from Point Roberts to the Sunshine Coast.

La Berengerie, 2806 Montague Road; (250) 539–5392. Restaurant nestled under the trees, serving Continental cuisine with an experimental (and expert) twist. Open nightly in summer, weekends in winter. Three guest rooms upstairs.

Madrona Lodge, 18715 Porlier Pass Road; (250) 539–2926. Cottage resort in treed setting by the sea. Fireplaces. Complimentary bikes and boats.

Max and Mortiz Spicy Island Food House, 322 Clanton Road, at the Sturdies Bay ferry; (250) 539–5888. Gourmet German hot dogs and Indonesian nasi goreng.

Mayne Island

Fernhill Lodge, Box 140, 610 Fernhill Road, V0N 2J0; (250) 539–2344. Outstanding inn on a wooded hilltop. Gracious service, comfortable rooms, enchanting gardens, dinners geared to historical themes. Full breakfast included.

Pender Island

Delia's Shangri-La Oceanfront Bed & Breakfast, 5909 Pirate's Road; (250) 629–3808 or (877) 629–2800. Oceanfront views. Private hot tubs. Filling country breakfasts.

Gnome's Hollow Bed and Breakfast, 4844 Cutlass Court Road; (250) 629–3844. Log home nestled in tranquil woodlands setting. Romantic outdoor hot tub near waterfall. Theme rooms, private bathrooms, guest lounge with fireplace, TV.

Sahhali-Serenity Oceanfront Bed and Breakfast Inn on North Pender, P.O. Box 83, 5915 Pirates Road, V0N 2M2; (250) 629–3664. Newly renovated suites and cottages. Private outdoor hot tubs, fireplaces, ocean views.

For More Information

BC Ferries, 1112 Fort Street, Victoria, B.C. V8V 4V2; (888) 223–3779; www.bcferries.com.

Hello BC, 300–1803 Douglas Street, Victoria, B.C. V8T 5C3; (800) HELLOBC; www.hellobc.com.

Galiano Island Chamber of Commerce, 870 Bluff Road, P.O. Box 73, Galiano Island, B.C. V0N 1P0; (250) 539–2233.

VANCOUVER ESCAPE SIX

Langdale to Lund

The Sunshine Coast / 2 Nights

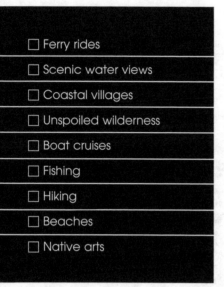

☐ Ferry rides

☐ Scenic water views

☐ Coastal villages

☐ Unspoiled wilderness

☐ Boat cruises

☐ Fishing

☐ Hiking

☐ Beaches

☐ Native arts

The 100-mile stretch of British Columbia coastline between Howe Sound and Desolation Sound is said to bask under more sunny days than anywhere else in western British Columbia. The stretch lives up to its nickname, the Sunshine Coast, drawing visitors who are lured not only by the weather but also by a wealth of outdoor recreation.

This itinerary provides a taste of the wilderness and seaside relaxation in a three-day escape to sheltered bays, fir-scented forests, and fish-filled waters.

Day 1 / Morning

Board an early-morning ferry at Horseshoe Bay, and travel north across Howe Sound to **Langdale,** a forty-minute ride. Under blue skies, the sea sparkles; if it's cloudy, with pewter skies and gray water, you feel that you're floating in a dream world of liquid silver.

Nearing the steep coastline, backed by massive, snow-cloaked mountains, you'll see private piers and cottages dotting the inlets.

From the Langdale ferry landing, it's a 2½-mile drive into the village of **Gibsons.** Grab a seat at the **Waterfront Restaurant,** 440 Marine Drive (604–886–2831), with waterfront views overlooking Gibsons Harbor. Large, savory breakfasts make the Waterfront a favorite with locals. The restaurant also serves light lunches and gourmet dinners using fresh fish in season, steaks, and barbecued chicken and ribs.

Gibsons faces Shoal Channel and the Strait of Georgia. **Molly's Reach,** at the top of the stairs leading to the boardwalk beside the government wharf, was the setting for the televison series *Beachcombers* and is now a restaurant. Shops line nearby **Molly's Lane.** Descend the steps toward Gibsons Wharf, and you'll see a path edging the waterfront. This easy, level walk will provide you with a pleasant, ten-minute stroll and a view of the boat traffic and sloping green hills around the harbor. Plaques posted along the route tell about Gibsons' founders.

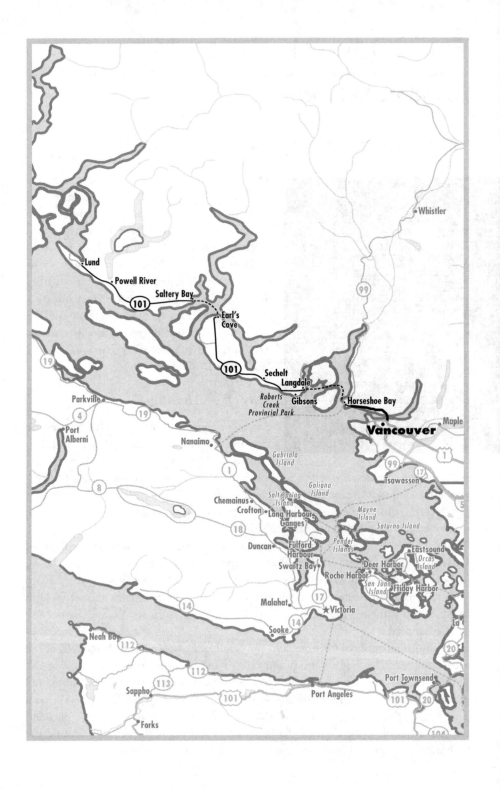

Elphinstone Pioneer Museum, 716 Winn Road (604–886–8232), houses Canada's largest shell collection as well as outstanding displays of historical items. Native stone hammers, spear points, cedar root baskets, knives, and arrowheads are on display, along with artifacts from pioneer life and the early logging, fishing, and canning industries. The museum is open daily in summer, and Sunday only from September through February.

Soames Hill, locally known as The Knob, lies off Bridgeman Road, between Gibsons and Langdale. A walk up this steep, 800-foot hill will test your leg muscles with its many log steps, but it's a short hike (forty minutes round-trip) and presents you with a glorious view of Gibsons, Howe Sound, Gambier and Bowen Islands, and the Squamish Mountains.

Return to Highway 101, the Sunshine Coast Highway, and drive north to **Sechelt.** You'll pass **Roberts Creek Provincial Park,** a waterside dell of dark cedars, sword fern, and bracken.

From the highway you seldom glimpse the water, since the view is blocked by forests so dense that they form a virtually impenetrable wall. To enjoy the real flavor of this scenic country, you have to get out on the water—your suggested afternoon excursion.

At the entrance to Sechelt, just off the highway, is the **Sechelt Indian Band's House of Hewhiwus** (hay-HAY-wus), including a small museum, a gift shop, and the **Raven's Cry Theatre.** Standing like sentinels before the hall are twelve totem poles, each carved to record major events in recent Sechelt Indian culture. The tribe's carving house is open to the public.

LUNCH: Pebbles Restaurant in the Driftwood Inn, 5454 Trail Avenue; (604) 885–5811. Savory seafood chowder, quiche, and salads served in an attractive dining room with a cheery atmosphere, overlooking the Strait of Georgia.

Afternoon

Follow the signs up Sechelt Inlet to picnic, swim, or canoe at **Porpoise Bay,** or hire experienced guides to take you sea kayaking or on an afternoon sightseeing excursion around nearby islands. You'll see the waterways and coastline from a different, dramatic perspective. Cruises include a five-hour trip to the tidal rapids at **Skookumchuk Narrows** and an evening ride in **Sechelt Inlet.** Any fish you catch will be smoked and canned for you to take home. (See "There's More.")

DINNER: Blue Heron Inn, 5591 Delta Road; (604) 885–3847 or (800) 818–8977. Quiet, romantic dining room with water view. Blue herons feed on the salt flats, while osprey and kingfishers swoop above. Fresh seafood includes lobster from the traps at the end of the inn's pier.

LODGING: Maritimer Bed and Breakfast, 521 South Fletcher Road; (604) 886–0664 or (877) 886–0664. Cottages, a loft, and two suites with private sundecks. Panoramic views of landscaped gardens and beyond, as far as Gibsons Harbor. Snack kitchens with minifridges and sinks.

Day 2 / Morning

BREAKFAST: Maritimer Bed and Breakfast.

Follow the highway north, passing moss-covered boulders, rocky outcroppings, and arbutus trees that twist at improbable angles over the sea bluffs. Scotch broom borders the roadside, its flowers bright yellow in spring.

Pass by the charms of **Half Moon Bay** and pretty **Secret Cove** and continue to **Madeira Park.** Stop at **Lowe's Resort,** 12841 Lagoon Road (604–883–2456), and board the boat for your scenic tour or fishing venture in **Pender Harbour.** Guides at this family resort are fishing experts. (You can rent a boat if you prefer.)

LUNCH: Box lunch on your charter trip, provided (at additional charge) by Lowe's Resort. Sandwiches, fruit, dessert, beverage.

Afternoon

The salmon or cod you catch will be frozen and packed at Lowe's Resort.

North of Madeira Park, take Garden Bay Road to **Mount Daniel** trail. The former logging road ascends about 1½ miles to the western peak of the 1,545-foot mountain, highest in the Pender Harbour area. Allow about an hour for the hike to the top. When you reach the summit, you'll have a panoramic view of lakes, islands, inlets, and Pender Harbour.

One of the lakes is **Garden Bay Lake,** which was considered sacred by the coast Salish Indians. Young girls, when they reached the age of puberty, would climb the eastern side of the mountain and spend four months there, communicating with the moon through circles of stone. When they returned to the tribe they were considered adult women. Evidence of their traditional rituals can still be seen on Mount Daniel.

Back on the highway again, drive to **Earl's Cove** and board the late-afternoon ferry to **Saltery Bay.** The ride around the tip of Nelson Island and across Jervis Inlet takes fifty minutes.

Drive another 18½ miles to **Powell River,** through thick forests interrupted by narrow, shady side roads that wind enticingly down to the sea and private homes. The town is dominated by an immense pulp-and-paper mill, one of the world's largest. Signs at an overlook along the highway list events in the history of Powell River and the harborside mill that created it.

DINNER: The Laughing Oyster, C4 Vandermaeden Road; (604) 483–9775. Steak, seafood, and vegetarian entrees to suit even the most epicurean travelers. Scallops, wild salmon—and, of course, oysters—are customer favorites. A gourmet buffet is offered every Wednesday. Also open for lunch.

LODGING: **Beach Gardens Resort and Marina,** 7074 Westminster Street; (604) 485–6267 or (800) 663–7070. Cabins and sixty-six rooms with private balconies overlooking the marina. Stone-and-cedar buildings under the trees. Indoor pool, sauna, tennis courts, boat rentals.

Day 3 / Morning

BREAKFAST: Ljubo's Bakery and Café, 6275 Marine Avenue; (604) 483–2089. Fresh-baked breads and pastries tease the senses as soon as you walk through the door. Enjoy the indoor cafe or its outdoor terrace in Powell River's Historic Townsite. Open daily.

In Powell River, stop at the **Powell River Historical Museum and Archives** (P.O. Box 42, Powell River, B.C.V8A 4Z5; 604–485–2222), across from **Willingdon Beach.** The exhibit explains Powell River's origins as a logging town and displays offbeat artifacts, such as the first piano in the district, a vest made of fishnet, a mastodon bone, and a reconstruction of the unique cabin lived in by an eccentric hermit, Billy Goat Smith.

There are several art galleries along Marina Avenue. **Gallery Tantalus,** 3 blocks north of the ferry terminal, shows paintings, limited-edition prints, pottery, native carvings, jewelry, and glass works. **Paperworks Gallery** features hand-painted silk scarves, jewelry, and kites.

Visit **Cranberry Pottery,** 6729 Cranberry Street (604–483–4622), in Cranberry, on the outskirts of Powell River. Cranberry is the starting point for an easy hike up Valentine Mountain. It is also the beginning of a road to Inland Lake, where an 8-mile, wheelchair-accessible trail circles the lake (see "There's More").

On the southern shore of **Powell Lake, Pacific Coastal Air** keeps float-planes available for business and tourist flights. For breathtaking views of the 30-mile lake, the steep green slopes of **Goat Island** (inhabited by mountain goats), the untracked wilderness and its multitude of lakes, and the rugged mountains that surround them, an airplane tour is ideal.

A half-hour flight will buzz you over the cove-scalloped lake and forests, fish farms, and log booms, to **Desolation Sound,** British Columbia's largest marine park. The area was named by Captain George Vancouver in 1792, when he explored here and was unimpressed, finding "not a single prospect that was pleasing to the eye." Today the sound and its many islands and inlets are considered jewels among the province's parks. The clear waters and rich undersea life make the area a favorite diving destination.

The plane flies above **Savary Island,** with its summer homes and miles of white-sand beaches, passes the smoking sawmill, and circles back to land on Powell Lake.

LUNCH: **Shinglemill Restaurant,** 6233 Powell Heights; (604) 483–2001. Bistro and pub. Good chowder, pasta, sandwiches, seafood, and ambrosial desserts. Open, bright setting on lakeshore, near float-plane docks.

Afternoon

Take the Sunshine Coast Highway as far as it will go, and you'll arrive in the out-post of **Lund,** about 17 miles from Powell River. You've reached the northern end of Highway 101, a ribbon of road that stretches 10,000 miles from Lund to Puerto Montt, Chile.

Established in 1889 by the Thulin brothers, who named it after the Swedish town, Lund is a relaxed, friendly community, favored by boaters and lovers of peace and quiet.

Visit **The Historic Lund Hotel** (hotel: 604–414–0474; restaurant: 604–414–0479) and local gift and craft shops. For a memorable outdoor adventure, charter a scenic cruise to Desolation Sound, kayak Cope Island, or take a water taxi to Savary Island. Both fine and casual dining, as well as a simple cup of cappuccino, are available at the hotel.

The renowned Jackie Timothy, a local native artist, may be carving above the dock at the Lund Hotel, a large white building that has dominated the village for a century. Prawn boats dock in front of the hotel with their catch in the afternoon.

Turn south now for the four-hour trip back to Vancouver. (The last summer ferry on Sunday and holiday Mondays departs from Langdale at 10:10 P.M. Check your ferry schedule for changes.) If there's time on the return trip, stop at one of the attractions you missed on the way up (see "There's More" for suggestions).

As you wend your way south on Highway 101 to Horseshoe Bay, it's a cer-tainty that you'll be planning your next trip to the splendid Sunshine Coast.

There's More

Canoeing, kayaking. Powell Forest Canoe Route travels a chain of eight wilder-ness lakes linked by portage trails with canoe resting racks and tent sites.

Ocean canoeing and kayaking are favorable in Jervis Inlet, Malaspina Inlet, and Desolation Sound Marine Park.

Pender Harbour and Three Lakes Circle Route is a 7½-mile trip through Garden Bay, Mixal, and Lower Sakinaw Lakes. You can see pictographs at Sakinaw Lake.

Pedals and Paddles, P.O. Box 2601, Sechelt, B.C. V0N 3A0; (604) 885–6440 or (866) 885–6440; www.sunshine.net/paddle. Sea kayak and canoe rentals.

Powell River Sea Kayaks, C-63 R.R. 2 Malaspina Road, Powell River; (866) 617–4444. Tours through Desolation Sound.

Diving. Powell River, considered the diving capital of Canada, has numerous div-ing spots with colorful marine life and intriguing shipwrecks. Mermaid Cove, the "Iron Mines" on Texada Island, Saltery Bay, Scotch Fir Point, and Okeover Arm are favorites.

Dive packages, Beach Garden Resort. Featuring the *Emerald Maiden,* a 9-foot-high bronze statue submerged off Saltery Beach Provincial Park.

Fishing and boating charters. Kaptain Wave Charters, 4210 Marine Avenue, Powell River; (604) 485–4380.

Sunshine Coast Tours, R.R. 1, S9 C1 Garden Bay; (604) 883–2280 or (800) 870–9055 for bookings; www.sunshinecoasttours.bc.ca. Scheduled marine tours. Also offers transportation to scuba divers.

Gift of the Eagle Gallery, 689 Gibsons Way, Gibsons; (604) 886–4899. Sunshine Coast and Northwest Coast art and genuine Native art, rooted in tradition and handcrafted by contemporary artisans.

Golf. Myrtle Point Golf Club, McCausland Road, C–5, R.R. 1, Powell River; (604) 487–4653. Eighteen-hole championship course.

Pender Harbour Golf Course, Highway 101, south side of Pender Harbour; (604) 883–9541. Nine holes. (Open daily.)

Sunshine Coast Golf and Country Club, 3206 Highway 101, Gibsons; (604) 885–9212 or (800) 667–5022. Hillside nine-hole course above water. Nonmembers after 1:00 P.M. weekdays, after 3:00 P.M. weekends.

Inland Lake. Unique to Powell River, Inland Lake is encircled by a wheelchair-accessible, 8-mile trail. A wide, level, graveled path winds through cedar, fir, and dogwood and around a lake that contains native cutthroat trout. Log cabins, fishing piers, picnic tables, and overlooks are all designed for wheelchair use. (Open mid-April to mid-October.)

Paper mill tours. Daily tours in summer of Catalyst Paper Mill, Powell River, are available. The minimum age is twelve.

Powell River Recreation and Cultural Centre. This remarkable, top-quality community facility holds a 25-meter pool, sauna, whirlpool, leisure pool, exercise room, two regulation arenas, meeting rooms, and a 725-seat theater.

Princess Louisa Inlet. This fjord lies in a majestic, glacier-carved gorge, with more than sixty waterfalls cascading down precipitous cliffs into placid inlet waters. Chatterbox Falls, at the head of the inlet, tumbles 120 feet; it's accessible only by sea.

Saltery Bay Provincial Park. Sixteen miles south of Powell River, this green park features ocean views, marine life, beaches, and campsites. You can swim, snorkel, and dive at Mermaid Cove, where a bronze mermaid rests 60 feet beneath the surface.

Skookumchuk Narrows. This is one of the West Coast's largest saltwater rapids. East of Earl's Cove, the tide turns in a narrow channel. There are cavernous whirlpools; on a 10-foot tide, 200 billion gallons of water churn through the channel.

Wilderness Camping. Tzoonie Outdoor Adventures, Box 157, Sechelt, B.C. V0N 3A0; (604) 885–9802. Tour boat up Sechelt Inlet, overnight camping, kayaking, mountain biking, scuba diving, fishing, access to Skookumchuck Narrows.

Special Events

Mid-March. Festival of the Performing Arts, Powell River.

Early July (biannual, in even-numbered years). International Choral Kathaumixw, Powell River. Weeklong choral festival with choirs from around the world.

July. Sea Cavalcade, Gibsons. Salmon barbecues, parades, dances, log burling, boat races, long-distance swims.

Mid-July. Texada Sandcastle Days, Powell River. Sandcastle competition.

Late July. Sea Fair, Powell River. Parade, ethnic foods, pancake breakfast, outdoor music, folk dancing, Indian dancers, canoe jousting, navy ship tours.

August. Festival of the Written Arts, Sechelt. Nationally renowned three-day gathering of authors, booksellers, journalists. Centered in Rockwood Lodge, restored heritage building with open-air pavilion.

Mid-August. Blackberry Festival, Powell River. Weeklong celebration honoring the ubiquitous blackberry: baking contest, wine tastings, desserts, pancake feeds.

Early September (Labor Day weekend). Sunshine Folk Festival, Powell River. Arts and crafts and music on outdoor stage.

Other Recommended Restaurants and Lodgings

Gibsons

Bonniebrook Lodge, 1532 Ocean Beach Esplanade; (604) 886–2887 or (877) 290–9916. Former boarding lodge 3 miles north of Gibsons, on Gower Point. Restored as small inn and fine restaurant, Chez Phillipe. French cuisine with West Coast influences.

Cedars Inn Hotel and Convention Centre, 895 Gibsons Way; (604) 886–3008 or (888) 774–7044. Modern hotel near shopping center, forty-five rooms, outdoor pool, sauna, meeting rooms.

Half Moon Bay

Rockwater Secret Cove Resort, 5356 Ole's Cove Road; (604) 885–7038 or (877) 296–4593. Newly renovated cabins and lodge with popular fine dining on a hill over the sea.

Madeira Park

Lowe's Resort, 12841 Lagoon Road; (604) 883–2456 or (877) 883–2456. Housekeeping cottages with one to three bedrooms, on cove of Pender Harbour.

Powell River

Beacon B&B and Spa, 3750 Marine Avenue; (604) 485–5563 or (877) 485–5563. Centrally located, across highway from beach. Three rooms, private baths, hot tub. Full breakfast. Great view.

Herondell Bed and Breakfast, 11332 Highway 101; (604) 487–9528. Country home on forty wooded acres with creek, pond, and river, 8 miles south of Powell River. Comfortable rooms, full breakfast.

Secret Cove

Jolly Roger Inn Pub and Restaurant, 101 Mercer Road; (604) 885–7860 or (877) 764–3746. Fully equipped town houses; kitchen, fireplace, television. Heated pool, views of a beautiful little cove.

For More Information

BC Ferries, 1112 Fort Street, Victoria, B.C. V8V 4V2;(888) 223–3779; www.bc ferries.com.

Hello BC, 300–1803 Douglas Street, Victoria, B.C. V8T 5C3; (800) HELLO–BC; www.hellobc.com.

Powell River Visitor Bureau, 4960 Marine Avenue, Powell River, B.C. V8A 2L1; (604) 485–4701 or (887) 817–8669.

Sechelt and District Chamber of Commerce Info Centre, 102–5700 Cowrie Street, Sechelt, B.C. V0N 3A0; (604) 885–0665.

Tourism Association of Southwestern B.C., Suite 204, 1755 West Broadway, Vancouver, B.C. V6J 4S5; (604) 739–9011 or (800) 667–3306.

VANCOUVER ESCAPE SEVEN

The Okanagan

Peach Blossoms and Wine / 3 Nights

- ☐ Sunshine
- ☐ Orchards
- ☐ Lakes
- ☐ Wineries
- ☐ Museums
- ☐ Stern-wheeler cruise
- ☐ Luxury resorts

British Columbia's Okanagan country, rich in fertile valleys, clear lakes, and frontier history, has one more enviable attraction: sunshine. People say there are more sunny days in this region than in any other part of Canada. Penticton proudly proclaims that while Tahiti receives 453 hours of sunshine in July and August, and Bermuda basks under 584 hours, the southern Okanagan Valley gets 598.

Thus it's not surprising that fruit orchards and vineyards flourish and outdoor recreation is a way of life in the Okanagan-Similkameen. Much of the area focuses on the water, for Lake Okanagan stretches up the valley for 80 miles, and there are a hundred more lakes and streams nearby. Three major ski areas draw thousands to the dry powder that falls east of the British Columbia Cascades.

Bicycling, boating, fishing, and sports events make the Okanagan an active vacationer's dream. This four-day itinerary adds other points of interest—such as museum tours, wine tastings, and a tour through ranching country—to the recreational fun.

Day 1 / Morning

Pack a picnic lunch and drive Trans-Canada Highway 1 east from Vancouver to Hope, 90 miles. Turn south on Route 3 to **Manning Provincial Park.**

Manning is a vast, green playground for nature lovers. There are boat launches, campsites, hiking trails, calm mountain lakes, wildlife, and wildflowers. Hike into alpine meadows in summer, and you'll walk among carpets of colorful blooms.

LUNCH: Picnic in Manning Park.

Afternoon

Continue north on Route 3, along the Similkameen River, to Princeton, where the road turns south toward **Keremeos.** Stop here for a look at the **Grist Mill and Gardens at Keremeos,** Upper Bench Road (250–499–2888). Built in 1877

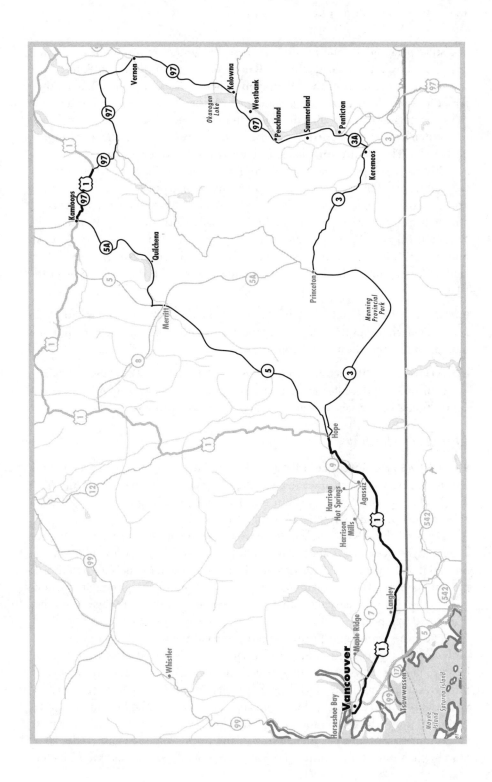

and still operating, it's one of the best-preserved waterpowered mills in Canada. Take a tea break in the Grist Mill Tea Room; then turn northeast on Route 3A.

You're in the heart of the **Okanagan,** where volcanic mountain ranges shelter a series of valleys, creating a unique microclimate. It ranges from arid desert in the south to a dry and mild environment in the north.

When you reach **Penticton,** on the southern edge of **Lake Okanagan,** check in at **The Penticton Lakeside Resort at Penticton.**

Stretch your legs with a shoreside stroll to the **Rose Garden,** where a miniature golf course full of castles and windmills may tempt you into a game; or take a cruise on the *Casabella Princess* (250–492–4090). The fifty-passenger stern-wheeler, which began service in Penticton in 1986, sails daily from the beach at the Penticton Lakeside Resort. Penticton has another stern-wheeler, the SS *Sicamous,* built in 1914, that plied the lake's waters for three decades. Now it rests on dry land, as a museum with displays showing the history of paddle wheelers on the lake.

DINNER: Theo's, 687 Main Street; (250) 492–4019. Greek food in Mediterranean atmosphere. Tables in courtyard with hanging bougainvillea and indoors under open beams and copper pots.

LODGING: The Penticton Lakeside Resort, 21 Lakeshore West; (250) 493–8221 or (800) 663–9400. Full-service resort at water's edge. Swimming pool, tennis courts, fitness center, sandy beach, restaurants, 204 guest rooms.

Day 2 / Morning

BREAKFAST: The Penticton Lakeside Resort. Two restaurants are located at the resort: The Hooded Merganser (named after the rare and elusive North American duck), which serves elegant fare at reasonable prices; and Magnums on the Lake, a cafe off the open, airy white lobby, with a lake view.

Drive north on Route 97 along the western shore of Okanagan Lake. On your left are high, eroded cliffs and pillars, while the ground slopes to the blue lake on the right. Small parks dot points of land beside the water. At the sign pointing to the Summerland Research Station, turn left and ascend the hill, through vineyards and fruit trees, to the agricultural center, where new varieties of grapes and other fruits are developed.

The area surrounding **Summerland** is second only to Kelowna in the fruit-growing and processing industry. Farms and orchards, world-class wineries, and heritage ranches all reside side by side here. If you are lucky enough to be driving through anytime from early July through late September, be sure to sample the harvest bounty: Cherries, pears, plums, and apples are some of the luscious and plentiful fruits grown here. Do drop by the numerous wineries to sip excellent wines.

Summerland center is a theme town done in the "olde" English Tudor style. Stop by the Visitor Info Centre for a pamphlet to guide you to Summerland's historical structures. Trace the history of Summerland at the Summerland Museum and Archives on Wharton Street, next to the library.

Take another self-guided tour, this time to the Summerland Trout Hatchery on Lakeshore Drive. Then visit the Summerland Ornamental Gardens, established in 1914. The Canyon View Path behind the main lawn presents breathtaking views of the Kettle Valley Railway Bridge and Trout Creek Canyon.

Step onboard the **Kettle Valley Railway,** which offers a two-hour journey from May to October on one of British Columbia's few remaining, fully operational steam railways. Constructed between 1910 and 1914, the Kettle Valley Railway was an engineering marvel, linking the towns of southern British Columbia as it climbed from 1,100 to 4,000 feet above sea level, and traveled over eighteen trestle bridges. Kettle Valley Railway's right of way remains largely intact today and is open for recreational use. The railway forms a spectacular cycling and hiking route, as it winds its way through mountain passes, valleys, towns, and tunnels and over the trestle bridges of Myra Canyon. Visitors should learn beforehand which bridges and tunnels along the route are no longer maintained and therefore unsafe to travel on.

For awe-inspiring views of Okanagan Lake and Summerland, hike the trails up to the summit at Giant's Head Mountain Park, an extinct volcano that resembles the profile of a man. A parking lot is conveniently located close to the summit. From here, two trails lead hikers to the summit. Continue north on 97 to **Peachland** and **Westbank** and watch for the signs to **Okanagan Butterfly World,** 1190 Stevens Road, Kelowna (205–769–4408). This outstanding exhibit, which has a coffee shop and wheelchair access, is well worth a stop. In exotic botanical gardens, hundreds of butterflies flutter. There are streams, birds, and a butterfly breeding area.

From here cross the bridge to **Kelowna,** a town on the east side of Okanagan Lake. Since this is orchard country, where most of British Columbia's apples, peaches, apricots, grapes, and cherries are grown, this is the place to see a working orchard and vineyard.

Drive out KLO Road to Dunster Road and **Kelowna Land and Orchards,** 3002 Dunster Road (250–763–1091). On this working farm, tours show visitors how orchards are run. Freshly squeezed apple juice is a specialty.

LUNCH: McCullough Station, on McCullough and KLO Roads; (250) 762–8882. The pub/cafe, built to resemble an old-time railway station, is adorned with historic photos of the Kettle Valley Railway. You can sit outside in the orchard or indoors by the fireplace.

Afternoon

Another tour, this time exploring the wine industry, is next on the agenda. Head for **Calona Wines,** 1125 Richter Street (250–762–9144). Calona, established in 1932, is the oldest and largest commercial winery in the Okanagan.

With a unique microclimate and soil of volcanic ash and clay loam, vineyards flourish in the region. Calona, known for its Riesling, gewürztraminer, and chardonnay wines, has garnered hundreds of medals in international competitions. It's noted for blended table wines. The winery offers tours, tastings, and souvenirs daily in summer and weekdays in winter.

In downtown Kelowna, at the foot of Bernard Avenue, you'll find lakeside symbols illustrating the Okanagan spirit: a soaring sculpture, *Sails,* by Dow Reid; an old-fashioned paddle wheeler, the MV *Fintry Queen;* an inviting green park with a public beach; and a whimsical statue of *Ogopogo,* Okanagan Lake's legendary sea serpent. The *Fintry Queen* (250–979–0223) offers lunch and dinner cruises daily. Beyond this is **Kelowna Waterfront Park,** with lagoons and walkways, adjoining the Grand Okanagan Resort, a large resort complex.

Purchase gifts and boutique items in Kelowna's quaint shops (with names like Teddy Bear Crossing and Scalliwag's) on **Tutt Street.** You might take tea here, in The Gathering Room.

Turn east at this point to Benvoulin Road, where the **Pioneer Country Market,** 1405 Pioneer Road (250–762–2544), is located. The old-fashioned market and museum stand where fields of onions once grew, planted by the pioneering Casorso family. The Casorsos grew produce and tobacco and ranched cattle, sheep, and hogs. John Casorso's great-granddaughter now operates the remarkable store, displaying antiques and heritage photos, as well as a wide variety of preserves and country crafts. It's a good place to buy locally made gifts and souvenirs.

Nearby is **Father Pandosy's Mission,** Benvoulin and Casorso Roads (250–860–8369). Father Charles Pandosy was the first white man in the valley. He set up a mission in 1860 and began Okanagan's fruit industry by planting the first apple tree. The home, church, schoolhouse, and blacksmith shop on the carefully maintained heritage site are open for self-guided tours.

DINNER: Hotel Eldorado. Lakeside dining in a light, upbeat atmosphere. Emphasis on seafood prepared with imagination (prawns with fresh papaya, three seafood mousses baked in puff pastry, salmon with saffron). Fresh seafood menu daily. Homemade gelatos and tempting pastries.

LODGING: Hotel Eldorado, 500 Cook Road; (250) 763–7500. Small, elegant country inn with twenty rooms, most with views of Okanagan Lake. Antiques, Jacuzzi tubs, original art, live music in the lounge, and an Art Deco flavor.

Day 3 / Morning

BREAKFAST: In the Hotel Eldorado sunroom. Try the toasted brioche with fresh fruit and syrup.

Drive north beside several small lakes for 28 miles to **Vernon.** You'll leave sagebrush-covered ridges to climb green, rolling hills, finally descending to a lush valley with mountains rising in the distance.

The restored Okanagan Post Office and General Store at O'Keefe Ranch.

Vernon is a small, rural town with lakes on all sides. Okanagan, Kalamalka, and Swan Lakes all have beaches and parks and offer good boating, fishing, water-skiing, and swimming.

Seven miles north of town, on Highway 97, is **O'Keefe Ranch** (250–542–7868), a significant piece of Okanagan history. On the sixty-two-acre site are ten buildings dating from the late 1800s. Each brings the past to life, through outstanding displays, demonstrations, and exhibits.

The General Store holds an array of merchandise from yesteryear: high-button shoes, harnesses, butter churns, bolts of calico. In the blacksmith shop, the big bellows keeps a fire blazing while the blacksmith forges tools (some are for sale in the ranch's gift shop). St. Anne's, a simple wooden church, was the first Catholic church in the Okanagan. Its first service was held in 1889.

The O'Keefe mansion illustrates the opulence of ranch life at the turn of the twentieth century, in contrast to the humble log house that was the first home of Cornelius and Mary Ann O'Keefe. The ranch the O'Keefes founded was run by the family until the 1960s.

Take Route 97 west after you leave Vernon. The 48-mile drive will lead you to Monte Cristo; from there it's 16 miles west to **Kamloops.**

Cool off in **Riverside Park,** a stretch of greenery along the Thompson River near downtown Kamloops. The park has an outdoor pool, a lawn bowling green, several tennis courts, playground equipment, and a long, sandy beach with lifeguard supervision. There are an old steam locomotive on display and a Japanese garden honoring Kamloops's sister city, Uji, Japan.

Back when water transport was used to reach British Columbia's mountainous interior, there were more steam-driven paddleboats on its lakes and rivers than anywhere else in the world, including the Mississippi River. Those days are long gone, but Kamloops has a boat that evokes nostalgic memories. The *Wanda-Sue* (250–374–7447) is a one-hundred-passenger stern-wheeler, hand built by a local retiree in his backyard. Two-hour cruises now travel the scenic waters of the Thompson River.

If you choose to stop early and stay overnight in Kamloops, stay at the newly constructed **Lazy River Bed & Breakfast,** 1701 Old Ferry Road (877–552–3377), situated on five acres along the Thompson River. Hardwood floors, custom-designed pine furniture, and marvelous views of the South Thompson River fashion a memorable resting spot. The area offers some of the best year-round fishing in British Columbia.

The **Kamloops Keg,** 500 Lorne Street (250–374–5347), located in the historic Canadian National Train Station, serves tasty steak dinners in a casual atmosphere.

After a satisfying breakfast, take Route 5A from Kamloops through a long stretch of rugged mountainous terrain to **Quilchena,** on the north side of Nicola Lake.

Afternoon

DINNER: Quilchena Hotel and Resort. Hearty ranch food in a quaint country inn.

LODGING: Quilchena Hotel and Resort, 6500 Merritt Kamloops Highway 5A; (250) 378–2611. Hotel built in 1906 on a 66,000-acre cattle ranch. Sixteen rooms share two baths. Victorian parlor, restaurant, peaceful setting. Fishing, sailing, horseback riding, and golf available. Closed December to April.

If the Quilchena Hotel and Resort is closed for the season, drop by the **Coldwater Café,** 1901 Voght Street (250–378–2821), in Merritt. While known for its prime rib and steak, this eatery also serves breakfast, beginning at 7:30 A.M. Built in a historic hotel at the turn of the twentieth century, the cafe is worth a stop just for its ambience. It is adjacent to a wine store that houses a collection of heavy horse gear and antique hardware.

Day 4 / Morning

BREAKFAST: Quilchena Hotel and Resort restaurant. If the Quilchena Hotel and Resort is closed for the season, drop by the **Coldwater Café,** 1901 Voght Street (250–378–2821), in Merritt. While known for its prime rib and steak, this eatery also serves breakfast, beginning at 7:30 A.M. Built in a historic hotel at the turn of the twentieth century, the cafe is worth a stop just for its ambience. It is adjacent to a wine store that houses a collection of heavy horse gear and antique hardware.

Join the Coquihalla Highway at **Merritt,** and drive south. It's 72 fast miles from Merritt to **Hope,** with one stop at the toll plaza. The freeway drive is both speedy and scenic, with craggy peaks rising high above the forested ridges on either side of the road. Waterfalls stream down steep, rocky ravines, while snowfields glisten on the mountainsides.

There's More

British Columbia Falls, Vernon. Off Silver Star Road, a gorgeous waterfall and picnic area.

British Columbia Orchard Industry Museum, 1304 Ellis Street, Kelowna; (250) 763–0433. One-hundred-year history of fruit industry in the valley. Open Tuesday through Saturday.

Davison Orchards, 3111 Davison Road, Vernon; (250) 549–3266. Family farm market selling numerous apple varieties and other produce. Hayrides, self-tours available July through October.

Fishing. Hundreds of lakes in the Okanagan and Shuswap regions offer good fishing for kokanee, Dolly Varden, and the world-famed Kamloops rainbow trout. Ask at Visitor Info Centres for local information.

Golf. Aberdeen Hills Golf Links, 1185 Links Way, Kamloops; (250) 828–1143. Challenging eighteen-hole course. Hillside views of Kamloops and the river valley.

Gallagher's Canyon Golf and Country Club, 2050 Campbell Road, Kelowna; (250) 861–4240. Eighteen-hole course under ponderosa pines, beautiful views.

Salmon Arm Golf Club, 3641 Highway 97B Street Southeast, Salmon Arm; (250) 832–4727. Eighteen-hole championship course in Shuswap Lake country.

Kalamalka Lookout, south of Vernon on Highway 97. Hike or bicycle to the lookout for a striking view of Kalamalka, the "Lake of Many Colors," which shimmers in brilliant hues of green and blue.

Kamloops Wildlife Park, 9077 Trans-Canada Highway East, Kamloops; (250) 573–3242. Largest nonprofit wildlife park/zoo in British Columbia. Exotic and British Columbia wildlife in natural surroundings, miniature train, picnic areas, concession stand. Open every day.

The Lloyd Gallery, 598 Main Street, Penticton; (250) 492–4484. Centrally located art gallery with more than 2,000 square feet of exhibition space. Works by noted Canadian sculptors and painters.

Munson Mountain, Penticton. Drive up the mountain on the edge of town, and walk the last few yards to the summit for a view of the long lake. It's touted as the "$100 view" because the scene was once depicted on the $100 bill.

Museum of Penticton, 785 Main Street, Penticton; (250) 490–2451. Considered to have the largest collection of western Canadiana in the British Columbia interior.

Red Bridge, Keremeos. This 1911-era covered bridge was left from the days of the Great Northern Railway. Mountain goats are sometimes seen nearby.

Secwepemc Museum and Heritage Park, 355 Yellowhead Highway, Kamloops; (250) 828–9801. Exhibits portraying all aspects of the culture of the Secwepemc Indians (European newcomers abbreviated the name to Shuswap).

Skiing. Apex Mountain Resort, P.O. Box 1060, Penticton, B.C. V2A 7N7 (forty minutes' drive from town); (250) 292–8222. Hilly course for the intermediate and advanced skier. Four lifts, fify-six runs. Condo rentals available.

Big White Ski Resort, P1 P.O. Box 2039 Stn. R, Kelowna, B.C. V0H 2A0 (forty minutes' drive); (250) 765–3101; in western Canada, (800) 663–2772. Highest ski resort in British Columbia. Warm temperatures, dry powder snow on 7,606-foot mountain. Sixty-eight runs, eight lifts (three high-speed quads), 16 miles of Nordic trails. Numerous accommodations and restaurants.

Holiday Inn Sunspree Resort, 7906 Main Street, Osoyoos; (250) 495–7223.

Silver Star Mountain Resort, Silver Star Mountain, 7 miles from Kelowna; (250) 542–0224 or (800) 663–4431. Ideal powder conditions, usually sunny November through April. Resort village in Old West style; ski shop, restaurant, saloon, condo rentals. Seven lifts, eighty-four runs. Summer chair lift to summit, 6,280 feet, for wide view of Monashee Mountain Range.

Wineries. Cedar Creek Estate Winery, 5445 Lakeshore Road, Kelowna, 9 miles south of Kelowna; (250) 764–8866. Landscaped grounds overlooking Okanagan Lake. Tastings daily, tours in summer.

Mission Hill Vineyards, south of Kelowna in Westbank; (250) 768–5125. Daily tours and tastings.

Sumac Ridge Estate Winery, Summerland; (250) 494–0451. Tours, tastings.

Special Events

Early February. Vernon Winter Carnival, Vernon. Largest festival of its kind in western Canada, with a parade, dances, sleigh rides, ice sculpture, and stock-car races on ice.

Early May. Spring Wine Festival, Kelowna and Penticton. A celebration of wine and food when new varietals are introduced.

Early June. Creative Chaos, Vernon. Crafts fair offering arts and crafts of regional artists.

Mid-August. Penticton Peach Festival. Ten days of music, contests, carnivals, parades, puppet shows, peach feasts.

August. O'Keefe Days and Cowboy Festival. Historic O'Keefe Ranch, Vernon.

Ironman, Penticton. Qualifying events for Hawaii Triathlon.

Early October. Wine Festivals, Okanagan Valley. One-week-long event. Twenty-five wineries participate in tastings, special dinners.

Other Recommended Restaurants and Lodgings

Hatheume Lake

Hatheume Lake Resort, P.O. Box 490, Peachland, V0H 1X0; (250) 767–2642. Log cabins and new cedar homes on mountain wilderness lake, famous for fly fishing. Caters to cross-country skiers, ice fishers, and snowmobilers.

Kaleden

Ponderosa Point Resort, 319 Ponderosa Avenue, P.O. Box 106, V0H 1K0; (250) 497–5354. Twenty-six snug log cottages and A-frames on Skaha Lake. Nicely furnished and immaculately clean. Shaded green lawns, pine trees, peace and quiet.

Kelowna

Earl's on Top, 211 Bernard Avenue; (250) 763–2777. Across the street from the lake and *Fintry Queen* landing. Outstanding food and unique Art Deco atmosphere, with lots of glass and plants.

Lake Okanagan Resort, 2751 Westside Road; (250) 769–3511 or (800) 663–3273. Full-service lakeside resort offering golf, tennis, boating, horseback riding, dining, 193 rooms.

Penticton

Granny Bogner's, 302 West Eckhardt Avenue; (250) 493–2711. Half-timbered former private home on landscaped grounds. Fine cuisine.

Royal Bed and Breakfast, 1929 Sandstone Drive; (250) 490–3336. Two rooms and a suite. With views of Okanagan and Skaha Lakes, and just five minutes from downtown Penticton. Outside deck with hot tub. Host Barb Akoi is a certified massage therapist who offers massage appointments. Breakfast includes fresh breads and pastries, Okanagan fruit, and a hot dish. Guests also can opt for a bagged breakfast to go or a continental breakfast (until 11:00 A.M.).

Summerland

Sumac Ridge Estate Winery, on Highway 97 just north of Summerland, is also home to the Cellar Door Bistro. Dinners are seasonally inspired, incorporating local ingredients whenever possible. In the summer, guests can dine at patio tables overlooking Lake Okanagan; in the winter, they can relax near the bistro's fireplace. Open daily, March through December.

Vernon

Castle on the Mountain, 8227 Silverstar Road; (250) 542–4593 or (800) 667–2229. Bed-and-breakfast and art gallery. Three guest rooms, use of kitchen, whirlpool tub on outdoor deck, barbecue area, spectacular view of lakes and valley.

Dimitri's Greek and Italian Restaurant, 2705 Thirty-second Street; (250) 549–3442. Steakhouse; well-spiced Greek foods.

The Eclectic Med, 3117 Thirty-second Street; (250) 558–4646. This charming, little restaurant creates innovative stir-fries and Italian classics.

Intermezzo Restaurant, 3206 Thirty-fourth Avenue; (250) 542–3853. Small place serving excellent Italian entrees. Veal, pasta, chicken, seafood. Takeout available.

The Italian Kitchen Company, 2916 Thirtieth Avenue; (250) 558–7899. One of Vernon's most popular restaurants, located in a fine old building with a tasteful interior that is complemented by a wine bar. Delicious Italian pasta dishes, seafood, and steaks. Reservations recommended.

Squires Four Public House, 6301 Stickle Road (off Highway 97 north of Vernon); (250) 549–2144. Multilevel pub with oak trim and hanging plants. Lunch and dinner daily. Traditional English dishes, daily soup-and-sandwich specials, chicken, pizza.

For More Information

Hello BC, 300–1803 Douglas Street, Victoria, B.C. V8T 5C3; (800) HELLOBC; www.hellobc.com.

Kamloops Travel InfoCentre, 1290 West Transcanadian Highway, Kamloops, B.C. V2C 6R3; (250) 372–7722 or (800) 662–1994.

Kelowna Visitor Info Centre, 544 Harvey Avenue, Kelowna, B.C. V1Y 6C9; (250) 861–1515 or (800) 663–4345.

Penticton Chamber of Commerce and Wine Country, 553 Railway Street, Penticton, B.C. V2A 8S3; (800) 663–5052.

Vernon Tourism, 701 Highway 97 South, Vernon, B.C. V1T 3W4; (250) 542–1415 or (800) 665–0795; www.vernontourism.com.

VANCOUVER ESCAPE EIGHT

Southeast Vancouver Island

Native Art and Edwardian Luxury / 3 Nights

☐ Ferry rides

☐ Scenic water views

☐ Native art

☐ Intriguing murals

☐ Fine cuisine

☐ Nature trails

☐ World-famous gardens

☐ Country mansions

☐ Luxury lodging

A rich mixture of British Columbia history is clustered around the bays and lakes of Vancouver Island's southeastern shore, in the Duncan/Cowichan region. Here you'll find settlers' farmhouses and rich men's mansions, proud displays of native art, wooded paths by quiet streams, and clear-cut hillsides that once were forest. This itinerary covers them all. Since the area covered is within a 50-mile radius and distances between stops are short, distance is only occasionally included.

Bring outdoor clothes and a dress–up outfit; this is a journey of contrasts.

Day 1 / Morning

Board a morning ferry at Tsawassen, south of Vancouver, headed for Swartz Bay (there are twenty round-trips daily in summer). The 24-mile ride takes an hour and thirty-five minutes, with the ferry cruising through the scenic **Strait of Georgia** and among the **Gulf Islands.** In spring and fall you'll see bald eagles and thousands of shorebirds, as well as sea lions and possibly orca whales.

From Swartz Bay terminal, head south on Highway 17 and follow the signs to **Brentwood Bay** and **Butterfly Gardens,** 1461 Benvenuto Avenue (877–722–0272), located at the intersection of Highway 17A and Keating Cross Road. When you enter the 12,000-square-foot conservatory that houses Butterfly Gardens, you're in an exotic world far removed from the Northwest. Here hundreds of multicolored butterflies live in tropical greenery. Open daily 10:00 A.M. to 5:00 P.M. March through October; 10:00 A.M. to 4:00 P.M. other months; admission charged.

You might choose to see Butterfly Gardens on your return trip, allowing more time to enjoy the nearby **Butchart Gardens** (800 Benvenuto Avenue, Box 4010, Victoria, B.C. V8X 3X4; 866–652–4422; www.butchart.com). It takes at least two

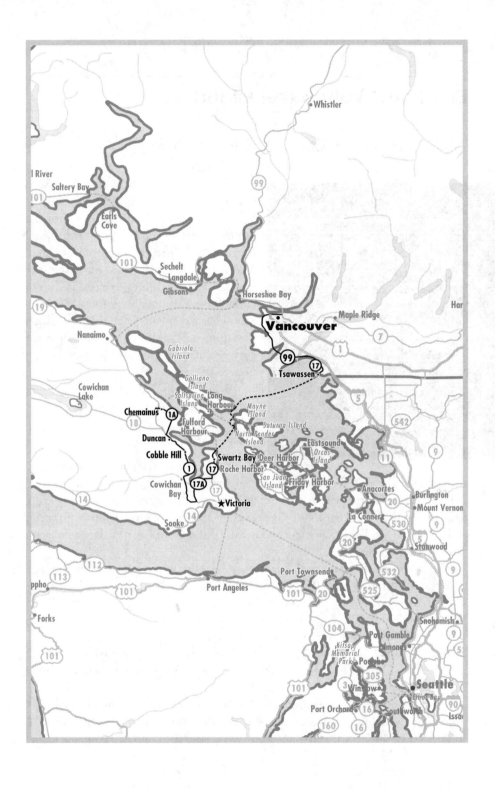

hours to explore the gardens, fifty acres of plantings carved from a former limestone quarry. This site is a must for any traveler who appreciates floral beauty and imaginative landscaping.

LUNCH: The Dining Room, Butchart Gardens; (250) 652–5256. A charming restaurant, once the home of the estate's owners, serves lunch, afternoon tea, and dinner in summer. Less expensive meals are offered in the casual, plant-filled Blue Poppy Restaurant. Reservations recommended (250–652–8222).

Afternoon

Catch the Brentwood Bay–Mill Bay ferry that crosses Saanich Inlet. After the twenty-five-minute ride on the little ferry, a contrast to the behemoths that ply the Strait of Georgia, turn north to follow Mill Bay Road, edging to the shore. You'll have views of the water, beaches, and Saanich Peninsula on the east.

When you reach the village of **Mill Bay,** you'll see a shopping complex, Mill Bay Centre, which has several interesting shops. **Asean Imports** sells intricate carvings and puppets from Indonesia, baskets, beaded shoes, and bags. Stationery, Mexican and Guatemalan imports, pottery, and watercolors are displayed in **Excellent Framing Gallery and Handcrafts,** while **Third Addition** is a browser's delight, selling toys, linens, gifts, and cards of high quality. The Centre has a sizable grocery market and an ice-cream shop, **The Creamery,** where you might settle at an outdoor table for coffee or ice cream and dip into the book you purchased at **Volume One Bookstore** in Duncan.

From here take Trans-Canada Highway 1 north to Cowichan Bay Road, turning northeast toward the pretty bay where the Cowichan and Koksilah Rivers join in marshlands at the northern tip of the inlet. The Cowichan Indians gathered here long before Europeans arrived, clamming and fishing for cod and salmon. Fishing is still a major attraction. **The Maritime Centre** (250–746–4955), home of the Cowichan Bay Wooden Boat Society and School, is open for tours. Its cedar buildings, set on a 300-foot pier, have exhibits showing the area's settlement and gradual change from agriculture and fishing to a recreational community. At the Centre you can watch students build and restore traditional and contemporary wooden boats.

Next to the Centre is a tiny art gallery, **The Red Door,** where pottery and weavings are displayed and sold.

Located 16 miles north of Victoria and 2 miles east of Sidney, off the Saanich Peninsula on Vancouver Island, **Sidney Spit Provincial Marine Park,** Sidney Island (866–768–1899), has hiking trails and wildlife viewing. Accessible by boat only. A foot-passenger ferry provides access to the island from the Sidney Wharf at the bottom of Beacon Avenue in Sidney. The park is open and fees for services are collected from mid-May to September 30. For information on departure times and locations, call (250) 727–7000.

Nearby **Hecate Park,** on the waterfront, has a boat ramp and picnic facilities. Look across the harbor and you'll see Mount Tzouhalem, crouching like a huge stone frog—transformed from a living frog, according to a Cowichan legend.

Past Hecate Park on Cowichan Bay Road is Theik Reserve Footpath, a choice place for flowers and birds. It has picnic tables and is close to a shorebird habitat. You may see otters.

Turning inland on Cowichan Bay Road, you'll see myriad birds in the wetlands near the South Cowichan Lawn Tennis Club. In winter they swarm with trumpeter swans and bald eagles.

Continue north on Cowichan Bay Road to Tzouhalem Road, which winds through the Cowichan Indian Reserve. Notice the old stone church on a hill to your left. It's empty and vandalized now, but it retains the quaint look of a stone country church built with care.

Before dinner at Quamichan Inn, make time for a visit to the **Quw'utsun' Cultural and Conference Center,** located at 200 Cowichan Way, Duncan (250–746–8119 or 877–746–8119), approximately 2.2 miles from Quamichan Inn. The center is a first-class tourist destination owned and operated by the Cowichan Tribes, the largest Aboriginal band in British Columbia. Situated on the beautiful Cowichan River, this hands-on reproduction of a native village is rich with learning opportunities that include visual arts, dance, music, and storytelling. A cafe, restaurant, art gallery, and gift shop are also on the complex. Call for seasonal hours.

On your way to dinner, stop at **Art Kinsman Park** on Quamichan Lake to see the flocks of swans, ducks, and Canada geese. The park has a grassy area, playground, and boat launch.

DINNER: Quamichan Inn, 1478 Maple Bay Road, Duncan; (250) 746–7028. Tudor-style restaurant on the east side of Quamichan Lake, noted for its continental cuisine in a linens-and-candlelight atmosphere.

LODGING: North Haven Bed and Breakfast, 1747 Herd Road; (250) 746–4783 or (800) 585–1822. A peaceful, romantic getaway in a 1914 heritage country home. Nestled among lush orchards and gardens with a pond and gazebo. Surrounded by pastoral views. Antiques-filled rooms with four-poster beds. Close to many activities, including water sports, golf, and hiking.

Day 2 / Morning

BREAKFAST: The menu varies daily at North Haven Bed and Breakfast. A full breakfast served on fine china might include blueberry pancakes, eggs Benedict, or eggs frittata.

Just north of Duncan on Highway 1 is the **Somenos Marsh Wildlife Refuge.** Here you'll see herons, ducks, geese, and other waterfowl in the fall, winter, and spring. There are observation points along the road and more under development.

Continue north and stop at the **British Columbia Forest Discovery Centre,** 2892 Drinkwater Road (250–715–1113 or 800–715–1113), where one hundred acres are dedicated to the history of forestry and logging. You can ride an authentic steam train once used on a logging operation and watch demonstrations of logging skills along the way. Open May through September.

Continue north on Highway 1, turning on 1A to reach the village of **Chemainus.** The "Little Town That Did" is 1 mile off the main highway and well worth a detour. Thirty-two scenes of the area's history, painted by Canadian, European, and American artists, cover the walls of Chemainus's buildings. In the early 1980s the townsfolk decided to rescue their dying economy by embarking on a program that would attract tourists. They chose historical murals.

Their plan worked. Visitors now flock here to follow the painted yellow foot-steps, which guide you past the murals to busy art galleries, quaint gift shops, and ice-cream parlors. See **Waterwheel Park,** the **Chemainus Valley Museum** (250–246–2445), century-old **Anglican St. Michael and All Angels Church** (open to tourists 1:00 to 4:00 P.M. Wednesday, Friday, and Saturday in summer; 250–246–4470), and **Locomotive Park.** Kin Park has a beach, a playground, and a boat ramp.

The big sawmill on the edge of town is a reminder of the area's logging history. Tours of the mill are available on Tuesday and Thursday afternoons in summer (250–246–3221).

Sa-Cinn Native Enterprises, Ltd. (250– 246–2412) features jewelry, carvings, pottery, prints, and other fine-quality native arts and crafts. At **Images of the Circle,** a working studio on Chemainus Road, you can watch the artists at work and pur-chase carvings, paintings, and jewelry.

Admire an ever-changing inventory of fine quality jewelry, carvings, pottery, prints and other fine-quality Native arts and crafts at **Sa-Cinn Native Enterprises, Ltd.** (250–246–2412). Drive along Chemainus Road, where seven mill houses dating from the late nineteenth century still stand adjacent to the **Chemainus Theatre.** This Italianate-style building, which boasts a majestic domed rotunda, houses the renowned **Chemainus Theatre Festival.**

If time permits, take a thirty-minute ferry ride to **Thetis Island,** where visi-tors are pleasantly surprised with excellent hiking trails that skirt wetlands and rock terrain, and a vineyard and winery that offers tours and tastings and—for the little ones—a small play farm.

LUNCH: Willow St. Café, 9749 Willow Street, Chemainus; (250) 246–2434. Housed in a one-hundred-year-old refurbished building. Choose from a selection of quesadillas, wraps, gourmet pizza, quiches, and freshly made soups and sand-wiches. Muffins, scones, and delectable desserts fresh daily. Full range of espresso drinks.

Afternoon

Drive south on Trans-Canada Highway 1 to **Duncan,** the commercial hub of the region. It's easy to find the **totem poles** for which the city is famous. There are about eighty throughout the city, especially in the downtown district, made by native carvers.

The Totem Pole Project, which began in 1985, honors an ancient Northwest Coast tradition and art form. Guided tours are available May through early September for groups of five or more; check at the Travel Info Centre, 381 Highway 1 (250–715–7100). Several totems stand near the Duncan Railway Station, which houses the **Cowichan Valley Museum and Archives** (250–746–6612). It contains pioneer possessions, a typical early-twentieth-century general store, and a gift and souvenir shop. Open Monday through Saturday in summer, Thursday through Saturday in winter. Hours vary.

On Craig Street, **Judy Hill Gallery,** 22 Station Street (250–746–6663), is a small shop with good-quality native carvings and jewelry. Stop for espresso or cappuccino at Gallows Glass Books on Canada Avenue, near the Cowichan Valley Museum and Archives; then take Cowichan Way south to the **Native Heritage Centre,** 200 Cowichan Way (250–746–8119), a complex of buildings where you can see how the famous Cowichan sweaters are made, watch a totem carver at work, and purchase fine native crafts. This is an exceptional visitor attraction, not to be missed. Owned by the Cowichan Indians, the largest tribe in British Columbia, it represents a rich and proud culture.

One mile south of Duncan on Highway 1 is Hill's **Native Art Kokosilah** (250–746–6731), one of several Hill's stores selling unique totems, ceremonial masks, leather moccasins, and Cowichan handknit sweaters.

DINNER: Bluenose Steak and Seafood House, 1765 Cowichan Bay Road, Cowichan Bay; (250) 748–2841. Prime rib and seafood in a pleasant setting on the water.

LODGING: North Haven Bed and Breakfast.

Day 3 / Morning

BREAKFAST: North Haven Bed and Breakfast.

From Duncan, take Koksilah Road south to **Bright Angel Provincial Park.** Walk the suspension bridge that hangs above the Koksilah River, hike the trails that wind through fir and cedar trees, and enjoy the rocky, riverside beach. You can swim (a convenient rope swing hangs from a tree limb, over the water) and fish.

Take Koksilah Road east to join Trans-Canada Highway 1 and turn south; past Dougan Lake, branch west on Cobble Hill Road. Driving through this rural area you'll pass a farm selling raspberries and blueberries in season. When you reach the little community of **Cobble Hill,** a variety of craft and antiques shops awaits you. Worth noting is **Cobble Hill Pottery,** 3375 Boyles Road (250–743–2001), a clay studio and galley with utilitarian stoneware.

Purchase a picnic lunch at the snack shop in Cobble Hill Country Furnishings and walk across the train tracks that lie at the base of Cobble Hill. Just behind the railroad shelter, a trail begins into **Quarry Wilderness Park.** Follow this trail (there are several offshoots; just keep going upward) to the top of the hill, and if it's a clear day you'll enjoy a sweeping view of the countryside. It takes about two hours to climb the hill. There are picnic tables at the summit.

LUNCH: Picnic on Cobble Hill.

Afternoon

After ambling back down Cobble Hill, you might take a refreshment break at the ice-cream bar in Cobble Hill Country Furnishings or in Cobblestone Inn, a Tudor-style pub with a full bar, darts, and evening entertainment on weekends. Then head south on Shawnigan Lake Road.

The country road goes to **Shawnigan Lake Village,** where you can check to see if the **Auld Kirk Gallery** (250–743–4811 or 250–383–1415) is open. The gallery, in a former church on Wilmot Avenue and Walbank Road, sells the pottery and textiles of local artisans. It's open weekends; weekdays by appointment only.

Continuing on East Shawnigan Lake Road, you'll come to Recreation Road, a right turn. At the end of the road is **Old Mill Community Park,** site of a former sawmill. In the early 1900s, when logging seemed unlimited, the mill handled 80,000 to 100,000 board feet a day. The last mill burned down in 1945 and was never rebuilt; now there are few remnants left among the trails that wind through the woods and along the lakeshore.

East Shawnigan Lake Road continues south to join Highway 1. At the juncture, turn north on the highway to Whitaker Road. Travel less than a mile on Whitaker, and you'll come to **Spectacle Lake Provincial Park,** a quiet, pretty park centered around a lovely lake. It takes about thirty minutes to walk completely around the lake. Part of the path is wheelchair accessible.

The Aerie Hotel and Restaurant in Malahat is near Spectacle Lake, off Whitaker Road, and is your destination for the night.

DINNER: The Aerie. Expensive, fine cuisine in a spectacular setting with forest, mountain, and water views. Try the pheasant in almond crust or rack of lamb with herbs, and save room for the heavenly chocolate-rum truffles. This is a special place for special occasions.

LODGING: The Aerie Hotel and Restaurant, 600 Ebedora Lane, P.O. Box 108, Cobble Hill, B.C. V0R 2L0; (250) 743–7115 or (800) 518–1933; www.relais chateaux.fr. Luxurious, Mediterranean-style villa on a hillside above Finlayson

Arm, with grand mountain and forest views. Twenty-three hotel rooms and suites, some with Jacuzzi tubs and fireplaces.

Day 4 / Morning

BREAKFAST: A full breakfast, included in the Aerie's room rate, is served in the dining room with fine china and silver.

Head north on Highway 1 to the ferry landing south of Mill Bay. If you have time to explore, drive into **Bamberton Provincial Park** for a last walk in the woods.

Catch the ferry to Brentwood Bay. Take Highway 17 north to Swartz Bay and board the ferry bound for Tsawassen.

There's More

Boating. Great Northwestern Adventure, 1705 Cowichan Bay Road, P.O. Box 5, Cowichan Bay, B.C. V0R 1N0; (250) 748–7374. Operates a unique fleet of classic sailing boats and tall ships. Offers a variety of excursions and overnight bed-and-breakfast packages from Cowichan Bay and through the Gulf Islands.

Centennial Park, at the end of First Street in Duncan, has a playground, tennis courts, and lawn bowling.

Chemainus Theatre, 9737 Chemainus Road, Chemainus; (250) 246–9820 or (800) 565–7738. Dinner theater, arts-and-crafts gallery.

Cowichan Lake, west of Route 18. Inland lake with fishing, picnicking, and hiking trails (much of the forest has been logged off, however).

Golf. Mount Brenton Golf Club, 2816 Henry Road, Chemainus; (250) 246–9322. Eighteen-hole course with fir trees and several lakes and creek crossings. Easy to walk but challenging.

Hiking. Cowichan River Footpath follows the scenic, wooded south bank of Cowichan River. The trailhead is shown on the large map at the Community Hall of Glenora, southwest of Duncan, off Indian Road. It's a 6-mile hike in to Sahtlam Lodge (see "Other Recommended Restaurants and Lodgings").

Kayaking. Cowichan Bay Kayak and Paddlesports, 1765 Cowichan Bay Road; (250) 748–2333. Full line of kayaks for touring the bay.

Jill's Galley and Marina, 2346 East Shawnigan Lake Road, Shawnigan; (250) 733–2547. Family dining on the lakefront and a marina with full boat services and fuel, plus water equipment rentals and tours.

Special Events

June. Cowichan Wooden Boat Festival, Cowichan Bay.

July. Annual Island Folk Festival. Sponsored by the Cowichan Folk Guild.

Mid-July. Duncan-Cowichan Summer Festival.

June through August. Festival of Murals, Chemainus. Outdoor theater, parades, puppetry, street music, folk dancing, food, music, swap meet, and arts-and-crafts demonstrations and sales.

August. Fine Arts Festival, Chemainus. Weekend celebration of contemporary fine crafts, showcasing artisans from around western Canada.

Other Recommended Restaurants and Lodgings

Chemainus

Birdsong Cottage Bed and Breakfast, 9909 Maple Street, P.O. Box 1432, V0R 1K0; (250) 246–9910. Bed-and-breakfast filled with Victorian whimsy and bird themes. Three suites and a hospitable innkeeper who lets guests try on her fancy hat collection. Cozy sitting room with a grand piano, harp, and pump organ. Full breakfast.

Chemainus Bakery and Deli, 2871 Oak Street; (250) 246–4321. Sandwiches and pastries in a bright, cheery space that's flooded with sun on clear days. Good chewy walnut cookies. Closed Sunday and Monday.

Saltair Porterhouse Pub, north of Chemainus on Route 1A; (250) 246–4942. Casual country restaurant in a rural, woodsy setting.

Cobble Hill

Cobble House Bed-and-Breakfast, 3105 Cameron-Taggart Road, R.R. 1, (250) 743–2672. One-level home nestled on forty acres of forest, with a creek running through the property. Three large guest rooms, each with private bath; one has a Jacuzzi. Full breakfast with a hot entree.

Cowichan Bay

The Inn at the Water Resort and Conference Center, 1681 Botwood Road; (250) 748–6222. Waterside hotel with fifty-five one-bedroom suites. Kitchenettes, a pool, and restaurant with ordinary food but great view of the bay.

Masthead Restaurant, 1705 Cowichan Bay Road; (250) 748–3714. Seafood and prime rib in waterside setting.

Rock Cod Cafe, 1759 Cowichan Bay Road; (250) 746–1550. Inexpensive spot with nautical atmosphere and marina views. Fish-and-chips and specials such as honey Dijon halibut with rice and salad. Serves breakfast too.

Duncan

Fairburn Farm Country Manor, 3310 Jackson Road; (250) 746–4637. A working bed-and-breakfast farm with seven rooms, set on 128 secluded acres. Homegrown vegetables, fresh eggs and butter, and freshly baked bread.

Oak and Carriage Neighbourhood Pub, 3287 Cowichan Lake Road; (250) 746–4144. English-style pub with comfy couches by the fireplace. A good place for lunch (generous hamburgers) and a game of darts.

Pioneer House Restaurant, 4675 Trans-Canada Highway; (250) 746–5848. Large log restaurant with friendly, prompt service and well-prepared steak, ribs, seafood, and chicken.

Sahtlam Lodge and Cabins, 5720 Riverbottom Road West; (250) 748–7738. Charming, old-fashioned lodge and rustic cabins scattered among woodland and gardens on the Cowichan River. Excellent meals; dinner served to the public, breakfast served to guests in cabins.

Vigneti Zanatta and Vinoteca Restaurant, 5039 Marshall Road, Duncan (250–748–2338), in Cowichan Valley, is a farm gate winery, which means that the wine is sold at the farm. Also on the premises is Vinoteca Restaurant, featuring simple Mediterranean-style cuisine. Restaurant information and reservations: (250) 709–2279.

Maple Bay

Brigantine Pub, 6777 Beaumont; (250) 746–5452. Eat outdoors on the deck at this friendly pub. A local favorite, it has the usual dartboard and television. A good spot for a light, flavorful meal; the mushroom soup is top-notch.

Mill Bay

Friday's, 3000 Cobble Hill Road; (250) 743–5533. Lively spot with a youthful clientele. The most popular item is pizza, cooked in open brick ovens.

Ocean Breeze Bed and Breakfast, 2585 Sea View Road; (250) 743–0608 or (877) 743–0654. Relax in a charming century-old home complete with ocean and mountain views. One block from the ocean, rooms with private baths and air-conditioning, twin and queen beds, full breakfasts. Perfect setting for fishing/outdoor adventures.

Shawnigan Lake

Marifield Manor, 2039 Merrifield Lane; (888) 748–6015. Spacious Edwardian home with six rooms, lake views, and hospitable hosts. Full breakfast included.

For More Information

B.C. Ferries, 1112 Fort Street, Victoria, B.C. V8V 4V2; (888) 223–3779; www.bc ferries.com.

Chemainus Visitor Info Centre, 9796 Willow Street, Chemainus, B.C. V0R 1K0; (250) 246–3944.

Duncan-Cowichan Information Centre, 381 Trans-Canada Highway, Duncan, B.C. V9L 3R5; (250) 746–4636.

Hello BC, 300–1803 Douglas Street, Victoria, B.C. V8T 5C3; (800) HELLO–BC; www.hellobc.com.

Tourism Association of Vancouver Island, Suite 302, 45 Bastion Square, Victoria, B.C. V8W 1J1; (250) 382–3551.